"If you're a leader who cares about developing other leaders around you, please read *Protégé!* It's practical, insightful   orehensive and rooted in real life. *Protégé* provide   or creating a culture—the fruit of whic'   no reproduce Christ-centered leaders.

Jim Mellado, president, Will

"Steve doesn't just know abou. what it means to have leaders invest in leaders; he has lived the reality of it. Here is a helpful guide in one of the great areas of the church's need."

John Ortberg, senior pastor, Menlo Park Presbyterian Church

"I sure wish I had had this book back when I was first figuring out leadership on the ground as a young church planter! Steve has made a remarkable contribution with this volume. Not only has he diagnosed the need of young leaders, he has offered some serious help in what to do about it. At the same time, Steve is dead-on right about some pitfalls and temptations that plague the dark side of young leaders. *Protégé* is a must-read for young kingdom leaders—and for those of us who work with them!"

Reggie McNeal, author, *A Work of Heart* and *Practicing Greatness*

"I wish I had received the kind of mentoring this book describes when I was a protégé. Now that I find myself as a coach in a season of investing in the next generation of leaders, this book equips me with wisdom, practical ideas and guidelines for a process that is by nature more an art than a science."

Nancy Beach, author of *Gifted to Lead: The Art of Leading as a Woman in the Church*

"When Steve Saccone speaks on leadership development I want to listen. He does not just write in theory in this book, but he has a proven track record of serving with young leaders. Our church had Steve consult with us and we modeled our intern program based on Steve's ideas. What you will read in this book has proven to be extremely effective. This isn't just another leadership theory book for unique and the extreme ideal situations. This is birthed and written from the front lines of working with young leaders in the reality of today's world."

Dan Kimball, author, *They Like Jesus but Not the Church,*
professor, George Fox University

"For an entire generation of church leaders (mine), this book is what you need for the final third of your ministry. The future of the church depends on its leaders taking seriously their responsibility and joy to mentor the next generation of leaders. As I read this book, I am amazed at the holistic approach Steve takes toward leadership development. He challenges more seasoned leaders to engage with younger leaders and plumb the depths of sin, healthy leadership, the gospel and the church. The result is an unleashing of God's amazing gifts into his world, through the men and women he designed to lead it. And I'm not just impressed with and excited about this very necessary book . . . I know Steve. I've worked with him and he authentically lives out the pages he has written. Perhaps that is the highest praise of all."

Nancy Ortberg, author of *Non-Linear Leadership*

PROTÉGÉ

Developing Your

Next Generation

of Church Leaders

Steve Saccone

with Cheri Saccone

IVP Books

An imprint of InterVarsity Press
Downers Grove, Illinois

InterVarsity Press
P.O. Box 1400, Downers Grove, IL 60515-1426
World Wide Web: www.ivpress.com
E-mail: email@ivpress.com

*InterVarsity Press® is the book-publishing division of InterVarsity Christian Fellowship/USA®, a movement of
students and faculty active on campus at hundreds of universities, colleges and schools of nursing in the United States
of America, and a member movement of the International Fellowship of Evangelical Students. For information
about local and regional activities, write Public Relations Dept., InterVarsity Christian Fellowship/USA, 6400
Schroeder Rd., P.O. Box 7895, Madison, WI 53707-7895, or visit the IVCF website at <www.intervarsity.org>.*

All Scripture quotations, unless otherwise indicated, are taken from the Holy Bible, New International Version®.
NIV®. *Copyright ©1973, 1978, 1984 by International Bible Society. Used by permission of Zondervan Publishing
House. All rights reserved.*

*While all stories in this book are true, some names and identifying information in this book have been changed to
protect the privacy of the individuals involved.*

*The author is represented by the literary agency of The B&B Media Group, Inc., 109 S. Main, Corsicana, TX 75110,
www.tbbmedia.com.*

Design: Cindy Kiple
Images: © Ron Hohenhaus/iStockphoto

ISBN 978-0-8308-3823-3

Printed in the United States of America ∞

Library of Congress Cataloging-in-Publication Data

Saccone, Steve, 1978-
  Protege: developing your next generation of church leaders / Steve
Saccone with Cheri Saccone; foreword by Mark Batterson.
      p. cm.
  Includes bibliographical references.
  ISBN 978-0-8308-3823-3 (pbk. : alk. paper)
  1. Christian leadership. 2. Mentoring—Religious
aspects—Christianity. I. Saccone, Cheri, 1977- II. Title.
  BV652.1S225 2012
  253—dc23

2012009662

P	20	19	18	17	16	15	14	13	12	11	10	9	8	7	6	5	4	3	2	1
Y	29	28	27	26	25	24	23	22	21	20	19	18	17	16	15	14	13	12

To Cheri:

What we have is more than I ever imagined.

We have dreamed together, cried together and laughed together.

Together, we have come to live in the fullness of love.

You embody beauty, life and joy in all their essence.

*The depth of who you are has propelled me
to become the person I long to be.*

Here's to an endeavor that has brought us together!

Contents

Foreword by Mark Batterson 9

The Protégé Narrative: *An Introduction* 11

1 Building Kingdom Cultures 21

PART 1: CHARACTER—
Four Deadly Sins of Emerging Leaders 29

2 The Sin of Imitation: *Envy* 33

3 The Sin of Performance: *Self-Reliance* 44

4 The Sin of Overconfidence: *Foolishness* 59

5 The Sin of Entitlement: *Greed* 70

PART 2: RELATIONSHIPS—
Three Critical Tensions of Relational Leadership 81

6 The Tension of Commitment: *Overcommitters*
and Underdeliverers 87

7 The Tension of Conflict: *Avoiders and Evokers* 96

8 The Tension of Attachment: *Overattachers and Detachers* . . . 116

PART 3: COMMUNICATION—
The Connectivity of the Poet 133

9 Developing the Gift of Communication 137

10 Communicating with a Missional Lens 150

PART 4: MISSION—
The Movement of the Gospel 167

11 Gospel Momentum 173

12 The Spirit of the Gospel. 180

13 Gospel Conversations 188

14 Gospel Community 201

PART 5: ENTREPRENEURIAL LEADERSHIP—
The Power of Possibility 215

15 Kingdom Entrepreneurs. 219

16 The Pre-church Experience 228

Epilogue: *One Last Thing* 239

Acknowledgments. 243

Appendix: *Fifteen Things to Do to Develop Leaders* 245

Notes 249

About the Author 251

Foreword

LEADERSHIP DEVELOPMENT IS A UNIVERSAL NEED, and there are a lot of voices out there speaking into that need. What makes Steve Saccone's book, *Protégé*, different is that Steve has a unique experience resulting from his creation of a customized, holistic leadership program that's been remarkably successful. It began as essentially an experiment, and blossomed into a substantial, effective, influential medium to take ministry leadership to the next level. Steve first imagined, then created and led, the Protégé Program based out of a church in Los Angeles called Mosaic.

I was fortunate to receive an invitation to speak to a couple different protégé groups. I found myself being really impressed with this young but high-caliber group of leaders. I was so intrigued after my interactions with the protégés that I felt compelled to find out more about this program. What began as me consulting and teaching them, ended up as me asking them questions about how this Protégé Program works. This led to more extensive conversation with Steve and other protégés about how we could do something like this at our church. So in 2008 we launched our own Protégé Program at National Community Church, and it has become a critical part of our community.

This was the beginning of an ongoing dialogue between Steve and me on what holistic leadership development really looks like in today's church culture, and in today's emerging leader. And I know other church leaders and pastors who have also gleaned unique insights from Steve on how to lead others toward authentic growth. We've learned that through intentional mentoring we can help maximize talents, foster spiritual gifts, equip with leadership skills, give direction on how to refine and test a leader's character, and ultimately how to help young leaders develop a walk with God in and through their ministry lives that abounds in depth.

This is an incredibly important conversation, one that Steve has been pioneering for more than a decade. His experience can teach all of us how to foster successes and learn from our failures, how to create innovative ways to become more missional and meaningful to the world around us, and how to provide practical hands-on training that will equip emerging ministry leaders to be a force in the future of the church.

As readers, we get the benefit of gleaning from Steve's unique experience, novel ideas, insightful understanding of the needs of next generation leaders, and new paradigms on how to cultivate authentic personal development in all of the protégés who surround us who are hungry and even desperate to learn. Steve Saccone is a leader of leaders. I know I've seen real differences as a result of his approach to developing protégés. And there aren't many things more significant than seeing real growth happen within the greatest movement in this world . . . the church.

MARK BATTERSON
Lead Pastor
National Community Church
Author, *The Circle Maker*

The Protégé Narrative

AN INTRODUCTION

WHEN I LOOK BACK ON MY LIFE, there's one pervasive theme that catalyzed my growth as a leader. It's a simple theme in a complex, larger story. It's so fundamental in nature, yet rare for a leader to experience in reality, at least to the depth that is necessary. This theme involves personal, customized development in the life of a leader.

The further I move into this whole leadership thing, the more I realize how lacking I myself truly am. I think that's what happens when you stick with something long enough—you realize that it's not as simple as you once thought it to be. Though much work still needs to be done with me, I'm most grateful for the people who took time to personally invest in my growth in individualized fashion. Without this investment, maybe I still would've made it, and maybe I even would've been successful externally—but I know I would not be the man I need to be to do what I do.

There are many people who made an intentional decision to take part in my leadership and personal development. I think back to when I was nineteen years old, when I initially stepped into ministry and had no idea where to even begin. Someone decided to help me figure it out. Marty has no idea how much he contributed to my growth. He was the first one to give me an opportunity to step behind what I believe to be the greatest platform on earth, the pulpit. Not only that, he spent time coaching and mentoring me with insight and compassion because he believed in God's call and gifting in my life. He believed in who I could become as a person, communicator and leader.

Fast-forward to my early twenties when I moved from my hometown to start an internship at a church I greatly admired. I was expecting to learn from a distance. Little did I know that I was about to be mentored in such deeply personal ways. It would change the course of my life.

Sheryl, the director of the internship program, walked alongside me through the highs and lows of my young ministry life. When I was particularly anxious about various things, she looked beyond the superficial causes and helped me discover what God was really doing in my life at the deepest level, and how he was trying to speak to me. When I struggled with my fear of failure, she reminded me of my true worth in Christ. When I didn't know where I needed to grow, she helped me see my strengths as well as my weaknesses.

Another mentor and supervisor at the time was Daniel. He was truly a gifted leader, and someone who played a huge part in my own development as I attempted to cultivate ministries and play a meaningful role within this larger-than-life community. And little did he know that we'd be part of the same family one day—I married his sister.

Being a ministry leader requires an intricate convergence of character as well as real-life skills, intentionality as well as accountability, execution as well as creativity. It also demands groundedness and imagination, innocence and shrewdness, humility and confidence, brokenness and wholeness. And so much more. The standard associated with this great calling is high.

So, how is someone to grow into the calling he or she was designed for, yet finds it so difficult to embody? And, how does each of us learn how to better engage other future leaders with a deeper, more customized approach to their own development?

THE PROTÉGÉ PATH

Throughout history, if someone wanted to learn a particular skill, he or she would find a master or mentor to guide them. This person seeking to learn and grow is called a *protégé*. And like any skill or trade, ministry leadership involves a set of abilities that must be developed and cultivated.

There are countless *protégés* simply waiting for an experienced master of their trade or wise mentor, but they so often become lost in the deficit of strong and developmental leadership that is so absent and misprioritized in today's culture, and in today's church. Where do these hungry protégés go to learn the skills and character they long to develop so that they can maximize their impact in the world? Who do they seek out to guide them on this critical journey?

A large majority of protégés within the church currently seek development from the educational system, predominantly from seminary. Others search for guidance from an influential, but distant, church figure, perhaps looking to imitate their success from afar. Although these tracks of learning and development are important, there are significant limitations when someone chooses either of them as their primary, even sole path.

Don't get me wrong, attending seminary can be (and was for me) a remarkable resource for attaining knowledge (of the Scriptures, church history, leadership, etc.). Do I believe seminary can play a significant role in a person's development? Absolutely. It has in my life, and in many others I know. So let me be clear. I am a believer in the value, and even necessity, of a theological education. However, research tells us that the overwhelming majority of seminary graduates don't gain the adequate hands-on experience necessary for effectiveness in the world outside those classroom doors. Ninety percent of ministers report that they were inadequately trained for pastoral ministry, and fifty percent admit that they feel incapable of meeting the needs of their current job.[1]

Although I greatly appreciate the seminary I attended (Bethel Theological Seminary in St. Paul, Minn.), it's still limited in its scope compared to what it takes for a ministry leader to develop in a holistic, customized fashion. I'm profoundly convinced that attending seminary without also receiving "on-the-job training" is the equivalent of a physician attending medical school without ever practicing their skills in clinical rotations. And this dilemma is not solved with a simple field education course, as good as it may be.

Think about it. Can you imagine being treated by a physician who possesses all the medical knowledge in the world after just graduating from several years in school but has absolutely no hands-on experience? Would you want him or her to go anywhere near you, or to be the person in charge of healing you or your child? Of course not! Any sane patient would demand a doctor who had examined real human beings and lived through the agony of genuine human suffering, not a doctor who only touched skeletons in a lab, solved case studies on their exams, and wrote papers explaining their perspectives and conclusions about their research.

Ironically, this is essentially what we do when it comes to the relationship between church leaders and the people we serve. We may have an enormous amount of head knowledge and even voracious eagerness to learn, but we often lack the experience, training and real-life perspective we need when it comes to interacting with real human beings, in real time, about real spirituality, that produces real transformation. And we also lack all the pain, mystery, wisdom and wonderment that go along with it.

Many protégés who attend seminary as their sole preparation end up stumbling around the church upon graduation and battling confusion and frustration. Why? Because they initially believe they've been properly prepared, trained and equipped for the demands ahead, but they soon realize it's not true. In actuality they were, more often than not, only given information instead of personalized and intentional development. We must join together to shift our paradigms on what it looks like to train and develop ministers, church planters, social entrepreneurs and other spiritual leaders. Our current system does a disservice to protégés when we tell them (or even imply to them) that education is enough, or that it's the primary path. We all know life doesn't happen in a classroom—it happens far beyond those walls. And it's only outside those walls that a more holistic process of leadership development is even possible.

FROM ICONIC LEADERS TO REAL MENTORS

Another common way that misguided protégés seek to prepare for ministry is through that iconic leadership figure in some far-off successful church or ministry. Protégés may have searched for ways to cultivate their skills but found no obvious path. So they begin to search elsewhere—like the megachurch pastor, charismatic leader, well-known nonprofit leader or prolific communicator. In a quest to fill their hunger for knowledge, they devour books, sermon podcasts, and attend any conferences they can (all of which *can be* an important part of development). And how can we blame them? Pursuing knowledge when a drive to learn strikes is commendable.

On the other hand, seeking development from masters of the trade who live nowhere nearby is remarkably similar to watching DVDs on how to take dance lessons. You could incessantly observe and study the flawless expert moves of a renowned dancer on a TV screen, but without someone training you in a non-virtual way, you will never come close to optimizing your maximum potential.

My father-in-law is an accomplished dancer, and I can attest to the difference between watching a video on how to dance and having my father-in-law actually stand next to me and walk me through the moves step by step. The difference is incomparable. And although I have no rhythm, he still can somehow help me avoid embarrassing myself on the dance floor—and that's nothing short of a miracle.

My point is simple. Being in relationship with a live personal mentor versus studying one from afar is the most significant way for a protégé to grow at the speed and depth necessary for them to reach their fullest potential. If protégés aren't under the close watch and care of a passionate, intentional, wise mentor, they'll always be one step behind. And, they may remain frustrated at their lack of ability and finesse in what they long to be great at, and what they yearn to accomplish through their leadership endeavors. I acknowledge that some people get very far in life and in ministry without ever having a mentor like this. However, I'm more convinced than ever that there are depths and nuances of a person that will never mature or become fully actualized without someone like this in their life.

So, how do protégés get one step ahead in a church culture that always seems to be one step behind? How do future ministry leaders become equipped to understand human nature through the eyes of God? How do these young but hungry leaders get set up to win, to excel and to do what the world so desperately needs the next generation of spiritual leaders to do—to lead the church into a better future that has a lasting, far-reaching and positive impact on society?

This quest begins when current leaders envision taking on the challenge to be not only masters of their trade, but to be mentors and coaches to the countless protégés around them. And if we're going to become the movement we long to be as the church, we must begin by raising up indigenous leaders rather than just looking outside our own backyards for people who are already where we want them to be. In the short-term, it may be easier to hire a ready-made leader from the outside; but in the long-term, we not only do a disservice to all the hungry protégés around us, but to the church's future. Her future will be shaped significantly by how we as leaders choose to engage the development process of the next generation of ministry leaders.

Any organism will thrive more under the care and nurture of its immediate environment than being transported into another one that may be manufactured to the point of perfection, yet remains unnatural and foreign. We as a living organism will serve ourselves best by nurturing our own environments and our own people, helping our little corner of the world thrive instead of die, influence rather than bow to outside influences, lead rather than just follow.

THE ORIGINS OF PROTÉGÉ

Along the way in my leadership journey, I wanted to do this very thing. I was serving as pastor at a church called Mosaic in Los Angeles. The lead pastor, Erwin McManus, had driven this conviction deeper within me—the need to raise up and develop those potential leaders within our community. He modeled this through his own way of leading and even in his approach to investing in me initially as a volunteer, and later as a staff member. The idea of *Protégé* was born from this conviction, as well as a place of gratitude for many who had invested in my life. And since I believed in the transforming power of the local church, I wanted to contribute to seeing her thrive in the future through the next generation of leaders.

I have personally received such incredible investment from more seasoned leaders and mavens who embody remarkable depth, giftedness, centeredness, vision, insight, as well as the truth and love of God. These have been women and men like Marty, Sheryl and Daniel, just to name a few. I wanted to pay it forward. In the same way the apostle Paul charged his protégé Timothy, I desired to pass on what had been given to me, entrusting it to reliable women and men to advance forward better prepared, formed, equipped and trained (2 Timothy

2:2). I had no idea how much this investment process would not only impact others' lives, but my own as well.

After dialoguing with Erwin about what it could look like to create a forum for developing young leaders both within our own church as well as beyond its walls, it took only a few months before we launched the Protégé Program at Mosaic in 2005. We set out to create a developmental experience for future ministry leaders, church planters, social entrepreneurs and ambitious spiritual catalysts. We began our prayerful search for women and men who were not only hungry for and ready to receive what we offered, but who had the gifting and talent potential to make a significant difference in the world.

We prayed that this program would provide young leaders with a different path of development—perhaps a more customized, personal and effective one than what we had seen. We wanted them to receive adequate skills training, intentional and personalized mentorship, a more diligent and individualized approach to spiritual transformation, as well as a holistic education that was rooted in a breadth and depth of theological understanding. Most importantly, we longed to create a place where protégés would experience the dynamics of true character transformation as the bedrock that would fuel their pursuit to become world-class, successful, morally and spiritually grounded kingdom leaders.

We yearned for this process to change the trajectory of these protégés' lives and ministries, to shift significant paradigms in their approaches to leadership and the local church, as well as open their hearts to a richer and deeper way of living life with Jesus. We wanted to do our part because we knew that the trajectory of the local church's health and effectiveness would be formed and transformed by who the next generation of ministry leaders became, and by how they decided to steward their gifts, talents, passions, relationships, character and abilities.

GOALS FOR THE NEXT GENERATION

One of our goals for the Protégé Program was to maximize intentionality and our focus in how we customized each individual's development process over two years—protégés were between twenty and thirty-five years of age. From a developmental perspective, we desired to accelerate their growth that otherwise might have taken a much longer time. We didn't try to force growth. However, we did strive to intentionally optimize the learning process, increase the intensity and continue to pay close attention to what God wanted to do in their lives. These were lofty goals but they were what God had set on our hearts to do.

Although I acknowledge that there are certain things that require life experience and time for certain aspects of growth to occur,[2] I'm convinced that we sell many growing church leaders short. I'm convinced that young leaders ought to be given more challenges to rise up to and more opportunities to step into as a significant part of their learning process. If lawyers can go through law school and med students can have residencies and fellowships that enable them to practice their disciplines as early as 27 or 28 years of age with professional excellence and effectiveness, why can't we train young leaders at that same level within the church to take on the daunting task of helping people navigate through the complex spiritual, psychological, relational and emotional issues of their lives? Perhaps our vision and faith are too small?

Along with these stated goals, the team that launched the Protégé Program also clarified what outcomes we desired. We created processes that we felt best facilitate those outcomes. This involved identifying the core areas of emphases that were critical for our developmental approach and philosophy.

From there, we decided to select twelve protégés annually, and invite them on a two-year experiment, I mean journey. Dozens applied each year, not only from here in the United States, but from around the globe—including Germany, Australia, Ireland, New Zealand, South Africa, and Canada. We partnered with Fuller Theological Seminary and Golden Gate Theological Seminary so each protégé could also receive an accredited master's degree in Global Leadership and Theology upon completion of the two-year protégé experience.

From our base in Los Angeles, the Protégé Program has made and continues to make a deep impact on many women and men who are aspiring to plant churches, lead spiritual communities and engage in social entrepreneurship. Although it wasn't our intention, at one point, more than forty percent of our staff at Mosaic had emerged from the

Protégé Program. In addition, we've now worked with a variety of churches to launch other Protégé Programs across the U.S. and Europe from a plethora of denominations and faith traditions.[3] Of course, the Protégé Program doesn't offer the perfect approach, as if that even exists, but I'm convinced that many of the developmental processes that we stumbled upon, experimented with and applied can play a significant role in the growth path of next generation leaders.

Personally, all this was a remarkable and unexpected adventure that expanded my perspective on what emerging spiritual leaders who want to bring change in the world need most for their development. I've watched dozens of protégés stumble, fall, walk and run as they've caught wind of what God was doing in their lives through this two-year developmental experience. Along the way, I've been given rare opportunities to observe critical core areas that need attention and development for emerging ministry leaders who are hungry to grow, who long to change and who desire to become true change agents. As the leader of the Protégé Program, I also stumbled and fell at times. It's never fun to learn the hard way. But in this case, I have the benefit of being able to pass on the successes that emerged from the failures, as well as the successes.

WHAT PROTÉGÉ OFFERS

Protégé describes what I believe to be the most critical growth arenas for future ministry leaders, including how we can better engage character development, foster emotional wholeness, build on biblical foundations, cultivate relational transformation, facilitate missional formation, increase communication effectiveness and raise up entrepreneurial leaders. For a generation that isn't interested in a standardized approach, this book covers various unconventional yet effective paths on how to mentor, train and coach others. I'll suggest ideas for sparking growth in protégés as well as new methods to enhance their spiritual formation. *Protégé* also instills a strong biblical framework to build on, which is foundational for all ministry leaders. If you're a mentor or leadership coach, you'll learn how to take people from a place of knowledge to experience, from learning to being, and from imitation to transformation.

Embedded in *Protégé* are practices that I've implemented and now want to pass on to you in hopes that you and many others will be propelled forward. We all face the daunting challenge to develop ourselves *and* to develop the next generation of leaders who will shape the future of the church. Improving our thinking, sharpening our theology, adapting our approach, changing our paradigms, and sometimes adjusting our methodology, can be exactly what we need to help catalyze the church into having greater impact on the culture in which it exists.

The local church is full of possibility. I believe in what it can become. I'm convinced that when the church gets it right (which starts with leadership) we can see God do the impossible through us to impact our world. I'm convinced that we can radically influence the culture in which we live—the church has done it before, and we can do it again. The hope of the church is to keep believing that we can make a real difference in our world. And most importantly, we've been entrusted to help usher more people into the kingdom of God and to see the kingdom of God bursting forth from the inside out.

The following pages will speak directly to both the protégé as well as the mentor—young and old, experienced and inexperienced. No matter what season of life and ministry you're in, you'll be challenged to take action as you learn or help others learn how to make the difference they feel called to make—and, how to become the kind of person that actually makes a difference. I won't offer a standardized approach to growth, but instead, a lens through which you can see the deficits that touch all of us and be moved to action to overcome them. After all, every one of us shares at least one thing in common—our humanity. And it is our humanity that can either project us into divine transformation or derail us into worldly darkness. Once these deficits are apparent, we can do something about them—*Protégé* addresses what we must do to change. With the help of one another and the power of God to reach our most broken places, every one of us can rise up to the level worthy of our callings. And as we begin this journey together, I say to you what the apostle Paul once said to another community of influencers: "I urge you to live a life worthy of the calling you have received" (Ephesians 4:1).

1 • Building Kingdom Cultures

I'M ALWAYS DRAWN TO INTERVIEWS where an actor who's been in the business for several years is asked what they would tell themselves twenty years ago. They're forced to look at some photo where they look a lot younger and way better (and a lot more naive). Then they have to come up with some profound answer on the spot as thousands watch them in a live interview. As uncomfortable as they may be, it offers a rare opportunity for reflection and honesty, and maybe even some wisdom for those watching.

Imagine that you had one chance to tell someone younger and less experienced what you would do differently in your life. What would you say? What would you tell yourself three years ago or five years ago, or even ten years ago? Would it be that you should have trusted God more, or that you should have valued people more, or that you should have lived with greater moral strength, or that you should have cared more for your family or for the poor or for the spiritually curious? The "should have" list could go on and on.

Some of the "should haves" are rooted in regret because you knew better. And some of them are simply due to naivety, lack of experience, or a deficit of guidance from wise and godly mentors. This is where the quest of a protégé originates.

Young leaders (both in age and in experience) throw themselves into the game of life with all the passion and raw talent in the world, and at times none of the personal development necessary to succeed in the right way, and for the long haul. On the other end of the spectrum, there are more experienced leaders who are pulled by a million important things soaking up their limited time and energy. They are gifted with competence and experience, yet often don't intentionally execute the responsibility to help teach, equip and guide those who are seeking to follow in their footsteps. We each have a rare opportunity to change the way we do things moving forward so we can look back on our lives in a whole different way.

As future ministry leaders, it is ultimately our personal responsibility to seek out a mentor(s) whom we respect and admire to coach or guide us. As more seasoned leaders, we are responsible to invite protégés to walk alongside us as we open our lives to them and share our insights, knowledge, wisdom and experience. We may not be able to look at that person we were years ago and tell them what to do differently. However, we can look at the people all around us who are in need of the invaluable lessons we've learned through the twists and turns God has brought us through thus far. We can share with them wisdom that could change their life trajectory and shape who they become.

We must remember that the mentoring process is not merely "information transfer" from one generation to the next, as if young leaders simply need to learn how the older leaders did it so they can repeat the same thing. Holistic leadership development is much more nuanced, and must be done with a much less standardized approach. In addition, the protégé learning process must be rooted in the context of the present culture and aligned with his or her unique personhood. And on the other side of things, young protégés must not fall prey to the mindset that previous generations have little to pass on to us because they just don't understand the new world in which we live, or they seem out of touch, or whatever other reasons we might have. There's a deeper, more multidimensional way of mentoring and being mentored that the church is in desperate need of if we desire to forge a new future together. That's what this book is about.

YOUR KINGDOM COME, YOUR WILL BE DONE . . .

At times, pastors can be quite blind to the realities in their own lives until they reach a breaking point and things start to fall apart. That's why we must learn to see things as they really are, and then ask God how he wants to change us into what we could be, as we learn to fight the temptation to be what everyone else thinks we should be.

If I were to step back, see with clarity and have the opportunity to tell myself five years ago what I should know, I'd start with what I see as the greatest enemies to the church's survival and what we as the next and future leaders of Christ's movement can and should do about it. My experiences and observations (as well as what research confirms) have revealed that four critical things that church leaders continually struggle with are burnout, moral failure, irrelevance to the surrounding culture and division within. I'm not normally one to emphasize the negative, but this is simply an honest assessment of some major ongoing deficits we have as a global spiritual community. Here's a snapshot of the research:

- 48% of all pastors will experience burnout or depression so severe that it will cause them to leave vocational ministry.[1]

- The 1,500 pastors who leave ministry each month is due to spiritual burnout, moral failure or contention in their churches.[2]

- Approximately 70% of people outside the church and between the ages of 16-29 consider the majority of Christians to be "out of touch with reality," "old fashioned," "boring" and "insensitive to others."[3]

- 80% of pastors say they have insufficient time with their spouse and that ministry has a negative effect on their family.[4]

I once heard someone say that it's so sad when someone dies before they ever really learn to live. I see a tragic parallel among church leaders. We have so much to give and so much to learn. We have so much life to live as a living, breathing organism created by God. However, death so often gets the church, or gets us, before life does. And people experience a dying church or a floundering pastor without ever experiencing a thriving one.

Death by burnout.
Death by moral failure.
Death by irrelevance.
Death by division.

The darkness of death shadows the radiance of life that is trying to break through the body of the church. I don't know about you, but I'm weary of seeing the same tired themes repeating themselves within the church. It seems almost inevitable that their death-stained tactics will continue to thrive in what should be a vibrant and healthy movement. Just read Genesis, then Exodus, and then keep on reading throughout the Bible. Sadly, you'll see that humanity is plagued with a self-inflicted disease of ingratitude and a denial of sin that hurts the movement of God over and over again. If it has been going on since Adam and Eve first tasted the forbidden delicacy of self-lordship, then who are we to think we can change anything, right?

The church is far from immune to the effects of sin. We hurt each other. We hurt ourselves. We hurt God. And we can't seem to stop. And if the story ended with this prognosis, it would be overwhelming and hopeless. Thankfully, the story doesn't end there.

Just as sin laces the pages of Scripture, so does another more powerful theme—*redemption*.

People meet God—*and they change.*

A person experiences grace—*and they extend it to others.*

A lost person encounters Jesus—*and they find their true identity for the first time.*

A woman ridden with self-hate feels the love of God wash over her entire being—*and she is finally free from the oppression of hatred.*

A man filled with greed is awe-struck by the generosity of his Savior—*and he gives all of his possessions away.*

A glory-hungry person catches a glimpse of the true source of glory—*and he gives his life away to serve others.*

A woman falls to her knees in shame—*and she receives forgiveness and freedom.*

Men, women and children have been experiencing the only thing that can overcome the strangling power of sin and death since the beginning of time. That is the life-giving power of salvation and redemption. The church is filled with these people. And God is determined to use them—*to use us.*

God has not given up on his church, and he has not given up on the world. Yes, we still hurt each other. But we also forgive one another. Yes, we still hurt ourselves. But now, we experience his grace. Yes, we still hurt God. But now, our growing love for him moves us to desperately want to stop.

Ministry leadership is always an uphill battle, a fight to the end. But, it's a fight that will ultimately be won. God has told us the end of the story. We must believe that we're part of his plan. We must join the prayer of Jesus and countless other saints who have prayed, "Your kingdom come. Your will be done, on earth as it is in heaven." Then, we must live out this prayer with action. That's our task as ministry leaders. That's our purpose. If we haven't been radically altered by this plea of the Son of God, then we aren't ready to be part of God's plan to change the world.

Dallas Willard offers a pertinent and relevant insight:

> So when Jesus directs us to pray, "Thy kingdom come," he does not mean we should pray for it to come into existence. Rather, we pray for it to take over all points in the personal, social, and political order where it is now excluded: "On earth as it is in heaven." With this prayer we are invoking it, as in fact we are acting it, into the real world of our daily existence.[5]

So how do we pray and act in a way that establishes *kingdom cultures*—environments that fly in the face of how humanity insists on doing things, where we are fueled by self-interest and complete unawareness of the sin that drives us toward death rather than life? How do we, as people and as ministry leaders who live the story of redemption, be what the Scriptures call the bride of Christ, and live in her full beauty and radiance? How do we as ministry leaders do the impossible, which is to reverse the power of death and its dark kingdom all around us?

ESTABLISHING KINGDOM CULTURES

Jesus Christ paints and embodies a beautiful picture of a kingdom culture in John 13:

> So [Jesus] got up from the meal, took off his outer clothing, and wrapped a towel around his waist. After that, he poured water into a basin and began to wash his disciples' feet, drying them with the towel that was wrapped around him. . . . "Now that I, your Lord and Teacher, have washed your feet, you also should wash one another's feet. I have set you an example that you should do as I have done for you." (John 13:4-5, 14-15)

Jesus declares, "I have set you an example that you should do as I have done for you." It wasn't just that Jesus "built" or "established" a kingdom culture; *he lived it first.* And living it is how he inaugurated it into existence. It can be the same for us.

There's hardly a more majestic image than when Jesus gets down on his knees and washes the feet of the disciples. There couldn't be a more revealing snapshot of what kingdom cultures look like in action. By this I don't just mean we should literally wash each other's feet. By this, I'm zeroing us in on the posture of Jesus' heart toward those he loves, and even one who he knows will betray him. Kingdom cultures are the opposite of what many leaders would imagine leadership to be, or what they actually desire to do with their leadership. Cultivating these kinds of environments is counterintuitive.

In our humanity, it seems our first instinct is almost always on the wrong track. When we should serve, we want to be served. When we should be looking out for others, our instinct is to look out for ourselves. When we should be giving, our desire is to take more. When we should be there when everything's falling apart, we want to run for the hills.

But there's this God who makes this gravitational pull that we have toward self very disturbing as he reveals its destructive nature. When we want to stand instead of bend a knee, we find ourselves alone and without meaning or purpose. When we want to command and control instead of serve and release, we often find ourselves less than compelled. However, when we allow God to change the natural course of our choices, to transform our very sinful nature, we begin to feel our knees weaken and, surprisingly, our faith strengthen. We throw the towel over our arm and say to God, "What next?" That's when he can begin to do his greatest work, changing the world through our lives through the cultures we pray for and participate in establishing in our world.

Protégés (as well as seasoned leaders) always need to be asking, "What next, God?" We're called to center our lives on the values where God centers his. That's counter to human nature. Here lies the great challenge of establishing kingdom cultures in our world and through our leadership. We need to align ourselves with what God calls good if we are to create good. We need to know what he's doing, or perhaps wants to do but simply needs a willing vessel.[6]

Seasoned leaders within the church need to recalibrate.

Emerging leaders need to calibrate.

As complex as faith is, and as many facets of God's truth that there are to discover, embodying the core values of Jesus' life here on earth is actually quite simple to understand. But as most of us know, they are much harder to live out. This book will guide us down a customized leadership development path that intends to draw us closer and closer toward this possibility becoming reality.

Although I focus on many integral areas in the two-year protégé experience, I'm unable to explore all of them in this book. For instance, although I strive to cultivate contexts for every protégé to receive a grounded theological education, I won't focus as extensively in this particular area, as many others have. In the Protégé Program, we put a heavy emphasis on the value of living a missional lifestyle of compassion, generosity and social justice, but we won't be able to go as deep on this topic as I'd like.

In this book we will, however, focus on five significant portals through which we as leaders can step if we want to establish and embody kingdom cultures in our life and leadership. In these spaces, we can invite God to stretch and mold us, as well as find tangible steps we can take to change the way we think, believe and ultimately lead. Broadly speaking, we will navigate through the everyday texture of our ministry lives by focusing on developing

1. character and spiritual depth

2. relational leadership

3. missional formation

4. transformative communication

5. entrepreneurial leadership

By zooming in on these five overarching themes, perhaps we'll catch the vision of what God is doing in the smallness of everyday moments.

Your kingdom come. Your will be done. On earth as it is in heaven.

IDEAS FOR MENTORS

Each of the following chapters will include a text box with ideas
that mentors can use to cultivate development among their
protégés. If you consider yourself a protégé and not yet a
mentor, you can still implement many of these ideas on your
own to help you foster personal development.

MENTOR TIPS

*Throughout the book, there will also be some quick tips I've
learned about mentoring others. These are more general applications rather than specific ones like those in the Ideas for
Mentors boxes. These tips don't necessarily directly correlate
with the chapter they follow.*

Character

FOUR DEADLY SINS OF EMERGING LEADERS

*We set young leaders up for a fall
if we encourage them to envision what they can do
before they consider the kind of person they should be.*

RUTH HALEY BARTON

*He who is noble plans noble things,
and on noble things he stands.*

ISAIAH 32:8 ESV

CHARACTER IS DOING THE RIGHT THING simply because it is the right thing to do, no matter the cost. That is the essence of true heroism and the defining mark of a Christ-centered leader. Unfortunately, character is not required to be an *effective* leader. Many leaders are remarkably successful while they choose not to engage the deeper and more critical quest for authentic character transformation.

On the other hand, character *is* what makes someone a leader worth following, and the church *is* in desperate need of ministry leaders who are worth following. When we choose to take a stand for what is right at the risk of losing what is perceived as more valuable to us, that's when we've become a leader worth following.

A character-driven leader is a leader who becomes *a person with something to say*. Their life compels others to listen because they embody heroic Christlike qualities. Ultimately, a hero understands that true character demands sacrifice of his or her own needs and desires for the sake of others. But in this heroic quest for character transformation, it is often unclear what it takes to actually see and experience character in our lives, not to mention what we must know in order to help others develop it in theirs. So, what does this look like and what can we do to spur this transformation process on in ourselves and in others?

STEAMED VEGGIES OR GARLIC MASHED POTATOES?

Most of us want to learn more about character like we want to order steamed vegetables with our dinner instead of butter-soaked, garlic-mashed potatoes. We know it's good for us. We know we want to fit in the same pants we wore in high school. And we know that it's going to be really hard to maintain. Let's run down the list of character-breaking agents: greed, envy, lust, deceit, selfishness, pride, bitterness, arrogance, addiction, hatred . . . just to name a few. If you're anything like me, varying degrees of these agents cycle through your spirit at full speed on a regular basis. They seem stronger than we are. The Scriptures tell us they wage war against our soul (1 Peter 2:11; Galatians 5:17). Even when we do beat them down, they wait just around the corners of our hearts, chomping at the bit for the next opportunity to worm their way in. Are you disheartened yet? You could blame me, but then you'd be exhibiting poor character. Life is tough, isn't it?

Now, allow me to hearten you. I remember watching the movie *Braveheart* for the first time. It was a little like falling in love. I can recall it more vividly than I remember my high school graduation ceremony. That's because my graduation was supposed to mean I was ready and prepared for life when all it really felt like was a long walk toward realizing how unprepared and confused I was about what life was supposed to be. Watching *Braveheart* felt like I was seeing what living life was really supposed to be about for the first time . . . sacrifice.

Braveheart is a story about a hero, William Wallace, who became one without even realizing it. Wallace inspired us, not because he set out to live a moral life, but because he felt compelled to fight for what was right, despite all the loss and pain and even horror it would bring. If you've seen the film, I know you remember that culminating moment when Wallace yells: "Freedom!" Who could forget that powerful scene?

That scene reminds us of a much more real, although invisible, freedom that we all long for. This is what the steamed veggie called character helps us find. It's almost as if God is playing the haunting bagpipes in the background, singing a more true and beautiful reality to our souls. We can hear it with our hearts. There is another way, a way that brings freedom rather than bondage, purity rather than profanity, a life calling rather than just a job, love rather than self-focus. This is the way of the hero.

If we attempt to be heroic in and of itself, we quickly lose heart, feeling the vacuum within us growing emptier with time. Sacrifice without intimately knowing the One we are sacrificing for is like dying in a war for a country we've never visited. We were practically built to give our blood, sweat and tears, but for *Someone* who has done the same for us—*actually, way more for us!*

There's no doubt that building character, and becoming heroic, requires great sacrifice. I'm convinced that it's worth every ounce of it because of the Savior we follow, know and trust. We must always remember not only the *who* we are becoming, but the *why* we are becoming.

Ultimately, we engage in this character-defining journey for two primal reasons: to grow more intimately connected to our Creator and to become more like him in essence as we travel through life. As we become rooted and transformed in our character, our lives will certainly produce remarkable results for us personally, and we'll no doubt become an inspiration and blessing to others. However, as ministry leaders, we must remember that it's not the results of ministry that we seek first and foremost. It is a life-changing, eternity-altering relationship with a freeing Savior that we're after. Ministry leaders, let's be the last people to lose sight of this.

Each time we surrender our personhood and choices to God, we draw a little bit nearer to him. And as we draw closer to him, he draws closer to us (James 4:8). This happens not only because he offers unconditional love, but because it reflects our spirit of surrender to him. When we live in daily surrender to Christ, God doesn't then take us captive. He redeems yet another part of who we are. As a result, we're able to be that much more intimately connected to him. This is the origin of the deeper journey that every protégé needs to embrace and embody if they are to lead the church into a new and better future. How do those steamed veggies sound now?

FOUR DEADLY SINS

I am convinced of four clear paths that can guide us toward becoming the kind of human being and leader we long to become—these paths will lead us to real freedom and true heroism. In the next four chapters, we'll explore four critical temptations that emerging church leaders face and we'll clarify how to engage the character-transformation quest to overcome them. These temptations are what I refer to as *The Four Deadly Sins of Emerging Leaders*.

Each of these four sins wages war against our character, and ultimately, against the sacrifices we must make to become leaders worth following, leaders with something to say. These sins can quickly derail us from our most noble pursuits. And when not dealt with, they will eventually diminish our influence and at times even cause us to leave ministry. When we fail to overcome these temptations, we fail to become the ministry leaders that God designed us to be. The challenges of this journey lie at the heart of true spiritual leadership, and they can have an unprecedented effect (for good or bad) on the future impact of the church on culture and society. I've seen these sins derail far too many leaders whom I know personally, and others I've observed from afar. However, I've also seen the power, freedom and impact of ministry leaders who have succeeded in overcoming them, as they became people of true Christlike character.

The four deadly sins of emerging leaders are:
1. The Sin of Imitation: *Envy*
2. The Sin of Performance: *Self-Reliance*
3. The Sin of Overconfidence: *Foolishness*
4. The Sin of Entitlement: *Greed*

2 • The Sin of Imitation

ENVY

ENVY IS NOT ONLY A DEADLY SIN, but probably one of the most uncomfortable sins, especially for emerging leaders as they're striving to distinguish themselves from everyone else. It's the lowest on the food chain . . . weak, needy, insecure. We tend to feel more comfortable sharing our struggles with "greed" or "selfishness" or even "arrogance." At least these traits emulate an air of "power" or "too much strength." Ever heard someone say, "He's a strong person"? And in reality, they're the most greedy, narcissistic, egotistical person you know?

In contrast, the characteristic of envy emulates an air of awkward jealousy, and worst of all . . . insecurity. Kind of like that kid in seventh grade who carefully observes the cool kid, trying to capture what makes him so much more likable and awkwardly imitate him. Instead of being more drawn to the imitator, one only feels more repelled by his poor attempt to be someone else rather than himself. It's hard to watch. It's even harder to live it.

Envy usually begins with caring too much about what the world and other people in your life find glamorous and interesting and sparkly. People are, undeniably, far too easily shunned or ignored simply because of external packaging. No one wants to learn from a boring teacher. No one wants to follow a passionless leader. No one wants to buy cologne from a smelly person.

If we are to spread our message and lead others with strength, we have to envelop ourselves with a kind of beauty that matches our worth within. In other words, we cannot completely ignore the importance of how we present ourselves, or how we develop our communication skills, or how we work on becoming more engaging to the world around us. It is essential to do all these things to some degree. However, we must not confuse personal development with imitation development. Far too often, I've seen the temptation to imitate derail young protégés as fast as any other deadly sin. And, it's perhaps the easiest temptation to rationalize in the name of "development."

IMITATION DEVELOPMENT

Personal development involves bringing who we are before God, and before those we trust and respect, and saying, "Here I am. Take me and mold me. Grow me. Expand my impact through the person I'm becoming." Notice the key word here is *me*. I think what we often do instead is imitation development, where we say, often without realizing it, "Here I am. I give you my essence to be reshaped into someone else's. Mold me into Mr. or Mrs. So-and-So (a.k.a., some leader we admire and want to emulate). You know, the guy who is everything I want to be but can never measure up to, the one who turns everything he touches into gold. Can you help me to be me, but really be more like him?"

Those words never leave your mouth, of course. But you'll find your silent prayers in the discontentment you feel when you're around someone more talented than you, more successful, more confident. You'll hear your desperate pleas to be someone other than you in your disappointment with yourself, with your constant attention to your weaknesses, your restlessness with your limited capacity and frustration with your failures. There is little room for mercy in your mental courtroom; you throw the gavel down on all the ways you are responsible for not measuring up to whatever the world defines as successful. What makes the jury especially fired up are the countless examples of other people who seem to make it all look so easy while you, let's face it, make it all look so hard.

Instead of owning the ugliness of our envy, we often busy ourselves with much more important work—imitating those who have what we want or are what we want to be. This strategy seems much more effective, giving us a sense of control over our helpless and paralyzing feelings of jealousy. Isn't it always better to first try it our way? Might as well give it our best shot first before bothering God with such petty things. In the process, we end up abandoning ourselves.

I believe this is one of the deadliest sins for emerging leaders because it is so unbelievably common and so incredibly easy to rationalize. Plus, we allow it to exist in the name of growth or learning from others, and don't realize the damaging effects of this sin.

Envy is a sin that affects every person at every stage of life, but it strikes particularly hard with ambitious and aspiring leaders when they're in early adulthood. As we enter our twenties, many of us emerge with unbridled passion to change the world, to make a difference, to be the one who rallies the troops and envisions the blind. It is an almost universal marker of youth . . . passion to fix what is broken and change the future. Women and men who see with clarity that the only way to do this is to join the movement of Jesus Christ are to be admired and affirmed. It is a narrow but beautiful path. Few plunge into it. And then sadly, many become quickly derailed by the deadly sin of imitation.

AN ACHING DISSATISFACTION

Young protégés in the church don't take long to spot the iconic figure of success as they define it in their own spheres of life and ministry. They may find this person close by, like behind the pulpit of their own church. Or they may find them further in the distance, like the dynamic, charismatic leader who seems to breathe magic into the air when they speak. It could even be a peer who has the career position that we desire, who gains stride with every step while we barely keep up.

At the core, envy is really an aching dissatisfaction with who we are, or who we are not. It breeds a way of life that involves constantly comparing ourselves with others and quantifying our successes and failures against our own self-worth. It is actually no way of life at all. This sin leads to a slow death.

Several years ago, I had been on staff for a couple years at a church when our lead pastor pulled more than twenty young leaders into a room—women and men, all under forty years old. We were kind of nervous because it seemed like we might all be in trouble—why else would he select a specific group of people that he *"needed to talk to"*? To our surprise, we all sat there as he shared his vision to move from being a *community of one voice* to a *community of voices*. In other words, he knew our community had become overly dependent on his preaching, and he wanted that to change. Not only that, but he had a growing passion to develop what he called "the next generation of world-class communicators."

He challenged each of us: "Prepare to give the best sermon you've ever preached and be ready to give it this summer. You're all going to get your chance to be on our speaking team. However, I can only bring four or five of you onto our team. I'm going to evaluate you as you speak to determine who that will be."

If you didn't guess it already, this quickly evoked competitive impulses. I'm not saying competitiveness was the right or best response, but how can you escape it in this context from a human standpoint? Our hearts were racing. Our palms were sweating. We all sort of looked at each other with much angst and awkwardness.

Personally, anxiety over the desire to stand out wreaked havoc within me. I became almost immediately aware of my deficit of character. I wish I could say that I was more concerned with sharing God's message and pleasing him than I was with wanting to do well in the eyes of others. I wish I had been confident enough in who God designed me to be rather than insecure as my abilities were held up against others.

I'd like to say that when I heard another person give a homerun sermon, I always celebrated them. But I didn't. I'd like to say that I refused to silently gloat when someone didn't do well. But I didn't. I'd like to say that when one of my best of friends did an incredible job where God used him in a supernatural way, I rooted for him without hesitation. But I didn't. I'd like to say I just sought to be myself and do my best and trust God to let the chips fall where they may. But I didn't. In fact, I actually found myself trying to be more like our pastor than being myself . . . and that wasn't the first time I had done this. That's a very small snapshot of the envy that resides in my heart, the envy that wins out far more than I'm comfortable sharing.

This whole experience surfaced an immense amount of ugliness in my heart—an ugliness that I'm convinced many young (and old) leaders rarely face with honesty and courage. Though a part of me didn't want to face it, I knew I had to look in the mirror and deal with my deep-rooted envy. I remember at one point feeling anger toward one of the speakers because he did so well. I remember feeling like my soul was being deflated, even dying a little. I also remember, after giving my talk that summer, a little heckler's voice inside that was taunting me and shaming me, telling me how badly I did, and how I wasn't going to make the cut, and that I didn't have what it took. I remember how strong my desire was to impress our pastor more than it was to please God . . . by far.

FACING THE UGLINESS OF ENVY

I hated that all of this was so real and raw inside of me. My spiritual immaturity had been exposed. But in light of all that, it was a critical growth moment for me in my journey as a spiritual leader. I began to recognize and face my issue of envy that ran much deeper and involved much more complexity than I'd originally thought.

As I invited God's Spirit to do a deeper work in me, I began to experience a renewed sense of freedom from wanting to be better than, and do better than, others as my primary motivation. I began to realize how ugly envy can be when it resides in our hearts, and how messed up we can become when we don't seek to unravel it, deal with it and face it head on.

My tendency to measure myself against others rather than embracing who God has made me to be was stronger, more intense and more difficult to manage than I thought it would be. But as the Scriptures guide us to "put on" certain Christlike characteristics, they also guide us to "put off" other traits that steer us away from Christlikeness (see Ephesians 4:24-25).

Each time we measure ourselves against someone else, we remove the power of God's opinion of us and replace it with humans' opinion. Scary isn't it? The internal courtroom quickly fills up with human faces painted with eternal frowns and unfeeling judges who sentence us to deep unhappiness with who we are. The voice of the critic inside our soul speaks against our true self, shreds our sense of worth, and heckles and distracts us from hearing God's divine whisper. The critic's voice that tells us all the ways we don't measure up is strong, seductive, deafening and powerful. I don't know about you, but that reality makes me unspeakably sad.

Whenever we seek to please others above God, we automatically relinquish the indescribable value God sees in us and gives to us through his approval, acceptance and love. We inevitably begin to imitate humans rather than God in an effort to quiet that relentless dissatisfaction with ourselves, paving a crooked path toward poor imitation rather than perfect originality as designed by our Creator.

FROM IMITATION TO ORIGINALITY

We must make this right in our own lives, then help those coming after us make it right too. If we don't, we will pass the baton to leaders who are spending all their time trying to be like someone else rather than becoming the person God designed them to be. If we ignore this subtle yet toxic disease of envy within humanity, we will inadvertently pour fuel on the internal flames of low self-worth and insecurity in the next generation of ministry leadership. This erodes churches from within. Sadly, most of the time it goes unnoticed as sin. Or at best, it gets noticed but not dealt with at the deeper level.

Instead of reinforcing the false message that success is defined by some elusive and removed figure, let us drive home the truth that "success" is defined by God. He is most pleased with us when we are most centered in him. This is where faith comes in (Hebrews 11:6). Then, God can do his greatest work, which is to make you the most *you* that *you* can be, the original masterpiece designed by the most gifted and brilliant Artist. The more we try to color in our spaces, the more we look like a kindergartner designed us. Envy drives us to take over who we are becoming—and we always, always mess up.

If the sin of imitation is rooted in envy, the antithesis is originality. Originality may just seem like a hip word, but it's more than that. It's intended to be the way we live, the way we surrender who we are and the unique way we've been wired to God so that he can continue his faithful work in completing us (Philippians 1:6). The origin of who we are is inseparably linked to the origin of who God is (Genesis 1:26-27). And the originality we crave is inseparably linked to the Original himself.

If we look to others for our originality, we will hit dead end after dead end. One of our first steps in this journey away from imitation toward originality is identifying who the people are we're trying to be like, and exploring through self-reflection why we want what they have or why we want to be more like them. We must explore this path of discovery to find the root of our envy.

There is a deeply eternal and spiritual longing in humanity to discover our unique and original self, and then to live in the freedom that this discovery brings. We ourselves do not create this uniqueness; rather we embark on a process of discovery, which is a gift from God. So how do we defeat the sin of imitation and live in the freedom of who we are, defined by the Origin of the original? It always begins with the question of what we are rooted in.

ROOTED

Do we embrace the fact that we were handcrafted by God in a certain way, with our design only fully realized when we surrender to him to continue molding and shaping us, or do we have our own ideas of who we think should be molding us? Are we identified by who we are in Christ, or are we defined by someone else's definition of success?

As young leaders, if we're ever going to be the original version of ourselves, we must stop fighting the parts of our truest selves that we wish were different. This is rooted in ingratitude and distrust in God. Instead, we need to embrace all of who we truly are with ever increasing gratitude and trust in God's work in and through us. If we don't learn to appreciate even the undesirable elements of ourselves (as we perceive them to be), we inadvertently displease the One who created us. We may even diminish the image of God in us. This is the journey to become fully human once again.

Sure, there are things about ourselves that we must bring before God to change, but most of us don't embrace the totality of our humanity in all its goodness and brokenness. As a result, we never fully grasp the power of how God sees us, knows us and how he desires to use us. God's heart is tender toward us . . . *every part of us*. Why don't we seek to have that same tenderness toward ourselves? And if we don't experience this same tenderness inside, how are we going to pass this on to others?

Let me make a distinction. If there are parts of yourself that are undesirable because they are sinful, then with God's help, you must continue to invite God to change those characteristics. In other words, if your struggle with yourself is related to bitterness or hatred, then you're responsible to rid yourself of that. Change is essential in your journey toward wholeness in Christ. But if your dissatisfaction is related to personality traits, or a talent you don't have, or a lower competence than someone else, or physical beauty or any number of insecurities, then it's time to let the internal disappointment and struggle fly away like a freed bird from its cage and never let it come back. Of course, it will try to come back. But just send it away again . . . and again . . . and again—by surrendering it to Christ. Learning to be deeply grateful for who you are is one of the most spiritually mature postures one can have. Eventually, your restless, insecure bird will visit you less and less. In the end, it will define you less and less.

Emerging leaders must lead the charge in living aware of our envy, and our desire to imitate, so that we can offer it up through daily trust and surrender to Jesus. As uncomfortable as it can be, seeing envy for what it is is the only way to surrender it to God and simply say to him, "Help me give this to you, and cover me with the absolute acceptance I have in you so that I can finally accept myself." Wouldn't that be a beautiful daily prayer that could fuel change in your character and essence?

LIVING AN ORIGINAL LIFE

Prayer is a nonnegotiable pathway that helps us learn to be our original selves, because through prayer we commune with the Original. We must trust Christ's ability to work deeply in us at his pace and in his way. Prayer is a spiritual portal through which this can happen. God isn't in a hurry, but he eagerly anticipates that you open your life to him so deeper transformation can happen. He longs to restore the originality, of which the raw material already resides in us, created by him, but remains hidden and undiscovered by us. This is the journey to become fully human once again.

Being original ought never to be about being cool or edgy or hip. It's about being grateful for how this God we believe in is perfect, that he made us and that he's committed to continuing to transform us into our most original, image-bearing selves. When we're our most original self, we become our most human self. Being original is about embracing God's design and rejecting the inflated importance of the world's design. It is about admitting that we aren't perfect and are never going to be, and that has to be okay. After all, that's what it means to be human. The quest toward originality and the fight against envy revolve around discovering a way of living where we learn to be comfortable in our own skin, grateful for exactly who we are, and where we remain rooted in Christ through introspection and prayer. This journey is about allowing the artistic and holy hands of God to mold his masterpiece as he sees fit. And maybe, just maybe, we will then have the eyes to see how absolutely beautiful that is.

> To be nobody-but-yourself—in a world which is doing its best, night and day, to make you everybody else—means to fight the hardest battle which any human being can fight; and never stop fighting.
> (e.e. cummings)

IDEAS FOR MENTORS

1. **Combat envy with celebration.** In your one-on-one time with a protégé who struggles with the sin of imitation, prompt or guide them to identify one person of whom he or she gets envious. Ask them to think of possible ways to celebrate that person's successes (i.e., share affirming words, express admiration of their work ethic/talents/success/etc.). Celebration can be a spiritual discipline that combats our envious tendency.

   Identify uniqueness. Help the person you're mentoring to discover what is unique about him- or herself and how it contributes to serving Christ in ways that no one else could. I suggest using a tool(s) of some kind to spark the conversation. You could walk them through the Gallup Strengths Finder Assessment (the book *Strengths-Based Leadership* includes a code for taking the assessment; visit Strengths.

gallup.com for more info). I also use the PRO-D, the Birkman method, the Myers-Briggs Type Indicator and the DISC profile quite often. As protégés discover their gifts, help them to see how these unique qualities and talents are playing out in their lives and ministry areas. Envy has more room to grow when we focus on wanting other people's talents rather than paying attention to the mystically unique way God has designed us.

2. **Leverage content.** To help a protégé go deeper on this journey of becoming his/her true and original self, read through a related book and discuss its content. Two core books I use are (a) *The Gift of Being Yourself* by David Benner—his insight into the "false self" versus the "true self" is brilliant—and (b) *The Me I Want to Be* by John Ortberg. He clarifies how we can become the best version of ourselves—what he calls You 2.0.

3. **Encourage surrender.** Have your protégé meditate on this Scripture: Romans 9:20-21. Praying through this truth will play a critical role in surrendering to the way God wants to use us, rather than trying to assert our personal preferences into his ultimate purpose. There is a sweetness that comes with surrendering our plans and purposes so we allow God to use us as he chooses. Whenever your protégé finds himself/herself struggling with envy, encourage him/her to recall this scripture, thank God for being aware of the jealousy and pray for his help. This will offer real help in real time.

4. **Superhero awards.** At certain times throughout the year, I make it a priority to affirm protégés publically. One way I have done this involves buying superhero action figures and giving them to protégés as an "award." I find a superhero whose powers remind me of the unique gifts and talents of a particular person, giving me an opportunity to affirm their individuality. This helps generate a kingdom culture of celebrating uniqueness.

MENTOR TIP:
SET CUSTOMIZED STRETCH GOALS

Help protégés set stretch goals. *For example, someone once asked me if I could help him improve in building and sustaining teams. When I met with him, I asked him to give me his perspective on what a good team-builder does. I wrote down what he said. Then, I asked him to rate himself on a scale of 1 to 5 in each specific area of team-building. I leveraged his own self-assessment as I explained where I thought he needed to grow, and together we set goals that would stretch him in his team-building skills. We revisited these goals in the coming weeks and continued to set more* stretch goals *as time went on.*

3 • The Sin of Performance

SELF-RELIANCE

MY WIFE, CHERI, IS FREAKISHLY SCARED OF WATER. Not the water that comes from a faucet, safely flowing in a slow stream. More like the water that's full of all sorts of scary-looking fish and plants. She's not one of those people who feels *one with the water*. She believes we humans should respect the deep blue sea and leave it alone. Her opinion is that if God wanted us to swim in the sea, he would've given us fins.

Cheri's fear is partially rooted in a movie she saw as a kid that she thinks should've been rated NC-17. It was about a shark that would squint his small eyes and swim around looking for human legs hanging in the ocean, in hopes of biting them off. Why our parents allowed us to see the movie *Jaws,* we'll never really know. Maybe they thought we needed a good scare before bed? I'm not sure. But what I do know is that this particular film forever marred Cheri's ability to swim without fear. At a young age, she was even just as afraid in little artificial lakes as she was in oceans. She just couldn't shake that image of her legs dangling under the water while Jaws, with his pointy teeth, lunged toward her. Being an adult hasn't really changed anything—she still has issues.

One time I wanted her to ride a WaveRunner with me at her family's summer cottage. Since it involved water, I knew she wouldn't do it. However, because we were newly dating, I thought she might be a bit more willing to do what she'd never do in her right, uninfatuated mind. On top of that, I knew if I were persistent, she'd probably cave in—and she did.

I found her fear of the water quite humorous. And like any good boyfriend, I wanted to make her hate me (in a flirting kind of way). I assured her that I would drive slowly and safely with her on the back, but the meaning of that promise was up for interpretation. Truth is, I hurled her around like a rag doll, which felt like a bucking bronco to her. Just as she'd look down at the water in fear, I'd turn a 180 or a 360, propelling her body into the air. I promised she wouldn't fall in. I broke that promise.

As she was thrown into the water, and her life flashed before her eyes, she probably made a mental note to leave me out of her romantic future. She later laughed at how silly she felt when she realized the water was only three-and-a-half feet deep, and that she could stand up. There were no dangling legs, no squinty-eyed sharks and no plants sharp enough to cut off her big toe. Not only was the water not scary anymore, it wasn't even interesting. She was expecting a little more shock and awe, something to really surprise her and validate her fear. But all she found was shallow water.

THE DISGUISE OF EXTERNAL SUCCESS

When it comes to the spiritual realm, we're often more fearful about exploring the spiritual depths than we are excited. Sure, it's great to go deep now and then, but we weren't meant to actually live there, right? After all, if we were, wouldn't we have "spiritual fins" so that we could survive the unfamiliar surroundings as well as thrive in an environment full of truth and life?

We often feel unequipped, afraid or overwhelmed when it comes to living deeply with God. So we swim around in the shallow waters, only to find that when we stand up we are barely touching the depths God has for us. It may appear vast on the surface, but underneath it is only two inches deep.

Kingdom-minded leaders are called to not only live a full and rich spiritual life themselves, but to cultivate a culture of spiritual depth for those entrusted to them. Jesus offers insight into cultivating this kind of kingdom culture:

> Abide in Me, and I in you. As the branch cannot bear fruit of itself, unless it abides in the vine, neither can you, unless you abide in Me. I am the vine, you are the branches. He who abides in Me, and I in him, bears much fruit; for without Me you can do nothing. . . .
>
> As the Father loved Me, I also have loved you; abide in My love. (John 15:4-5, 9 NKJV)

Jesus paints a clear picture here of how we are to live life with God and the life we can invite others into if they want to experience authentic spiritual and character transformation. To "abide" literally means to "stay at or with" (in this case, Jesus), or to "continue in" or "remain in."

Jesus also reveals the consequences of not living this way: You are "like a branch that is thrown away and withers" (John 15:6). If we want to embark on creating a kingdom culture of character transformation, we ourselves must be rooted in the One who has envisioned what a life of transformation looks like. *We'll never see God-honoring fruit produced in our lives if we are not abiding in Jesus.* We may see external success and growth, but never the true fruit of the Spirit.

THE PRODUCTIVITY MINDSET

There's a mindset among Christ followers and church leaders everywhere that pushes up against this idea. It's the mindset of *productivity.* This mindset has deeply influenced the way we live our spiritual lives as well as the way we lead our ministries and churches. It is one of the most pervasive values embedded in how we work. It cleverly moves into every fabric of our thinking, believing and being. This mindset involves believing that success will be the direct result of our own work ethic, planning and competence. If we articulate a clear goal, craft a solid plan that has measurable milestones and diligently execute on all the deliverables, we will essentially guarantee our success. This is how the marketplace gets the job done, meets the bottom line and operates daily.

In ministry leadership specifically, productivity is characterized by a conviction that if we have all the right pieces to what makes up a successful ministry, and if we assemble them in the right way with the right amount of diligence and strategy, we'll produce the results and growth we desire. And we almost always assume this is what God desires. Do it the right way, do what you're supposed to do, and your ministry will inevitably grow into what you (and God) want it to be. In essence, we're the producers who determine our ministry's growth. When our primary goal becomes performing and producing rather than abiding and being, we commit the *sin of performance.*

This productivity mindset is fueled by the concept of self-determinism, that we create our own destiny. We have the power within us to be as successful as we want to be and produce the results that we want to produce. We are the determiners, releasing our human potential and activating our dreams through human effort. We think our success (or failure) in life, ministry and spirituality depends almost entirely on ourselves.

Although a productivity mindset isn't inherently negative, when it gets out of alignment, we miss what's most important when it comes to growing our ministry and even our own lives—that is, fruitfulness. Authentic, God-honoring fruitfulness happens when we as ministry leaders make abiding in the Vine our first priority.

MORE LIKE A FARMER

Emerging ministry leaders need to adjust their mindset about what it means to "produce." Consider the mindset of a farmer. Do you know that farmers don't actually make anything? They aren't the ones who produce the avocado or banana. That's not *their* job. Instead, farmers cultivate environments where life has the possibility to grow. They partner with the powers of nature (water, sun, soil, etc.) to prepare a place for seeds to germinate and grow. Of course they do their part in planning and working hard, but ultimately the results of growth (bearing the fruit) are not in their control.

When it comes to bearing fruit in our ministries, we certainly have a role in growth. However we must not forget that we aren't the ones who produce the fruit. While a productivity approach can manufacture a wide variety of things that look like growth, or even are some form of growth, it rarely yields the deepest kind of authentic transformation that's rooted in the way of the kingdom. In fact, if we have external success due to our productivity, we often instinctively think it's of God, which can be dangerous. If productivity is the primary thing that drives us, we're inevitably setting ourselves up to be frustrated when all our best efforts don't produce exactly what we want.

I've observed so many twentysomething leaders who get so focused on what they themselves can produce because they're trying to prove themselves, or prove their worth. They cannot separate their value from how they think their production is perceived or received. This sets them up to come crashing down when things don't go exactly like they hope. Imagine how the future of the church would be affected if emerging leaders shifted their primary focus from results produced by human effort, and instead sought after the focus that God invites them to have when it comes to productivity, or "fruit-bearing."

I'm an extremely driven and active person, and productivity, without question, appeals to me. On the one hand, striving to be productive is a very good thing; it just should never be the main thing. At times, I've too closely associated productivity with activity. I used to think the idea of fruitfulness was passive in nature—many others feel the same. Not true. The distinction I've learned to make isn't about the kind of effort we should or shouldn't give. It's about focus and emphasis. It's about keeping our mindset and approach centered on the ultimate prize. And that's much easier said than done.

Being a fruitful ministry leader involves the diligent work of cultivating an interior environment where the mystery of God's Spirit is welcomed to grow in you, speak to you, change you and lead you. This is the quiet and sometimes solo journey of character transformation. But when this is the essence of a leader, everything changes—our perspective, our focus, our emphasis, and without question our approach to productivity and fruitfulness. Not only that, but we're reminded that God is the One who deserves the credit for fruit bearing, not us. We learn to stop seeking the spotlight and to quiet the seductive pull to have our egos stroked by how much we ourselves accomplish. We learn how to minimize our self-obsessions and recalibrate our own pride. We posture ourselves to stay on track, to stay centered in engaging the depths with Jesus Christ, and ultimately to grow in Christlike character. Life and ministry become less about our accomplishments and more about what God is doing.

THE ROTTING TREE

When I read John 15, I imagine a large tree that's rotting from the inside and no longer growing. One trap that next-generation ministry leaders fall into involves allowing our insides to rot because we aren't truly abiding in the Vine. We get swept up into all the distractions and activity around us and lose sight of what it means to abide. We drift from of our once established priority of staying continually connected to God's presence.

When we notice that we're not producing fruit as we desire, it's as if we start frantically running around, attaching fruit to our branches with scotch tape. We focus on appearances and become consumed with producing for others. We zero in on what things look like on the surface, rather than what's really going on underneath. Often, we aren't even aware of what's going on in the depths of us. We're rotting and don't even know it. Jesus is essentially saying, "Stop taping fruit to your branches and start connecting yourself to me; until you're rooted in my love, you'll be frantically keeping up appearances and dying on the inside all the while."

I've been painfully reminded of the effects of a life detached from the source of life. A friend of mine was a highly successful pastor, which was especially impressive due to his relatively young age. By *successful* I mean that he was an extremely dynamic communicator and visionary leader, highly sought after by other ministry leaders, and the numbers at his church had been increasing steadily for the last few years. I watched him as he glided effortlessly through complex leadership questions from others, as he preached with gravitas and with a commanding presence, and as he so beautifully cast vision about what the church could and should be. He's the kind of guy who at times I have even struggled to root for in my human depravity because he makes it all look so easy. But he's so likeable. Everyone who knows him would affirm his charm, charisma and pastoral heart.

Unfortunately, his strategy of taping fruit to the branches was exposed. It came out that he's been having multiple affairs, living a double life. He left his family and ministry in the wreckage of his sin. When we hear stories like this, we sit there scratching our heads, wondering how it could come to this. Why would someone who seems to be thriving in his life calling ever choose to throw it all away? Why can't we separate the illusion of external success from the reality of internal success? There are disastrous results that stem from this false kind of thinking and living. And ignoring the roots of our spiritual life will not only lead to personal and moral failure, but will also damage our role in God's purpose as leaders called to infiltrate this dying world with the undying love and presence of Christ. And once again, we're forced to watch the theme of moral failure replay in the church as a result of leaders who focused on producing more than abiding.

Abiding in the Vine is core to building a kingdom culture of spiritual depth and character transformation. This is where true internal change really happens. The Scriptures demand that the "fruit" of our lives and ministries flow from the inside out. We must demand no less of ourselves. No one needs a leader who is externally successful but remains detached or rotten inside.

ATTACHMENT ISSUES

Abiding involves attaching ourselves to him in all things. By abiding, we're inviting his life to flow in and through us. The temptation of every human being is to attach themselves to earthly things rather than heavenly things in order to find the life and meaning they're searching for. Every time we attach the deepest part of ourselves to *anything* but God, we cease to abide in him. This is a human problem rooted in our sinful nature. All must face this great dilemma.

This dynamic of attaching ourselves to the wrong things runs deep. It intersects the life of *every* ministry leader. Many ministry leaders whom I've interacted with on a deeper personal level aren't keenly aware of how these kinds of issues affect their lives, their ministries and even their emotional well-being. As a result, these leaders end up attaching themselves (unknowingly) to the wrong things.

The journey of abiding is more complicated than it may first appear. As leaders, we must realize that one of the greatest enemies to abiding in Christ is buying into the lie that we already are. We can easily mistake light bulbs for the sun if all we're doing is looking for some version of light. But they are altogether different. We might find a false sense of life and meaning through indulging in the sin of performance. Perhaps we're even addicted to performance. If we fail to face this issue, we neglect the deeper walk with Christ necessary for true spiritual leadership. In an effort to create a kingdom culture of spiritual depth and character transformation, we can offer this powerful gift of abiding at the deepest level to those we serve.

THE ROLE OF IDENTITY FORMATION

One of the most fascinating frameworks established in psychology is Erik Erikson's stages of psychosocial development. He determined that there are eight defining stages where we encounter life-changing dynamics, and end up being defined by one of two characteristics. For example, the first stage we embark on begins with birth and lasts through eighteen months of age. He categorizes this stage as *trust vs. mistrust*. It's quite simple. If our parents (or caregivers) provide reliability, care and affection, we end up being defined by our ability to trust. If these fundamental needs are not attended to, we end up falling in the mistrust camp. Make sense?

The stage of development that always interested me most takes place in adolescence, between the ages of twelve and eighteen. This stage is called *identity vs. role confusion*. It's about our need to develop a sense of self and personal identity. Success leads to an ability to stay true to ourselves, while failure leads to role confusion and a weak sense of self.

The thing about this stage is that the need for identity doesn't end at a certain age. It lasts a lifetime. Interestingly enough, Erik Erikson changed his last name to Erikson when he became an American citizen. He did so to define himself as a self-made man, Erik, son of Erik. He was essentially saying, "I created myself." His search for identity seemed to be monumental in his life, and the answer to that search, he thought, lay within himself.

I agree with Erikson that if we're successful on our search for identity, we will achieve that enviable state of staying true to ourselves. If we fail, we will sink into that despairing state where we are confused and maintain a weak sense of self.

Humanity seems to continually wrestle with who and what we find our identity in (perhaps this is one reason why the words to "Amazing Grace" are famous to this day: "I was lost, but now I'm found"). Although many of us know on a cognitive level that our deepest sense of personhood is found in God, we continue searching for who we really are and what makes us matter. This is a critical issue that emerging church leaders must be equipped to navigate through in their lives as well as in others' lives.

One particular protégé in our Protégé Program embodied this search for identity. Jared was young, talented, charismatic and eager—one of those guys who can snap you out of your daze simply by talking to him. I couldn't help but allow his passion to inspire my own.

At first glance, it might appear that he didn't struggle with identity because he seemed to have a strong grasp on who he was and where he was going. Guys like Jared seem like they don't need anyone to help them feel found because they think they already are. He charged ahead right out of the gate when beginning the Protégé Program. He was everywhere and knew everyone. He quickly gauged the ministries with the most buzz around them and dove in. Jared was confident that he'd be the cause for momentum and growth in the ministries that he served. What happened along the way surprised me not only on an external level but also on an internal one.

To put it bluntly, Jared didn't succeed at any endeavor he put his mind to, at least not on a visible level. Other protégés who didn't even have as much natural talent and gifting, and who began more slowly, quickly outran him. It seemed that failure followed Jared everywhere he went. This didn't impact his place as a protégé, or in our group's affection and respect for him. But unfortunately, that wasn't the gauge Jared was using for his own success, nor is it usually our gauge for success.

His gauge was based on numbers, outcomes and notoriety. What happens when none of these things happen? What happens when you perceive yourself as a failure in the eyes of God, in the eyes of others and even in your own eyes? Your sense of identity comes crashing down—that's what happens.

The strong self-image that Jared projected began deconstructing. He became more reclusive and downcast. His anxiety increased and joy levels decreased. He even started to have health problems related to stress. Ministry burnout was his future trajectory. He was plagued by the terrifying question, Who am I if I'm not the person I thought I was and if I don't have the competence I thought I did?

Along the way, I tried to guide Jared in certain directions, and even cautioned him about where he derived his worth. But it was difficult to break through his tough exterior. In essence, he didn't really see it. When I noticed Jared beginning to unravel, I had a good idea of what was going on. The reason I could recognize it was because I've been there—too many times to count.

In the Protégé Program, we held monthly one-on-one meetings where we discussed everything from leadership strategy to skill development to dating and romance, from emotional struggles to spiritual formation to nitty-gritty ministry details. In light of Jared's journey, I decided to probe deeper in an effort to guide him. I asked thoughtful and caring questions about why he felt increased anxiety and stress and why he felt like a failure more than a success. Taking time to ask and engage with poignant, thoughtful and reflective questions with our protégés is one of the most effective mentoring practices. In fact, asking the right questions is undeniably more important than giving the right answers if we desire to leave lasting impact.

Some of Jared's answers stayed on the surface, as is often the case. So I probed deeper and listened intently. At appropriate times, I steered the conversation where I sensed God wanting me to lead it. In essence, I guided our conversations toward him recognizing his own search for identity and described the effects of attaching his sense of personhood to ministry success that's defined by others (or himself), rather than by the love of his Father. This is often a greater struggle than many young leaders are initially aware of. One of the reasons is because when we're in our twenties our drive to prove ourselves as capable is as intense as ever. The role of the mentor or coach is often to simply help them see and gain clarity around this issue—that's at least where a deeper conversation starts.

It didn't take long for Jared to put the pieces together . . . the depression, the withdrawal, the health issues and the unexplainable sense of lostness. Up to this point, he had been splashing around in three feet of water, dwelling on more shallow dreams of success and surface-level happiness where he was always the winner, and where everything he touched turned to gold. He was far from being a bad guy, just on the wrong path, misaligned. Jared was attaching himself to a big earthly idol of human-defined success, rather than attaching himself to the One who calls him son. I'm convinced that every leader has lesser things that we attach ourselves to, otherwise known as idols. Our great dilemma involves identifying what these lesser things are and then dealing with them. For Jared, this happened to be the thing God wanted him to deal with at the time. And as his mentor, that's what I sensed God doing, and as a result I attempted to nudge him toward dealing with it.

I can honestly say that Jared became a different person through those two years as he dove more intentionally into dealing with his core issues of where he found his identity. He didn't shrink back from the uncomfortable conversations around this issue. And he committed to living in the volatile and unpredictable territory of God's presence in a deeper way in order to face the darkness he was discovering inside.

Jared leaned into his earthly failures and found that at the end of that road there was a door—a door that led him into the unfailing love of his Father. That was the fuel for him to engage a much deeper dimension of his own spiritual journey. That was the beginning of a newly transformed way of abiding in the Father. And as ministry leaders now and in the future, we must remain in touch with what God is trying to say to us at the deepest level. Sometimes those issues don't look that bad on the outside, but can derail the very trajectory where our lives should be headed.

Jared emerged out of that difficult season a more spiritually, and even physically, healthier person. Through his failure, he discovered what he had not recognized before—that his identity was unknowingly wrapped into lesser things, idols in fact. It didn't take long before Jared was seeing more progressive growth in his walk with God than he ever had. He began to see the nuances of his character being formed. Plus he started seeing growth in the ministries he was leading, sometimes in numbers but more importantly in spiritual depth and authentic transformation in the lives of others. Why? Because there's a direct correlation between seeing God working in the depths of our soul and seeing what he's doing in the souls of others.

Perhaps the next generation of churches will relinquish their grip on performance, numbers and notoriety, and will instead zero in on spiritual depth, character formation and life-change such as we've rarely seen in churches. For Jared, the contrast was clear. Before, he was self-reliant, restless, self-promoting and lost. He quickly changed courses and became more humble, God-dependent and clear about who God was to him and where God was leading him.

As Jared's core motivation shifted and he became more centered in finding his identity in his heavenly Father, he finally started to see the fruit of his hard spiritual labor in ministry. Jared began to speak, lead and live with spiritual authority that people recognized and were compelled by. People responded to his leadership like never before, not because he was a charismatic and gifted leader, but because he was a living example of what it looks like to find one's identity in the Father and rely on God for one's sense of true worth. Multiple people expressed to him that he was living proof that a person can actually live from that place where their ultimate worth remains strongly connected to God instead of being attached to and driven by idols of success and status and the pleasure or displeasure of others. The ministry that emerges from living this way of life is the kind of ministry that builds and establishes a kingdom culture.

We must rid ourselves of trying to control our appearances and search beneath the surface until we find what we're all truly looking for—a vibrant, meaningful, life-giving relationship with God. It sounds so simple, but far too many ministry leaders drift from this once-existing significant reality in their lives. The world needs a new generation of spiritual leaders who carry the vision and conviction of this biblical truth: *Apart from Jesus, we can do nothing of kingdom value.* Then, if we long to see people with a vibrant and ever-deepening faith, we can help lead them into the living water that we are actually experiencing ourselves. It's from that place where we can teach them with integrity how to dive deep and experience authentic spiritual transformation. Not just once. Not just twice—but over and over again for the rest of our lives.

ELIMINATION DOESN'T WORK

So then, how do we actually live in the deep? How do we overcome this sin of performance? The reality is, the sin of performance cannot simply be eliminated. Instead, it must be replaced. You can't just kill it off, because it will regenerate itself. It'll find its way back into your life. Your heart will attach itself again.

The only way to be freed from and overcome the attachment to performance is through an ongoing, deepening and growing connection with God that integrates our emotions, motivations, thoughts, attitudes and actions. To be sure, this kind of deeper transformation can't be limited to the religious duty of "having a daily quiet time." It must revolve around authentically encountering God in and through everyday life, in an integrated moment-by-moment kind of living, and in a way where we learn to depend on God rather than self.

As emerging leaders, our job is not only to face these issues in our lives, but to help others recognize what we're attaching our identity and worth to, where we're elevating performance over abidance, and where we're taping fruit to rotting branches instead of watching the fruit of the Spirit emerge from a healthy core. From there, we can become spiritual guides who remind people of the only Name who gives them real worth, through whom they discover their true identity.

Every day I do something to center myself in God and remind me of my dependence on him for my worth and identity. Each morning before the chaos, temptations and earthly dust fly at my face, I close my eyes and say a short prayer. "Lord, you are the one true God. The Father, the Son and the Holy Spirit. . . . I am your beloved. I will depend on you." I cling to the truth as written in Scripture: "I am my beloved's, and his desire is for me" (Song of Solomon 7:10 NASB). As those words float out of my inner being, I take a deep breath. Inhale. Exhale. It's as if God's breath is entering into me as I speak these transcendent words. I find life over and over again in the truth *I am loved by my Father.* And that's enough. It has to be.

The search for who we are, and why we matter, has been with us from the beginning. And it will be with us until the end. As leaders, this search resides inside every person whom God entrusts to our influence. And there's only one way to allow God to shape who we are and to be reminded of where our worth comes from. That is to attach ourselves to his presence and love every second of every day—kind of like a branch attaches itself to the vine. The Father is the Vine. And here's what he's saying to you and to me in every moment of our lives both now and forever:

You are my son. You are my daughter.
You are loved.

IDEAS FOR MENTORS

1. **Abba Prayer.** One of the prayers I encourage protégés to pray
   is what some call "The Abba Prayer." I didn't come up with it;
   I just use it. It's quite simple. It involves allowing yourself to
   sink deeply into God's love, letting the words from Song of
   Songs 7:10 wash over you and settle into the deepest part of
   your soul. "I belong to my beloved, and his desire is for me."
   Encourage protégés to pray this (or something similar) daily,
   perhaps even before they stumble out of bed or fall asleep at
   night. Have them pay attention to how it centers them, woos
   them to depend on God and even changes them. For those
   guys who think they're too tough and macho, they're wrong.
   And they're missing out on perhaps the greatest eternal truth
   we could discover. Just tell them to man up! To offer them
   richer context and depth, you could also encourage them to
   read either *Abba's Child* (by Brennan Manning) or a series of
   books called Theodyssey (by Dave Smith, see <www.theod
   yssey.org>). These are core books that I use to stimulate
   deeper dialogue and growth around God-dependence,
   abiding and the deeper spiritual journey. These layers of conversation are essential to discipleship. These resources directly relate to the deep places in which we derive our motivations and from which we lead our ministries.

2. **Identity formation.** Have protégés make a list of the things
   they find their identity in. For example: my job, how successful I am, concrete growth, how liked I am, etc. Have protégés discuss these with you and how they play out in their
   everyday lives. Help them explore what it would look like to
   detach from these false identities and instead attach to God.

3. **Rotting tree or spiritual fruit.** Lead a reflective exercise asking
   protégés where they see growth in their ministries. Have
   them reflect on whether this kind of growth is the product of
   self-reliance or the result of abiding in God. Is this fruit taped

to a rotting tree, or is it fruit produced by the Spirit? Is it self-reliance? Help them discover ways they can depend on God rather than themselves, and how they can better discern the difference in their ministry and personal lives.

4. **Encourage solitude and sabbath.** Encourage protégés to practice solitude on a regular basis. This provides a place where they cannot perform, produce or do. They can only *be*, *abide* and *center themselves* in Christ. Solitude is often uncomfortable because we come offering nothing but ourselves, unable to perform or create. We're simply the created, dwelling in the presence of the Creator. This time will provide much-needed perspective on how we need God, and how he is ultimately calling us to be in relationship with him, first and foremost. Keeping a sabbath is in the same genre. We must set time aside where we stop doing, and practice being. Otherwise we will fall into the performance trap over and over again.

MENTOR TIP:
ADAPTIVE LEARNING METHODS

When I'm thinking of resources to recommend for a protégé's development, I often ask them: Are you a light reader, medium reader or heavy reader? Then if they're light, I give an article. If they're medium, I may give them a chapter or two from a book. And if they're heavy, I give them a book to read. Others learn best through podcasts, videos, verbal processing or even tactile learning. Knowing and adapting to someone's learning styles will strengthen our impact on them and enhance their growth and development.

4 • The Sin of Overconfidence

FOOLISHNESS

WHERE DO WE DRAW THE LINE BETWEEN healthy confidence and unhealthy overconfidence? Where does the balance lie between knowing you have specific gifts to offer, and thinking you are better than you are? And how does knowing the difference actually *make* a difference?

The apostle Paul masterfully sums up overconfidence, the third deadly sin of the emerging leader, in Romans 12:3: "For by the grace given me I say to every one of you: *Do not think of yourself more highly than you ought*, but rather think of yourself with sober judgment, in accordance with the measure of faith that God has given you" (emphasis mine). I can practically hear Paul whispering these words to each of us. Sadly, there are far too many spiritual leaders who have let overconfidence (and pride) get the best of them. It causes damage to so many.

Paul is highlighting the reality that we as human beings tend to see ourselves inaccurately—better than we really are, more than we really are. We think flippantly about our true selves and how that relates to what God is trying to reveal to us. As smart and interesting and talented as we may believe ourselves to be, we're still lightyears away from seeing an accurate picture of who we are and seeing the holy perfection that is embodied in who God is. There the sin of overconfidence begins to unravel . . . in a good way.

When we see someone who is overconfident in action, it's like watching a bad movie. You just want it to end because you know it's not going to go well at all, yet you can't bring yourself to look away. Has the main character ever been you? Unfortunately, I've been there more times than I'd like to admit.

I remember my stormiest season of overconfidence. I was that karaoke singer who thought I was a rock star. I was the one who thought more highly of myself than I should have. Looking back, I can see more clearly what was lurking behind the overconfidence—it was foolishness. I was kind of like an annoying teenager who thinks he knows everything, when in fact I knew practically nothing. Unfortunately, I'm not alone. This disease has infected far too many leaders in our churches. And most of the ones who are infected don't even know it.

SOPHOMORIC THINKING

The Greeks articulated the paradox of having knowledge without having wisdom through the term "sophomore." The word *sophomore* actually means "wise fool"—meaning that they have gained a lot of knowledge yet are still incapable of behaving wisely. We see this reality everywhere. If we're honest, we can see it in ourselves.

Foolishness stems from overconfidence that we know what is right without having to seek the counsel of others, without being willing to do the hard thing and ultimately without seeking the wisdom of God. We think that all this brilliance swirling around our brains is enough to figure out life, and even enough to please God. Of course most of us probably wouldn't categorize ourselves as foolish, but if you've ever done any of the following, you may be more of a card-carrying member than you first thought.

Being aware of our sin and deficits is the first step toward character transformation. And often, young leaders in particular don't take time to identify their tendencies toward foolishness. As a result, they find themselves making avoidable mistakes. So let's take a quick assessment together. Read these verses and nod your head if you ever exhibit these traits:

• A person is a fool who denies the existence of God (Psalm 14:1).

• A person is a fool who trusts in his own heart (Proverbs 28:26).

• A person is a fool who despises wisdom and instruction (Proverbs 1:7).

• A person is a fool who is quick-tempered (Proverbs 14:16-17; Ecclesiastes 7:9).

• A person is a fool who scoffs at sin (Proverbs 14:9; 10:23).

Have you ever denied the existence of God? I'm not talking about dramatically throwing your fist into the air and yelling, "You don't exist, God!" I'm referring to much more subtly isolating him from your daily decisions and ignoring his voice in your life, as well as his commands stated in Scripture. This is the disguised way we ignore God's existence, therefore denying his aliveness in every moment we are breathing. It is foolish. And too many spiritual leaders are guilty, yet remain unaware of this reality in their lives.

Have you ever trusted in your own heart? It's a rhetorical question. Trusting in our own heart is probably the easiest doorway that we walk through to foolishness. We're tempted to walk through it a million times a day. I know people who refer to their heart as "he" or "she" in order to deeply validate its voice. I know people who say they follow God and are making horribly destructive choices that say, "If my heart says it's right, how could it be wrong?" I know myself, who subtly surrenders to the desires of my fallen heart rather than submitting my desires to a holy and trustworthy God.

The prophet Jeremiah tells us something critically important about the heart: "The human heart is the most deceitful of all things, and desperately wicked. Who really knows how bad it is?" (Jeremiah 17:9 NLT). Trusting in our hearts is like trusting in a dirty politician. It will tell us anything in order to gain popularity and indulge its desires. Of course there are beautiful and wonderful dimensions of our hearts, but for every fiber of goodness there lies a fiber of darkness around it. We must trust in and depend on a more pure Creator to guide us, a completely perfect God who desires to redeem, restore and transform our hearts. When we don't, it is foolish.

Have you ever despised wisdom or instruction? Again, rhetorical question. There is a deeply rooted resistance in our spirits toward any kind of criticism, instruction, authority or feedback. Many people hesitate to offer advice for fear that we will immediately throw up walls, forever excommunicating them from our internal lives. Other people throw out advice freely and perhaps need a bit more hesitancy. But either way, a lot of us are terrified of receiving advice, at least any advice that implies we may be lacking in an area we feel competent in. Our fragile ego trembles due to deep fears of not measuring up in this life. People just can't get near our oversensitive ego. Many times God can't even get near it because we just don't allow it. And spiritual leaders are especially guilty. But remember, only a fool rejects wisdom and instruction.

Have you ever been quick-tempered? Some of us are already aware of our temper because we struggle with controlling our emotions, and often explode with feelings such as rage, anger and hostility. We might groan with frustration over our inability to keep our cool. Others of us are more of the quiet type, silently brewing within and imploding rather than exploding. We are just as quick-tempered but much less externally expressive with it, often trying to hide from others who we secretly know we really are. The more observant type knows when the silent brew is happening and usually stays away. Others are less fortunate. They become victims of our silent rage. Whether you explode or implode, the undercurrent of sin is the same . . . foolishness.

Have you ever scoffed at sin? In other words, have you ever diminished the power and darkness of sin, or flippantly allowed it to take root in your life despite God's clear commands against doing so? It's much easier to diminish the weight of sin. Living in constant awareness of our weakness against it can be unbearable. But in diminishing the weight of sin, we also diminish the holiness, grace and power of God. Scoffing at sin is foolish because it allows darkness to inhabit our hearts more easily than God's light, therefore affecting every single choice we make. This kind of foolishness has indescribably destructive consequences in our relationship with God and with others, and it extends into our ministry area.

These are just a few examples of what foolishness looks like in our personal lives and leadership endeavors. Some struggle with this sin more than others, but—make no mistake—we all have the capacity to display the foolish behavior fueled by overconfidence. Overconfidence can creep up on us, and before we know it we've damaged others and even our own soul. And one of the greatest challenges is that we usually don't see it. Maybe all of us should just consider ourselves a bit foolish and overconfident and in desperate need of wisdom. In fact, I think ministry leaders ought to seek wisdom the most, because after all, they are often the ones speaking on God's behalf the most. They are the ones who are often entrusted with the greatest levels of spiritual authority and responsibility.

THE CHALLENGE OF CHOICE

Too often we as Christ followers talk about what to run away from rather what to run toward. It's not enough to reject foolishness. We must pursue wisdom . . . relentlessly. We must face our sin of overconfidence, realizing there's so much we don't know, so much that it is actually frightening, even paralyzing at times. Often younger leaders don't know how much wisdom they actually need, so they fail to seek it as they should. It's later when they've been through a painful or overwhelming experience that they realize how desperate they are for wisdom. Unfortunately, that's also when they finally realize how foolish they've been.

Countless questions on how to make wise choices in our lives weigh us down, choices that include: how to handle difficult people, how to know what is morally right and true, how to discern between good and evil, what career to pursue, how to spend our time and resources, how to approach people who believe differently than us, what step we should take next in our personal relationships, how to know who can be trusted with our hearts, how to express our emotions without being negative or toxic to those around us, how to share the truth without alienating and wounding others, how to lead those who are entrusting a large part of their spiritual journeys to us. Mentors and protégés ought to be engaged in intentional conversations about matters like these, including not just what the best decision is, but also what process is healthy and wise and biblically grounded.

These are not simple questions and they do not have easy answers. Choices like these require wisdom. And what we do with these choices contributes to the sum total of our character. And character *always* has a direct effect on our ministry, even when we don't see its effects immediately.

AN ISAIAH MOMENT

Where do we begin the quest for wisdom? There are a few Scripture passages that unlock the doors to the mystery of wisdom. Proverbs 9:10

tells us, "The fear of the LORD is the beginning of wisdom, and knowledge of the Holy One is understanding." If we are to pursue this remarkable gift, we must first acknowledge that God is not only the source of all wisdom, but that he is holy, perfect and all-powerful. He is to be revered, surrendered to and worshiped.

Many of us have experienced what I call an "Isaiah moment," where we catch a glimpse of God that essentially brings us to our knees and breaks our hearts in agonizing love. We encounter him with such awe, humility and repentance.

> "Woe to me!" I cried. "I am ruined! For I am a man of unclean lips, and I live among a people of unclean lips, and my eyes have seen the King, the LORD Almighty." (Isaiah 6:5)

We feel so exposed, while at the same time so blessed to see God's holiness and majesty. We feel ruined and healed simultaneously. This is what Solomon is referring to when he uses the word *fear*. We will never be wise if we don't first grasp the absolute chasm between our lack of holiness and knowledge and God's perfection and omniscience. Only when we see our need will we pursue the only One who can meet us in that place.

Step one: Fear God.

THE FORGOTTEN PRAYER

Once we see clearly that God is the only One who can ultimately bring us internal clarity, we must do one simple thing: *ask him for wisdom*. James 1:5 (NIV 2011) says, "If any of you lacks wisdom, you should ask God, who gives generously to all without finding fault, and it will be given to you." What is most revealing about this verse is that wisdom is not some elusive and exclusive spiritual gift. It is not something that God makes a mystery of where to find. Rather, it is freely given to anyone who asks for it from God himself.

I don't know about you, but this captures me. This is a hand-delivered promise from God saying that wisdom is ours for the taking. He couldn't be any clearer on how to attain it. The path to wisdom isn't some secret maze we have to fumble through and constantly guess which way is the one that will lead us in the right direction. We simply have to ask and then believe that God will keep his promise.

I have a mentor named Marty who taught me many things about leadership and ministry. One of the most significant and memorable insights he told me came after I asked him, "What's the most important lesson you've learned about doing ministry and leading others?" His answer was, "Never stop asking God for wisdom, and then thanking him when he gives it." It was simple, but I'll never forget it.

It's almost as if God so desperately wants us to gain wisdom that he is making it completely accessible. But ask leaders how often they actually ask for wisdom, and the responses won't be as consistent as you may think. We must never forget that we have a free pass to probe the mind and heart of God, to ask for spiritual clarity where there is human fog, to request discernment where we lack the knowledge to know the difference, to know the depths of his commands and the reasons why he asks us to surrender things to him (1 Corinthians 2:11-16). This is the next level of spiritual depth. This is transcendent knowledge. This is how we put on the very mind of God. This is the path to yet another dimension of character transformation.

If emerging leaders made this forgotten prayer in James 1:5 a daily ritual, just imagine how it would affect our leadership, our relationships and our entire lives. Just imagine how much different we might lead the church into her anticipated future?

Step two: Ask God for wisdom.

WISDOM EXPOSED

There's a passage in Scripture that paints a vivid picture of wisdom trying to capture humanity's attention. It almost haunts me.

> Does not wisdom call out? Does not understanding raise her voice? At the highest point along the way, where the paths meet, she takes her stand. (Proverbs 8:1-2 TNIV)

This image of wisdom, literally "raising her voice," is easier to see in other people's lives than our own. It seems that we are sometimes forced to watch people we love make destructive and foolish choices despite the spirit of wisdom holding a giant megaphone, pleading with them to turn toward an understanding not of their own and obey the voice of wisdom instead. And all they do is walk on by, happily plugging their ears and singing songs of their own folly. How maddening to watch! Oh, how I wish we could see ourselves when we're doing exactly the same thing. It would be painful, but at least we would get a good kick in the right direction.

Cheri and I went to Rome a few years ago. We were looking forward to seeing the Colosseum, and we were not disappointed. It was spectacular. We could almost tangibly feel the history as we climbed the two-thousand-year-old steps. As we stood on the highest step in the pouring rain, we felt as though we were connected to an era that defined the culture of its time.

Then we saw something we will never forget. Under the flooring of the Colosseum lay a maze. And only from the top could one see the way out. We later found out that the Romans would release lions and other dangerous animals into the maze to chase down their prey . . . *human beings*. This was entertainment for the civilized, the elite and the fortunate ones.

Floor of the Colosseum

Have you ever felt like you were watching someone you love running frantically through a maze? And that only you could see the way out? Maybe they refused to listen as you desperately tried to show them the way to their freedom, the way of wisdom. It is as if Satan is chasing them down. But his power is only fueled by our own ignorance, pride and foolishness. There is God, reaching his hand toward us, calling us toward him, desperately trying to be heard as he cries out, "Turn this way . . . not that way . . . your freedom is near." We are running into dead ends, wasting precious time, listening to the wrong voices, and making choices out of fear, pride and foolishness rather than out of the truth, knowledge of God and wisdom.

As we are driven deeper into fear and confusion, we may even become entertainment for the world around us. Our agony is their relief. Our destruction is their success. It is a disturbing thought, but just look at the world around us. It does not seem as barbaric as the Colosseum events revealed, but human nature has not changed in two thousand years. We're just better at masking it. Our greatest comfort often comes from someone else's demise. We know we are messed up and don't have it together, so seeing someone else fall relieves some of our own pain. It's as if we know how easily it could be us in that maze. Maybe we are in denial that it *is* us.

So much of gaining wisdom has to do with us unplugging our ears and looking toward the source of truth rather than painfully twisting our heads around until we can safely ignore it. We overcomplicate things. We think that if something were just said to us in the right way, we could finally understand. Or if we could do the same for others, then they would see the truth, as if the substance of wisdom lurks behind mysterious corners and only speaks in whispers and riddles.

This is not how Solomon describes wisdom. This is not how God designed the pursuit of wisdom. It couldn't be more opposite. There is the concrete, unchangeable truth in the Scriptures that we can, and must, turn to for wisdom (see 2 Timothy 3:16-17). There is the voice of the Holy Spirit, guiding us through tough and complicated terrain, revealing what steps we should take next (see John 16:5-15). There is the counsel of wise and trustworthy mentors, pastors, elders and friends (see Proverbs 12:15).

When we seek all three, when we actually listen and take action, when we lean on God to give us the clarity and courage and ability to keep walking in his commands, we will find wisdom. We will no longer remain *sophomores* filled with knowledge yet void of wisdom. We are now out-of-the closet fools, ready to admit we need help from the one true and perfect God, every step of the way. That's a picture of wise living. That's the core of real spiritual leadership that will inevitably evolve into real spiritual authority and power.

IDEAS FOR MENTORS

1. **Wisdom collectors**. Two friends of mine got engaged. In an effort to gain more wisdom, I challenged them to meet with ten married couples whom they admired. Their goal was to learn what it takes to have a great marriage. In the same spirit, guide and challenge your protégés to identify five to ten people possessing areas of wisdom (leadership, parenting, communication, marriage, etc.). Have the protégés initiate getting together with them to ask for input, advice and/or expertise—on whatever areas they feel led to grow in. If possible and applicable, you can help connect your protégés to wise people you know.

2. **Create a character feedback loop**. Challenge protégés to create a feedback loop about their character where they can receive honest evaluation and analysis from peers, co-workers, friends, etc. One way you could do this is by using <www.surveymonkey.com>. Invite protégés to create a "character survey" and send a list of "survey questions" to five to ten people that know them well and care about their growth. Perhaps you can help them come up with a list of ten to twelve questions. (A sample question might be: From your perspective, which of these three sins seem to be a greater struggle for me: pride, envy or foolishness—can you briefly explain?) Work hard to frame questions in a way that generates helpful responses. The protégés can even gather the information anonymously if they feel that fosters more honesty from people. Seeking feedback takes great courage

and a willingness to find wisdom in a vulnerable way, but protégés I know have gleaned much value from this process.

3. **The spiritual practice of asking.** Encourage protégés to meditate on James 1:5 and pray for wisdom consistently as a spiritual practice. You could even challenge them to read prayerfully through Proverbs. Challenge them to trust God's promise that he will give wisdom to those who seek it. Encourage them to pay attention to how God grows them in wisdom.

4. **Character matrix assessment.** Sometimes it's difficult for someone to gauge where some of their character deficits are. One tool I created and frequently use is a self-character assessment. I look for opportunities to give this assessment to protégés and circle back to discuss it. Sometimes I even do it with groups. It helps me understand their own view of their character, and it also tends to increase their own urgency and desire to grow in character. After administering the assessment and engaging in discussions, I encourage protégés to develop a growth plan and to set goals of what areas of character they desire to grow in. If you'd like access to this assessment, e-mail me at steve@stevesaccone.com.

MENTOR TIP:
SHARING THE STORY OF YOUR LIFE

One way of mentoring that really impacts protégés is when a mentor shares a current struggle, even a vulnerable one. In other words, how are you growing in overcoming the sin of imitation (envy), or how are you currently changing in your approach and theology of mission? In essence, use your personal and current experience to help inspire and guide others on similar journeys. Sharing your struggles will almost certainly propel your relationship toward greater depths.

5 • The Sin of Entitlement

GREED

GREED IS DEADLY BECAUSE IT TAKES more than it gives. It consumes rather than creates. It is never satisfied. What makes it worse is that greed is difficult to recognize and acknowledge within yourself. I've never run into anyone who openly admits, "I'm a greedy person." At the same time, we all know our world is full of greedy people . . . and this certainly doesn't exclude Christians. In fact, it seems that there's hidden greed inside the hearts of many ministry leaders that has been left undealt with. As a result of going unchecked, in ways we don't realize greed begins to fuel and pollute our ambitions, the very ones that look good on the outside but end up wreaking havoc in our marriages, ministries and personal lives.

When Cheri and I were vacationing in Italy, we found ourselves in St. Mark's Square in Venice where an uncomfortable number of pigeons linger. In the spirit of fun, I took a handful of birdseed and tossed it toward Cheri. Instantly a dozen pigeons flocked around her. Yes, she was angry with me. And it got worse. They wouldn't leave her alone until we actually left St. Mark's Square. Unfortunately, she didn't think it was as funny as I did.

Have you ever fed a pigeon and lived to regret it? Most people are too smart to do so because they know that pesky bird will not be grateful for the bit of fast food or birdseed you threw its way. It will, in fact, only be less satisfied than before it was fed. It will peck at your feet and bob around your space. Pigeons don't ask nicely, because they just assume your life goal is to give them more of what they want. Sound like anyone you know?

When someone feels entitled to something, it's not motivating to do things for them. Their response is kind of like the pigeon's response: "You were supposed to do this thing, or give that thing, so why should

I thank you?" They have pigeon-like qualities. I confess, I can resemble that bird once in a while myself.

Greed often presents itself as a form of entitlement. Entitlement lives and breathes for one purpose—to consume, gather and take. It is ugly. However, it cleverly disguises itself as ambition, drive and a healthy dose of assertiveness. One thing entitlement doesn't project is gratitude.

In fact, entitlement is the antithesis of gratitude.

We learned an important rule in kindergarten—always say "please" and "thank you." We also learned to ask for a bathroom pass before leaving the classroom. We still obey the please-and-thank-you rule because, let's be honest, we would look bad if we didn't. Saying thank you is part of civility, but is often not part of the fabric of our hearts. Instead of feeling grateful, we often feel entitled. Behind this pigeonish quality of entitlement and lack of gratitude is greed. We're greedy for more stuff, more status, more talent, more position, more everything. We humans just can't seem to get enough; in fact, the more we gain, the less satisfied we are.

THE SPIRIT OF THE PIGEON

I remember my first car. Wow, it was bad. So bad that I would get a sick feeling in my stomach when I had to drive farther than ten miles, or on the freeway, or in the snow. So I'd have that sick feeling almost every time I drove it. The radio didn't work when it was cold. I had to manually spray Windex on my windshield due to a leaky windshield-wiper container. It had absolutely no pick-up. I had to learn to cope with being the most hated car on any given road, because my little Mitsubishi Precis couldn't clear forty miles per hour. It was all very bad for my self-esteem.

I was convinced that all I needed to be happy was a car that could keep up with the speed limit and didn't break down every two seconds. When I finally got a real job and real money, I knew right where to go. Carmax, here I come. I walked in there thinking, *just buy what you need, not what you want.* I'm happy to report that I bought a used, very reliable Nissan. But only after I stood salivating over a brand-new sporty Mustang for about an hour. It was way out of my price range, way out of my league and exactly what I wanted. I could just see myself driving it. I actually thought for a moment that it could bring me an unimaginable level of happiness. A pretty piece of metal that cost $30,000—yeah, that was going to do it.

I finally snapped out of my greed coma and realized that it was unwise to buy this car: it would just end up as another material casualty of my short-lived satisfaction with stuff. Soon I would want something better, faster and more expensive. I won that battle, but I'm afraid I'm nowhere close to winning the war of greed in my own heart. I have bought the lie that stuff brings happiness a million times. And every time I have failed, my sense of entitlement shot up with it. I was less easily content.

The obsession with material things in our culture is only a snapshot of the overall greed we inhabit within. We are greedy emotionally, relationally, spiritually. Do you ever take more than you give in a relationship? Do you ever get angry because someone didn't meet an expectation you had for them? Do you ever want more than you deserve? Do you ever wonder when the obsession with earthly treasure will end? Do you ever wish you were different, even free from this insatiable appetite for more and more and more? It makes sense why Jesus told his followers: "Watch out! Be on your guard against all kinds of greed; life does not consist in an abundance of possessions" (Luke 12:15 TNIV).

We are created to desire, to long for and even to obtain. At the very heart of this endless greed lies a deep truth about humanity. Instead of leaning into this truth, we violently swing our arms around grasping for stuff, power, status and riches. We say it's because we need to feel secure. Or we even tell ourselves that God wants us to have it.

We believe that one day it will be enough.

We don't understand why it never is.

That is until we hear that still small voice among the deafening noise of our self-constructed palaces crashing in on us. We hear it say, "You are looking for happiness in things, security in your abilities and resources, intimacy in your relationships alone, love from the things you buy with cash. Joy and contentment will not meet you there, for all of it is void of anything that mirrors the divine. All of these things can be swept away by time and calamity. Your fulfillment will only meet you through the everlasting love of your Savior. In his arms alone will you experience the security, the strength and the no-strings-attached love and contentment that you crave.

OVERCOMING THE OBSTACLES OF GREED

Remember the words of the phenomenal spiritual leader, the apostle Paul.

> I am not saying this because I am in need, for I have learned to be content whatever the circumstances. I know what it is to be in need, and I know what it is to have plenty. I have learned the secret of being content in any and every situation, whether well fed or hungry, whether living in plenty or in want. I can do everything through him who gives me strength. (Philippians 4:11-13)

Paul's context is different than ours. But no matter your context, don't you wish you could say these words and that they would be genuine to who you are and to how you relate to God and others as a leader? I have been careful not to let my greed be too obvious, and my entitlement too recognizable, but it is there. Hidden is my quiet discontentment with what I don't have, my desire for more and nicer and better things—and I don't just mean material things. Sometimes I find myself subtly demanding from God a bigger ministry, a promotion or special acknowledgment as if I'm entitled to these things. Relationally, I fight the constant temptation to take more than I give, to emotionally draw what I want and discard the rest. The rest is sometimes people. There is no corner of my inner or outer world where greed and discontentment has not played their dirty part, including in my ministry.

My good friend Andrew was recently confronted by one of his team members. She told him, "I've been concerned lately and even a little irritated about how our conversations have gone. Every time we've gotten together in the last few months, I know you're going through a hard time, but you really only talk about yourself. Even if I share something that is happening in my life, you find a way to steer our dialogue back to yourself. I don't know if you've noticed or not, so I just wanted to express how I perceive it because it's bothering me."

Although he was a little pricked emotionally, he welcomed what she shared with humility and grace. It was done in the context of love, which included her being candid and direct. He later told me, "Although I was defensive internally and didn't want to believe what she was saying was true, I knew she was trying to help me grow and hoping it would build our friendship stronger. I also knew it took courage and vulnerability for her to share what she did. Believing that she wanted the best for me, I welcomed it."

In my analysis, she was basically saying, "You've been relationally and emotionally greedy lately."

Sometimes when people are going through hard times, they feel they have a free pass to take more than they give. Perhaps that's okay in certain scenarios, but all of us need to monitor our inner spirit. Are we taking more than we're giving? Are we always demanding something from someone emotionally or relationally, and not really giving back in return?

I was impressed with Andrew's response. Instead of reacting in anger or spite, "I'm going through a lot right now and you should be there for me," he acknowledged his emotional and relational greed. He owned it. For him, this was one more area that he was willing to surrender to God so he could become a more generative, selfless person.

I'm not sure I would've handled it that way. Maybe I would've just been upset and defensive and angry. If so, I would've missed out on an important conversation about how to move from greed to generosity of spirit, and how to rid myself of relational and emotional greed.

It would be easy to grow discouraged and simply accept that human nature will always want more, no matter how much it already has. But when I read Paul's words, I am reminded that it is possible to have what seems to be impossible to possess—contentment. Drawing from God's strength rather than one's own is a theme in Paul's life. How strong is God's love to us? Is it stronger than our possessions, our stuff, our status and our adult-sized security blankets we carry tucked underneath our chins everywhere we go?

Leaders, what really drives you? The answer to that question is the only way out of our deeply rooted greed.

I can just imagine the sadness God carries over our obsession with worldly things when he can see so clearly that it is dust clouding the eternal treasure that lies in his face. I remember watching my two-year-old son, Hudson, surrounded by countless toys, still grabbing the one toy my one-year-old son, Holden, was playing with. I am not exaggerating when I say that it broke my heart to see him showing the early signs of possessive greed. As a parent, I wanted to tell him that none of those toys will bring him happiness—that sharing them would. That looking into the loving eyes of his mother or father would. But all of us parents know that simply telling him won't work. Only the experience of a greater divine nature will. He, I, we, must live in God's strength if we are to let go of the things we are spending all of our affection on. We must be transformed by him. We must be driven by and for him. Or as the apostle Paul once told the church at Colossae, "Set your hearts on things above. . . . Set your minds on things above, not on earthly things" (Colossians 3:1-2). Two verses later he has a list of sins and tells us, "Put to death"—one of those sins is greed (Colossians 3:5).

UPSIDE-DOWN GREED

This is an image I can easily wrap my mind around.

> Today the heart of God is an open wound of love. He aches over our distance and preoccupation. He mourns that we do not draw near to him. He grieves that we have forgotten him. He weeps over our obsession with muchness and manyness. He longs for our presence.[1]

Often, the way to develop character is by practicing the opposite of the vice. And some may say the solution to greed is to give more. Of course in some respect, giving more is absolutely virtuous and crucial to the development of our character, including overcoming some forms of greed. However, giving more is not where the primary cure to our entitlement disease originates.

Greed is a desperate attempt to grasp and hold on to *worth* through means of our own. Drawing near to *Worth* himself is the kind of greed we need to have more of. We need to be more discontent with how easily we settle for earthly trinkets rather than divine treasure. Strength. Love. Security that is eternal. Worth. Contentment. Divine ambition. Where do we find such things?

> Do not store up for yourselves treasures on earth, where moth and rust destroy, and where thieves break in and steal. But store up for yourselves treasures in heaven, where moth and rust do not destroy, and where thieves do not break in and steal. For where your treasure is, there your heart will be also. (Matthew 6:19-20)

When we store up treasure in heaven, not only will we find we're finally fulfilled, we will inhabit a spirit of undeniable gratitude and strength. We will live in acute awareness that if we have anything at all, we have already been blessed. We will realize we have been given a gift that outshines any glittering earthly possession, God's love and his perspective on life. Thankfulness will spill from our hearts. For how could we not be joyful in the face of such extravagant blessings from the Giver of every good thing? We will turn greed upside down and from our grateful and content hearts will flow generosity. We will stop this pursuit of "muchness and manyness" and instead become present with *the Presence*. Eternity will press into our earthly space and break our hearts wide open with gratitude that cannot be doused by the sparkle of dust. We will finally know the difference between earthly and heavenly treasure the moment we allow him to be our greatest prize. Only then will we put those pigeons to shame with our greed-free souls and entitlement-void hearts.

MINISTRY GREED

Have you ever found yourself consistently discontent with your current position? Have you ever found yourself perpetually preoccupied with receiving a promotion or rising in the estimation of others? Are you notoriously known for talking more than you listen, and as a result people distance themselves from you? Maybe you've found yourself secretly wanting more attention and limelight, and never feel you're getting enough. Have you ever wanted to benefit from others or leverage what they have for yourself significantly more than you want to benefit them or leverage what you have for their sake? Truth is, leaders always find ways to rationalize this stuff in the wrong direction.

When you experience the kind of contentment that Paul addresses in the New Testament, it wages war against a greedy heart and combats greedy behaviors. Your perspective is transformed. You don't live with the posture of always asking for more or wanting more than you should appropriately expect in a relationship. The compulsion of your heart actually changes, and you begin giving more—relationally, emotionally and spiritually. Generosity flows from the core of who you are—your character. And soon that becomes the place from which the core of your ministry flows. You become stronger, freer and, in a phrase, empowered by God.

Being content doesn't mean we don't strive to bring change, improve things or challenge the status quo. This is what leaders do. They always maintain a bias toward action that brings change. But the very essence of a discontent heart (wanting more than you should) differs from a content one. Discontentment is about wanting something for personal gain (status, money, position, etc.) or being driven by selfish ambition (Philippians 2:3-4). Contentment is about wanting gain for the kingdom and seeking to give to others from a grateful and generative heart and spirit. It's about living a life that's always postured to generate good and serve others as God calls and directs us. This way of life and leadership begins with a content heart and a perspective of gratitude.

Emerging ministry leaders ought to pursue becoming the most generative, grateful and content Christ followers we know. If we pursue this, the way we do ministry will change for the better, flowing from Christ's generosity being formed inside of us. The world will become a better place. It will look more and more like the kingdom of God. We will begin building a kingdom culture of gratitude, contentment and generosity. People will be better served, and we will begin to more fully embody the spirit of Jesus who didn't come to be served, but to serve and give his life as a ransom for many (Mark 10:45)! The measure that we learn true contentment and gratitude will be the measure of our generosity that will flow though our lives and into our ministry.

IDEAS FOR MENTORS

1. **Practice secrecy.** Do a good deed and try to make sure no one finds out. It could be an act of generosity or love for your spouse, for one of your kids, a friend or someone at work. Remember, serve anonymously. It will grind against greed that exists in your heart. Encouraging protégés to do this as a spiritual discipline can help form the character trait of generosity.

2. **Cultivate a generative spirit.** Invite protégés to do one or more of these:

   - *Relational*—Identify where you do more taking than giving in your relationships with others. Be more intentional about serving someone this week. Make sure you are listening more than talking. Perhaps you can practice relational generosity in some way by expressing gratitude or affirmation to others you know. Or maybe you give a gift to someone just to show someone your appreciation.

   - *Financial*—Consider adding 10 percent to your already faithful tithe this week. Give it to your local church, or find a creative place of need to be generous.

   - *Time*—Carve out significant time this week to do something generous and meaningful for someone. Perhaps serve a meal to a family or person in need. Maybe spend time with someone you know is lonely, whether it's someone you already know well or someone you don't. It could involve going to a nursing home or homeless shelter to spend time with someone who just needs a listening ear or someone to be present with them. This can be a spiritual discipline that cultivates the spirit of generosity, and even contentment within.

3. **From meditation to transformation.** One spiritual discipline that shapes who protégés will become involves meditation.

In effort to facilitate meditation in a protégé who struggles with entitlement or greed, challenge them to meditate on these verses and ask God to speak to them about contentment, entitlement, greed and generosity: Philippians 4:11-13; Matthew 6:20; 2 Corinthians 8:7. Perhaps you want to spend time discussing or studying these passages together in a one-on-one or even a group setting.

MENTOR TIP:
THE MENTOR'S PLAN

1. *Build an authentic relationship with your protégé on a foundation of trust. Part of building trust is making sure you're being invited to mentor that person and not just assuming that he/she wants your investment. No one wants a mentor to impose themselves on them.*

2. *Discern the growth need(s) and desire(s) of the protégé—and make sure this is a dialogue, not a monologue.*

3. *Develop a growth plan together with concrete next steps— help them identify their own deficits and set their own goals. It will enhance their motivation.*

4. *Provide a clear accountability structure, follow-up plan and feedback loop. Make sure the expectations are clearly communicated and understood.*

PART 2

Relationships

THREE CRITICAL TENSIONS OF
RELATIONAL LEADERSHIP

Do nothing out of selfish ambition or vain conceit.
Rather, in humility value others above yourselves,
not looking to your own interests but each of you
to the interests of the others. In your relationships
with one another, have the same attitude of mind
Christ Jesus had.

PHILIPPIANS 2:3-5 TNIV

Accept the fact that we have to treat almost
anybody as a volunteer.

PETER DRUCKER

A NEW COMMAND I GIVE YOU: Love one another. As I have
loved you, so you must love one another. By this everyone will know
that you are my disciples, if you love one another" (John 13:34-35 TNIV).
I wonder if Jesus was referring to what he was observing in real time, or
if he was casting a vision for his followers? Were the disciples living
proof of God's existence by their expression of love toward one another?
Or were they struggling to even understand what the true definition of
love was? Was Jesus trying to tell them that if they failed to love each
other, the world would fail to recognize their leader?

There's probably no more overused word than *love*. There's probably
no more abused thing than relationships. There's no end to the confusion
of what love is in its true form. If you don't believe it, look around.

I remember when my best friend's father left his family when we were in seventh grade (as if junior high isn't hard enough). Before he left, he told his family that he loved them, but that he wasn't happy and that he was sure they'd understand one day. Really? How does any child (or even adult) ever understand the word *love* in the face of abandonment?

Love is often just a word—sadly, we humans make sure of that. There are more examples than grains of sand on the seashore. A blanket of darkness covers our relational world that threatens to swallow it up completely. Maybe that's why it's so compelling when Jesus takes such a complex thing like love, and links it to the proof of his presence in our lives. In the depth of influence that we long for our lives to have, our own relational health will be the greatest catalyst, or the greatest inhibitor.

Love produces light. Light reveals the truth. Truth sets people free.

Love may sound so glamorous, but in actuality, living it out is highly unglamorous. Relationships are messy, unpredictable, invasive and unwelcome mirrors of our ability to give or withhold love. We may long to be like those stars that Paul refers to in Philippians 2:15-16: "You will shine among them like stars in the sky as you hold firmly to the word of life." We may long to magically light up the dark sky and reveal the glory of our God. However, the everyday realities of selfishness, fear and myopia sideline our longing. We're plagued by shortsightedness, only seeing what is in front of us instead of the bigger picture. We're afraid to let people in. We're consumed with consuming.

And the lights flicker out.

This conversation is especially relevant for leaders in the church. The disciples were the leaders in their day. We are the leaders in ours. We have a responsibility to be living, breathing evidence of the God we talk about, preach about and proclaim boldly. According to Jesus, people are indeed watching. The bewildering thing is that Jesus thinks we can actually pull this off. He thought his disciples—who were unschooled, ordinary men almost certainly in their twenties when Jesus walked on earth with them—could pull this off as well. It appears that he's convinced we are capable of loving each other remarkably well, just as he loves us. And I don't think he's referring to the kind of 101-level love that we are quite comfortable with—like being nice when we can, putting on a good face around others, giving now and then to those in need, befriending a person easy to be friends with, glossing over difficult issues and calling it "peacekeeping," smiling and nodding in affirmation when people talk to us, being sociable even when we don't feel like it. Not that these are bad things; however, these can be just a few of the ways we cheapen love by calling it what it isn't. Often we are simply trying to behave well, however we humanly define that. That isn't what Jesus meant by love (see Luke 6:27-36).

UNCOMFORTABLE RELATIONSHIPS

What is Jesus talking about when he frequently speaks to this idea of loving one another? There is in fact another level of love that he calls us to—a level that often makes us feel very uncomfortable. His call to love entails increased levels of sacrificial commitment. Not only does he challenge us to love our neighbor as we love ourselves, but he later calls us to even love our enemies. In John's Gospel, Jesus commands us to love "as I have loved you" and makes it clear that love often demands self-sacrifice, even unto death—greater love has no one than this, to lay down one's life (John 15:12-13).

Leaders, emerging as well as seasoned ones, are surrounded by people who have endless relational expectations, even demands. They want to be loved and cared for. As a leader, you're under constant pressure to not only love others well, but to create cultures where those you are leading also learn to love others well. Some moments you may find yourself feeling overwhelmed by someone's emotional needs, so you're tempted to pretend they aren't as bad off as they really are. Other times you're in a relationship with someone who has unhealthy demands on you as a ministry leader, and you give in rather than lovingly draw boundaries. Some of us struggle with minimizing the value of the very people who serve tirelessly under our leadership, and who help us make our great vision a reality. Others of us can't bear to face one more unhappy person, one more disgruntled volunteer or one more resentful friend. They all blend into one. We start seeing everyone as a potential enemy rather than people we are called to love.

In ministry, leaders can very easily slip into a relational vacuum where we get sucked into the strongest force, or to remove ourselves so completely that we become virtually inaccessible to the very people we're committed to leading. Love, once again, becomes just a word. And we forfeit our calling to be part of the living, breathing proof of God's existence. That's what happens when we allow relationships to die a slow death, or when we allow them to suck all the life out of us. We stop relating. We stop loving. We stop proving that God is at work in our churches, our communities and our world.

Surrendering to mediocre and false versions of love is not an option if we want our impact to go far and wide and deep. We must lead by example first, and inspire cultures where God's love stops being just a word and becomes a reality. To do that, we must learn how to navigate three critical tensions in relational leadership that guide us down the path of knowing how to love in deeper, stronger and healthier ways. Although there are many ways in which we can grow in love as it is biblically defined and envisioned by Jesus, I've concluded that these three tensions are absolutely core to effective, God-honoring ministry leadership.

NAVIGATING THE EXTREMES

When it comes to relational leadership, we must hold on to a dynamic tension that's often not reached. Ecclesiastes 7:18 speaks pointedly to that part of the human condition that seeks to live in the extreme rather than holding true to the tension of two extremes.

> It is good to grasp the one and not let go of the other. Whoever fears God will avoid all extremes. (TNIV)

We find it easier to hold on to one way of thinking, one way of being or one way of relating, than to hold on to other aspects God calls us to. How can we understand God's grace if we don't also understand his need for justice? How can we hear God call us to engage conflict if all we hold on to is his desire for harmony? How can we strive for good if we don't understand our capacity for darkness? What almost seems contradictory is actually complimentary. And it's the moment we go to one extreme that we lose the essence of who God is and how he beckons us to relate to one another. But the goal is not to strive for balance either.

Striving to live in this tension isn't some disguised form of diluted compromise. It's quite the opposite. It's in the holding on to both extremes that we find an ability to exhibit a nuanced and textured form of love, which mirrors that of our heavenly Father. You may be one of those fiery leaders who pride themselves on being extreme. Or you may be one of those Zen-like leaders who pride themselves on being a "go-with-the-flow" type. Wherever you fall on the spectrum, there's growth to be made and a new kind of tension to hold on to if you desire to live out the love Jesus calls each of us to.

Within this framework lie the three critical tensions that I've observed when it comes to how leaders relate to others and do ministry. As I've developed leaders, I've consistently seen them gravitate to one extreme or the other. So, I've guided many in seeing more clearly the value in the other extreme and then developing a more centered approach toward relationships. Of course none of us ever achieve perfection in this, so remember to give yourself (and others) grace along the way in your growth process.

Most of us tend to easily recognize which extreme we lean toward. If we address this problem head on, we'll see relational (and emotional) health flourish not only in our ministry endeavors, but in our personal lives as well. When we catch an accurate glimpse of how we ought to love others, and what type of relational culture we're creating (because the cultures we create inevitably stem from our own strengths and weaknesses), we will have a real shot at deepening and widening the way we love.

As we explore these three leadership tensions, assess where you fall on the spectrum. Be mindful about which extreme you lean toward, remembering that we tend to want to justify the behaviors of the way we prefer to love and relate, and sometimes demonize the other extreme. There's great value in leadership to realize the good on both sides, as we strive to hold both in tension together (and again, it's not about a neutralizing form of balance but living in the tension that allows for a meaningful balance that combines extremes). God may want to challenge each leader to hold on to one without letting go of the other. These tensions remind us that all leadership in the kingdom needs to be centered in relationships, but the way we engage relationships can look quite different. We are still God's grandest plan to redeem humanity. Remember, Scripture tells us that others will know we're his disciples by our love for one another.

The kingdom of God is all about relationships. Creating a culture of relational health is all about love. Our leadership must be all about relationships and love. So, are you ready to take your relational leadership to the next level?

6 • The Tension of Commitment

OVERCOMMITTERS AND UNDERDELIVERERS

THE FIRST CRITICAL TENSION of relational leadership revolves around commitments we make in our relational world. We'll begin with the infamous *overcommitters*. They are a lovable bunch, mostly because they'll do anything and everything. There's only one requirement. Just ask. The overcommitter is practically incapable of saying, "No." They treat the word *no* like it's a curse word only to be uttered by pagans and naysayers. Relationships mean more commitments, more obligations and more duties to fulfill. Overcommitters would rather die than let you down. And since dying isn't all that desirable of an alternative, they'll rise to the occasion once again.

Overcommitters equate loving with doing. As a result, they take very little time to themselves. They are stretched so thin you could use them as a tightrope to walk across. These kinds of leaders are frequently drained, exhausted and overwhelmed. They may have an unhappy spouse, and feel neglected while everyone else's needs are taken care of. They often live in a constant state of guilt over not doing enough. The only thing stopping them from doing more is time. If they had more, they would most definitely give it. But they're exhausted, even if they don't realize it. Not only do they have an impossible list of demands to meet, there's also no end in sight. Because if they are to love well, they must keep doing, doing, doing . . .

We met with a couple once who were high-level leaders in our church, out-of-the closet overcommitters. They needed an intervention of sorts. Jake and Shannon were overdrawn in their ministry and relational responsibilities. They didn't know how to stop committing to any and every request that came their way. They're the kind of leaders that everyone loves because they'll give and give and give, without ever asking anything in return. But the big questions that overcommitters struggle with are, "Will we still be sought after, and valued, if we start saying no?" or, "Will people still feel valued if we don't give endlessly?"

These were the questions Jake and Shannon were asking, even though they didn't fully realize it. We guided them through a process that involved getting to the root of why they felt the need to endlessly commit to being on the Sunday connection team, leading a small group, starting a new outreach ministry, organizing retreats, doing counseling, all at the same time. They also both worked other full-time jobs. All the while, they felt guilty for taking anything for themselves, or even for stepping back in their commitments. We didn't uncover every last reason for why they would overcommit, however we did discover enough for them to be convinced that they had a problem, and that they needed to do some deeper introspection. Issues like these always come from a deeper part of us that we struggle to grasp fully and clearly. Intentional reflection and self-evaluation is necessary.

Practically speaking, we helped Jake and Shannon come up with a plan on how to start saying no and how they could begin to draw much-needed relational boundaries. They cringed as we gave them our suggestions. Together, we mapped out the strategy of whom to start saying no to, and what relational boundaries were healthy ones to draw. Even though they hated that they were living on empty all the time, they had come to believe this was the godly way of relating to others. Saying no pushed up against a deep-rooted conviction that had built over time.

Underneath it all, there also lurked another fear. They couldn't imagine a relationship could exist that didn't demand everything of them, an unconditional love that was based on nothing but the inherent value of who they were. It was almost impossible for them to believe in. Our empathy for them was strong but we knew things must change if they were going to remain in ministry for the long haul. I have seen too many ministry leaders burn out because they didn't deal with their issues of overcommitment and look more deeply at their interior life to figure out why they do what they do.

THE RELIGION OF NEVER SAYING NO

The motivation for this young couple's overcommitment is similar to that of many other ministry leaders. On the surface, it appears to be saintlike sacrifice; dig a little deeper, and it's a struggle with people-pleasing. Go even deeper, and you may find that the overcommitter is racked with an irrational fear that he or she doesn't feel worthy enough to be loved if they don't keep doing. They're frightened to disappoint almost anyone. So they work and work and work. They think if they jump off the spiritual treadmill of service, they'll be knocked off for good, and never welcomed back to the only meaningful existence they can imagine.

So they run, and keep running. If they don't have the energy for it, they keep going anyway. If they are overwhelmed, they put their heads down and run harder. If they are warned by family and friends that they are burning out, they simply shrug them off as not understanding the belief and conviction they have to serve. When the whole time it is not really about serving. It's about earning. Earning love and finding worth. It's also about our trust levels with God.

Overcommitters have some wonderful qualities, but they get misaligned internally. The extreme emphasis is on doing and earning and pleasing. At some point, this leads to burnout, a complete sense of resentment, or perhaps even moral failure—because it's the only way to get out, so they sabotage themselves. They're so afraid to not be needed that they make sure that's never the case. What almost always begins as a noble virtue of serving and caring for others slowly morphs into an addiction to doing. The obvious tragedy here is that the more the overcommitter commits, the more he or she believes the lie that love is bought and earned, not given and received. The core of the gospel message is lost in the background of good works and the religion of never saying no.

As uncomfortable as it is for overcommitters, the challenge for them is to say that dreaded word "no." As this kind of leader draws boundaries and nurtures the atrophied truth of grace in their souls, they'll find the original beauty of sacrifice once again. One that's not based in a lie that says grace must be earned, rather one that's based in the perfect sacrifice Jesus Christ made for us. Once the extreme focus isn't merely placed on the value of service, a sacred balance is struck. Over-committing will cease. The true essence of serving will take its place, as we learn to navigate through the inner challenges that drive our overcommitment. Then, love will move further away from being just a word, and will start touching those surrounding the servant leader, who now understands that grace is given, not earned, and that their commitment or even lack of commitment doesn't change that fact.

FOUR GUIDING PRINCIPLES IN LEARNING TO SAY NO

1. **Limits:** Remember that you have limits—and that Jesus in his humanity did too. Be clear on these limits of time and relational capacity, embrace them humbly and then use this clarity to inform whom you spend time with and how often. Sometimes you also need to communicate your limits to people so they understand why you're saying no (see Ephesians 4:25; 5:13-14).

2. **Priorities:** Clarify your priorities in life and in ministry. Saying yes to one means saying no to another (always). Instead of letting others determine where you spend your time, take initiative to spend it in ways that align with your priorities and core values. Be less reactive and more proactive. This is your responsibility, no one else's. For instance, if your family is your top priority, your behavior should be congruent to your stated value. Monitor this consistently.

3. **Margins:** Far too many ministry leaders live maxed out, meaning they don't leave space in their life for interruptions, which can often be divine interruptions that we don't have time for. Make sure your schedule can breathe so that you can respond to crisis, or emergency, or needs that ought to be responded to. Jesus lived this way. One example of a margin involves practicing sabbath, and my experience shows me that far too many pastors don't obey this teaching of Scripture. Another example is to leave one hour of each

workday open as you schedule your weeks. This margin allows interactions, coversations or even personal space to be had that need to be had.

4. **Counsel**: Ask a couple close friends or your spouse to give you honest input on what they think you say yes to and perhaps shouldn't. Find someone who is especially courageous and also willing to speak directly to you about what they observe. Much wisdom may follow.

THE UNDERDELIVERER

Now, let's examine the *underdeliverer*, which just sounds bad, doesn't it? If you have to be on one extreme, wouldn't it look better to overcommit rather than underdeliver? Although this may sound unappealing, many things about the underdeliverer actually look good at first glance. For instance, this kind of leader tends to cast beautiful visions and make those around them believe in the impossible. However, if the overcommitter's problem is that they're too reliable, the underdeliverer's problem is that they're not reliable enough. They are often great at inspiring us with how things could and should be, but they may struggle with making that inspiring vision a concreate reality.

The underdeliverer tends to be very popular, thus rallying tons of relational energy around them. They're kind of like the kid running for school president who promises free lunches and longer recesses. There's no way they're going to follow through with it, but they genuinely believe they are going to in the moment. And what kids are going to follow the candidate who promises more realistic results, like an extra ten minutes in homeroom, or discounts on textbooks for kids who achieve honor roll status? Most of us would vote for the underdeliverer every time.

The kind of leader that's always making promises can be very attractive to others. These leaders create a culture of idealism, vision, enthusiasm and even hope that things can be different (maybe school can actually be fun instead of boring). They have no shortage of followers. Who doesn't want to commune around such idealism, optimism and what appears to be innovation? But to maintain this kind of enthusiasm, momentum and ongoing vision, underdeliverers need to be remembering to partner with people who can help them keep those promises they keep making.

What happens when that leader cannot keep his or her promises? What happens when the weight of reality crashes down on the illusion of perfection? What happens when school doesn't get out early and lunch isn't free? The once profound adoration for the underdeliverer quickly disintegrates into distaste when those promises are broken. As sincerely motivated as the underdelivering leader was when making those vows, it matters little when he or she simply doesn't deliver. This lack of follow-through wreaks havoc on relationships and church cultures. Followers become disillusioned. People become angry. Trust is broken. People leave churches. Promises lose their meaning. As a result, relationships are fractured.

MOUTHS OF INACTION

What does God have to say about underdelivering?

> It is better not to make a vow than to make one and not fulfill it. Do not let your mouth lead you into sin. And do not protest to the temple messenger, "My vow was a mistake." Why should God be angry at what you say and destroy the work of your hands? Much dreaming and many words are meaningless. Therefore fear God. (Ecclesiastes 5:5-7 TNIV)

This passage breaks down the problem of the underdeliverer's mindset.

First, "Do not let your mouth lead you into sin." Solomon is basically saying that we allow words to come out of our mouths without action to back them up. We should always measure our words, because if we don't they could lead us down a race we cannot finish. As leaders, we can easily make the mistake of talking flippantly about things we plan on changing, implementing or creating, while not truly having the intention to follow through with it. We should resist the temptation to talk a good talk, make grand promises and cast impossible visions. If we don't follow through with our word, we sin. It's as simple as that.

Second, "Do not protest" when the work of our hands is "destroyed," and simply chalk it up to being a "mistake." I think this is all-too-descriptive of so many young ministry leaders' modus operandi. We make promises and don't keep them. Our work (peripheral or central to the promises) is destroyed, or at least fractured, which we would see in the form of either relational distress or obstacles in our ministry efforts. And we do two things. We protest and question. Why should God get so angry over a little thing like unfulfilled vows? I meant well. Sometimes things just don't work out. Why should I be blamed for an innocent mistake? And if we're doing a good thing, how could it be wrong to be idealistic in how we talk about it? The world needs a little more of that, don't you think, God?

It's real clear: God doesn't want us to promise what we can't deliver. He wants us to promise what we can deliver. And when we don't, there are consequences. But not just from him—from us. We think God destroys the work of our hands, but the irony is that we are often the destroyers. If we as leaders cannot turn our words into reality, who can? We crush the very idealism we preach. And much worse than that, we crush the relationships we have built around our false promises. Trust dissolves, and our impact diminishes. Truth is, the consequences are often far worse than we realize.

LEADERSHIP INTEGRITY

At the core of the underdeliverer's sin is a lack of integrity. We may perceive it as the shadow-side of idealism, or a casual personality flaw. But in actuality, it's usually a poor attempt at rationalizing a lack of integrity. When we gloss over the severity of breaking our word, no matter what form it takes, we open ourselves up to relational breakdown—not only with others, but with God.

We as leaders may not start every sentence with "I promise . . . ," but if the implication is that we will do something, then we must keep our integrity and do it. If we can't, we need to confess to those that we verbally commit to and seek forgiveness for not fulfilling our word. Otherwise, people in our circles of influence will stop trusting us. Our words will become meaningless. Our credibility will be always in question. If we are to create healthy relational cultures, where we value others as God does, we must honor others by keeping our word. That's an example of love lived out. And that's the path toward developing spiritual authority.

Solomon ends the passage brilliantly: "Much dreaming and many words are meaningless. Therefore fear God." I see these words as powerful keys for the underdeliverer to use as they unlock the mystery of what's holding back their relational influence. It's as if Solomon is saying to us, "What do dreams and words matter if you can't keep your integrity?" All your idealism and vision are meaningless against the background of broken promises. Here's how to stop allowing your mouth to lead you to sin. Fear God. Understand that he holds us accountable for our leadership as it relates to the promises we make—good intentions or not. When we break our word, it hurts the people we claim to love. It hurts the church. And God sees that. It's about time we do as well.

IDEAS FOR MENTORS

Mentoring the overcommitter. Encourage an overcommitter to take some time to reflect on how they can set better relational boundaries. The book titled *Boundaries* by John Townsend and Henry Cloud is a phenomenal guide to take you deeper into this conversation with protégés. (I also use the book *Choosing to Cheat* by Andy Stanley to guide and stimulate this conversation.) Instruct protégés to identify where they need to say no more often, and perhaps even identify more clearly what drives their lack of boundary setting (fear of rejection, fear of disappointing others, etc.). Create an accountability structure to revisit this conversation so you can help them grow over time. In other words, revisit what they commit to saying no to, and ask them how well they've kept that commitment. Setting relational boundaries is critical for young leaders to get a hold of if they want to avoid things like burnout, failed marriages or other significant issues down the road.

5. **Mentoring the underdeliverer.** Challenge an underdeliverer to stop overpromising and start overdelivering. Challenge him or her to actually *do more* and *talk less*. Before protégés talk about what they're going to do, have them do it. Set up

an accountability structure for them where they share with only you what they are going to do, or what responsibility they're taking on. Then, when they complete the task(s) or project(s), ask them to let you be the first to know.

MENTOR TIP:
A COACH'S ESSENCE

The best coaches embody these five things:

1. *presence and availability*

2. *support and encouragement*

3. *willingness to challenge people honestly and directly*

4. *offering the appropriate dose of direction according to what someone needs and desires*

5. *asking the right questions*

7 • The Tension of Conflict

AVOIDERS AND EVOKERS

> *Change means movement. Movement means friction.*
> *Only in the frictionless vacuum of a nonexistent abstract*
> *world can movement or change occur without that*
> *abrasive friction of conflict.*
>
> SAUL ALINSKY, **RULES FOR RADICALS**

IT'S IMPOSSIBLE TO DISCUSS RELATIONAL HEALTH without addressing the ever-present reality of conflict. Many of us have a love-hate relationship with conflict. We know it can be good. But we also know it can be really bad, and really hard. It can bring people together and make them grow. Or it can sever their love forever. It is terribly dangerous territory with huge potential for the kind of saving that so many of us need.

It is difficult enough to deal with conflict in our personal lives, much less our ministry lives. Since most of us aren't exactly the poster-child for healthy conflict resolution skills, we must look honestly at the effects of unresolved or mishandled conflict in our ministry relationships. Facing conflict and engaging confrontation is far from comfortable for me, and probably for many of you. But one thing I've learned in my life and leadership is that not facing conflict has far worse long-term consequences than we usually consider. Plus, I've also learned how much real growth can happen when conflict is faced and resolved in increasingly healthy ways. As a mentor, I try to remember that one of my roles in mentoring protégés involves reminding them to face the conflict in their lives, and then holding them accountable for doing so. Hardly anyone likes to do this. But it must be done.

The way we handle conflict is so essential to the health of our ministries and the relational cultures we create. If emerging ministry leaders don't determine in their hearts to develop conflict resolution skills, ministries and churches will remain dysfunctional, stunted in their growth, and in some cases even become relationally and emotionally toxic if they're not already. If we leaders don't set the right example in our approach, which none of us have perfected, our bad habits will inevitably trickle down to the relational spheres underneath us. Our ministries will continue to be places of increased division instead of the unity that Jesus envisioned for us.

One way we embody a more mature version of love is through how we handle conflict. If we're ever going to optimize relational impact and depth in our circles of influence, learning to engage conflict in a healthy and biblical way is crucial. And to establish kingdom cultures of relational health in our churches and ministries, most of us need to rethink our approach to conflict. So, let's take a deeper look at two of the extremes of how people tend to handle conflict, and consider how we can hold both of these extremes in tension as we learn from both the conflict avoider and the conflict evoker.

THE CONFLICT AVOIDER

On one end of the spectrum, we have the avoider. But before we pick on the avoider, let's look at the good qualities. Conflict avoiders often have a gift for not harboring the little things, for finding common ground and for knowing how to maintain harmony in their relationships. Maintaining harmony is not just important relationally, but commanded biblically. The Scriptures tell us to "make every effort to live at peace with all" (Hebrews 12:14). You usually don't see a lot of quarreling and bickering in their relationships—almost none in fact. Their silent mantra is "keep the peace." That can be one remarkable contribution they make to the body of Christ, and the body of Christ certainly needs peacemakers. Jesus even says that peacemakers are blessed. For those of us who have come from backgrounds where we had a lot of chaos, violence or anger (family, ministry, etc.), these kinds of leaders are a sight for sore eyes.

There are different variations and degrees of conflict avoidance, some less extreme and harder to detect, while other forms are more obvious and evident. In general, you don't have to worry about setting off avoiders for some unknown reason, or about what mood they're in, or whether or not you're going to need a counseling session after meeting with them. The avoider tends to be kind, gracious, easy on the nerves and always on your side (even when they aren't). You could be fired by them and may not even know it. You may even think that you just got a promotion because of how nice they were. Or you could be like me who got dumped by one of them but had absolutely no idea until she vanished like a ghost.

The problem with the technique of avoiding conflict is that it feels nice, tenderhearted and kind at first. But eventually it catches up with you. Although some conflicts are good to avoid, there are others that must not be avoided. If they're avoided, internal tension builds, which sometimes blows up in our face later. In most cases, when we avoid conflict, we're not really avoiding, rather we are simply putting off the consequences of dealing with it. Quite often, the consequences are worse down the road, or at a minimum, they hinder the health of our own emotional and relational world.

Avoiders are often the kind of leaders who flood others with encouraging, affirming and positive words. But if confrontation becomes necessary, they fear saying the hard truth or bringing up an uncomfortable issue. They often choose the comfort of avoidance over honesty and courage. We may see them as gracious truth-avoiders. They may graciously pretend that everything is all right, or that they aren't angry when they really are. They often rationalize their decision to avoid because facing the truth produces unnecessary anxiety they don't want to face. Sometimes avoiders even think they're *loving people* by keeping the peace, but in truth, they might be failing to step into a whole arena of life that can produce spiritual transformation in others and even in themselves. True love may be lost.

A friend of mine who is in vocational ministry recently shared his experience with me in relation to the avoider technique. Brad worked at a church that he loved. He couldn't believe how well everyone seemed to work together, and how friendly the high-level staff were. Brad enjoyed the harmonious work environment and almost always felt like things were going well. He assumed that someone, anyone, would talk to him about it if he wasn't meeting their expectations. He learned the hard way that this wasn't the case.

One day Brad was casually talking to John, his supervisor, when John kindly gave him shocking news. As they discussed normal ministry stuff about the church, John casually shared with Brad how well this other staff person was doing in his new role. The weird thing was that the new role he was talking about was actually Brad's exact role. In other words, Brad had been unknowingly replaced by another staff person, and this is how Brad found out.

In the same casual conversation, John quickly articulated how excited he was about Brad's *new role*. Again, this was how Brad found out about *his* new role. Brad's new role was presented as if it were a promotion, even though it wasn't that at all. John was friendly, nice, even casual about the whole thing, but of course it really bothered Brad. As Brad walked away, he allowed the words and reality to absorb. It felt like a strange way to get demoted.

John believed he was doing Brad a favor by glossing over the demotion, and essentially pretending it was a promotion (so Brad would "feel better"). Though John seemed to be patting him on the back and shining a five-star pastoral smile his way, Brad felt quite the opposite. When reality set in, it ended up being very upsetting, even hurtful. Since trust was broken, a rift formed between them. Honesty and truth had been swept under the rug.

There was no real or honest conversation about this major role change. This left Brad in an awkward spot. And not only was he demoted, he was never given any constructive feedback on how he could or should have improved, or even what he did wrong. He was never told in an evaluation that he was not meeting the expectations and goals of his job. In truth, he never had a chance to succeed because he didn't even know he was failing in the eyes of his superiors.

Yes, Brad enjoyed a serene and gracious working environment, but at the cost of honesty and openness. He quickly saw the price to be paid for the unending niceness he experienced—eroding trust and ongoing skepticism about what the real truth was. In avoiding conflict, the relationship lacked honesty and the kind of feedback that could produce genuine growth. As you can imagine, all this made the situation a more painful experience and created unnecessary, lingering tension between Brad and John.

Brad now knew that things had to change, and that facing this conflict was inevitable if he wanted to bring resolution here. In the spirit of obeying Jesus' words in Matthew 18:15, he approached John and expressed his disappointment and hurt feelings on the matter. John was quick to politely acknowledge that he was sorry that it hurt Brad's feelings (which wasn't an acknowledgement of doing anything wrong, and therefore not really an apology . . . don't you love those?). Then John shined another five-star smile, while proceeding to change the subject with lightning speed. Brad was later told by another high level staff member that he should simply do what he's told and not make waves with his supervisor. The message that this sent to Brad was that it's not okay to bring up conflict, and instead he should just deal with it on his own. Once again, the effects of the avoider were at play.

Although the scenarios may look different, there are many staff and team cultures that don't affirm the importance of appropriate, honest conversation when a conflict arises. These cultures are rampant in churches, and they are not the way of the kingdom. According to Matthew 18:15-17 there are appropriate, biblical ways to face conflict that may be countercultural, but they paint a picture of a kingdom culture.

Still, Brad attempted to probe deeper into resolving the existing relational tension, as he had attempted to do in other awkward or tense scenarios. However, he eventually came to accept that the relational dynamics were not going to change with John and the existing culture of that staff. This was, in essence, the last straw for Brad. Although avoiders can contribute in positive ways, John's avoidance patterns were just too dysfunctional for Brad to embrace. There had been systemic conflict avoidance on this staff team that over several years had not been looked at or acknowledged. As a result of all this, Brad resigned. He was unwilling to stay where the truth was hidden and where relational honesty was pushed away, even frowned upon. He didn't want to stay in an environment where his commitment to engage conflict was perceived as antagonistic rather than helpful. Whether that was true or not, he'll never know. But what he did know was that avoiding conflict was the only option in this church staff culture. That isn't the way of the kingdom, and it's not the way to build a culture of relational and emotional health. Brad didn't want to remain where he wasn't free to tell the truth, no matter how nice, harmonious and friendly everyone seemed to be.

THE HARD TRUTH

Avoiding conflict creates unhealthy relational cultures for two main reasons. First, it diminishes the value and need for relational honesty, which fosters pretending. Second, it stifles the relational courage and vulnerability necessary for healthy relationships to exist.

There's no doubt that the truth can be incredibly difficult to hear—whether it has to do with offense taken, or critical feedback given, or if it has to do with something you're protective of. We often don't like to hear truth, and many don't even like to tell it. We know we're stepping on the equivalent of emotional glass. Emotions are extremely fragile. Insecurities are easily flared. And the relational glue seems to be disturbed to a frightening degree. No wonder so many of us avoid it. Who wants to take those kind of relational risks? Is honesty really worth the fallout? Is vulnerability really worth the rejection we may face? The answer is yes. It is worth it. With one disclaimer: It's worth it if it's done the right way. But that doesn't mean doing conflict resolution perfectly, because that pretty much never happens.

As leaders of teams, we need to affirm people's attempts at resolving conflict the right way, the biblical way. We will look at what Jesus has to say about how to engage conflict in a moment, but first, we have to examine the cause of withholding truth.

Fear stops us from telling the truth. We're afraid of so many things. Afraid that those we care about will be angry with us or disappointed in us. We fear the volatile and unpredictable emotions of others. We dread the unknown results of raising an issue. We're afraid we will second-guess ourselves when we're told we are wrong, allowing doubt to silence us. We think we're inarticulate, unable to share our thoughts that will inevitably cause friction to the one we're communicating with. Most of all, we fear rejection. Will our friend, family member, employee or ministry partner be so angry or hurt that they'll abandon us or write us off for good? The thought is unbearable to us. So what do we do?

We avoid.

If we're ever going to be honest (in a God-centered way), there's one trait that we cannot live without . . . courage. Avoiders lack courage like a car engine lacks fuel. We just can't move forward because we're so afraid. Courage will only be possible when we do one essential thing—when we determine to do relationships God's way.

All too often when people face conflict, they try to force the result they want or try to manipulate the situation. If our sole intent in facing conflict is to produce a certain favorable result, we have failed before we've even begun. If we're doing it because it is the right thing to do, not because we want a certain selfish outcome, then we'll be able to lean into the uncomfortable territory of living in relational truth.

We learned in kindergarten that not everything we think should be said out loud—and that is certainly true. And even those things that ought to be said out loud in honesty are not always welcome. So how do you know when God wants you to engage conflict through telling the truth? Well, if you struggle with avoiding, and need points of reference to guide you in when it's time to say the difficult thing, here are a few markers from Scripture to consider.

1. Are You Taking Responsibility of Your Own Emotions?

First, it is always wise to get clarity about your own emotional state, and then deal with what's going on inside of you. For instance, if you find yourself marinating in an offense that has happened against you, or you just can't shake the anger or even bitterness ruminating inside, remember the words of the apostle Paul:

> Get rid of all bitterness, rage and anger, brawling and slander, along with every form of malice. (Ephesians 4:31)

By "get rid of," Paul doesn't mean for us to suppress our feelings. Instead, we must take healthy steps to process our emotions by thorough reflection or with friends or some type of counselor or mentor. Identify why they exist. Be honest about where and how we've been wronged and where you may be oversensitive. Reflect on what part of our thinking is right and what part is unhealthy and misguided. Our emotions always signal something. We ought not shame ourselves for having an emotion, but certainly shouldn't avoid dealing with it either. Our responsibility is to pay attention to our emotions, and invite God and trusted friends to help us identify what our particular emotions are signaling to us. Don't ignore them. Don't even try to "kill them off." Pay attention to what's going on. Prayerfully consider the root of those emotions. You could even read and pray through the Psalms as a way of helping you express yourself to God.

As a protégé, if you desire to become emotionally healthy and whole, you must not neglect self-care in your emotional world. I could say much more on this, but for now, I simply challenge you to pay closer attention to what's going on inside and take responsibility for dealing with your emotions in the healthiest way you know how, trusting God and wise counsel to help lead the process.[1]

2. Are You Withholding What Someone Really Needs to Hear?

There's a second biblical marker to guide the avoider. When someone in your life is open to your influence and you are withholding insights that could help him or her grow in Christ, remember: "It is better to correct someone openly than to have love and not show it" (Proverbs 27:5 NCV). Let's say the scenario involves someone who's under your leadership. You see things in their life that need to change, or areas in need of growth. Like Brad's supervisor John, maybe you have expectations but are not sharing them because you're afraid the person will be upset. You're avoiding appropriate truth-telling. Even when it would be so much easier to avoid facing the conflict, remember that the biblical way is to share life-giving correction with them.

Now, I don't mean we go around sharing anything and everything we see. I'm directing the application here to people with whom we have established trust and relational credibility. When we do offer life-giving correction, Scripture tells us that the person who allows it to permeate their exterior defenses will be on the path toward ever-deepening wisdom.

This also means that when we withhold what conversation we need to engage, the other person loses the chance to become wiser. Sharing a difficult truth with someone always creates an opportunity to grow.

3. What Do You Do When Someone Who Has Authority Over You Sins?

A third marker for the avoider relates to how we respond when we observe a person in leadership living in sin. The kingdom way is to approach them, and to do it using humility, tact, love and wisdom. We see a priceless example of this when Nathan approaches David about his adulterous relationship (see 2 Samuel 12:1-13). This is the same David who had humble beginnings as a shepherd and who had risen to power as king. But David lost his way. He began abusing his power and didn't see it. He got off track, and didn't deal with it. By the time Nathan came to David, there had been one abuse of power after another. For one, David took a woman who wasn't his wife and killed a soldier in an effort to clean up his mess. That's where Nathan comes in.

This is pure speculation, but I imagine Nathan did not want to confront King David. However, we do know that Nathan was moved by God to speak with conviction and courage to someone who had the power to end his life with one simple command. God may have called others to speak truth to David, but no one else had the courage and deepest kind of unselfish love to do so.

Nathan tactfully used a metaphor to communicate to David, who had sinned heinously. David's eyes were suddenly opened to the ugliness of what he had done. His heart was broken with repentance and regret. It was as if these words Nathan spoke unlocked a steel door between David and the truth of his own heart. David was finally free to be honest before a friend and before God. He was free to move forward and receive forgiveness. And although there were horrible consequences (the baby born from the adultery was killed), David was once again back on the path toward wholeness.

Conversations like these are never easy, and they almost never come at a good time. Plus, there's always a compelling reason to avoid a confrontation. People who have these conversations with us almost seem like our enemies. But they can be our truest allies.

Once in a while a person comes along who speaks life into that future we so desperately want to believe can be true. They help us find our way back to forgiveness, wholeness and freedom. Sometimes that person needs to be us, and that's why we cannot remain as avoiders if we want to be the best kind of spiritual leaders.

In this case, Nathan uses a metaphor to communicate to David in a way that's not accusatory; he uses tact and wisdom to tell the truth in a way it may be more likely received. Conflict resolution almost never works well when it's driven by accusatory comments or a judgmental, arrogant posture that some even disguise in spiritual language. Instead of being accusatory or proud, choose to walk humbly, love mercy and remain gracious in the midst of your honesty and confrontation. Nathan clearly thought about *how* exactly he'd communicate this truth to David. His tactful, wise approach paid off. Will we have this kind of courage when it's called for? Will we use the same level of tact and wisdom, as well as humility, mercy and grace? Will we be willing and courageous enough to be a Nathan for someone who has lost their way?

4. Do You Have Unresolved Tension?

There's a fourth marker that can guide the avoider. When you observe, or sense, an ongoing tension between you and another person, initiate a conversation around the source of friction. Sometimes you don't even know what exactly is going on, or what you did wrong or why that person is upset with you. You just sense that person has something against you. According to the Bible, it must be addressed.

Ministry leaders too often allow conflict to remain underground. If we allow this to continue, it will directly affect the health of our ministry. Jesus teaches us what to do with unresolved tension and conflict with utter clarity. His advice is simple to understand, but extremely hard to do. As spiritual leaders, we must not only choose this path in our lives, we must guide and encourage others to do the same.

> Therefore, if you are offering your gift at the altar and there remember that your brother or sister has something against you, leave your gift there in front of the altar. First go and be reconciled to that person; then come and offer your gift. (Matthew 5:23-24 TNIV)

So, if you realize that you've sinned against someone, be the first to initiate. Apologize. Initiate reconciliation. Take responsibility. Be courageous.

5. What If You Get Sinned Against?

One final marker for the avoider is revealed when someone has sinned against you. Once you establish that there's an offense or sin between you and another, or you know there's a conflict that needs to be engaged with someone, use Matthew 18:15-17 as a guide. This passage instructs us on what to do when *sin* is involved.

> If a brother or sister sins, go and point out the fault, just between the two of you. If they listen to you, you have won them over. But if they will not listen, take one or two others along, so that "every matter may be established by the testimony of two or three witnesses." If they still refuse to listen, tell it to the church; and if they refuse to listen even to the church, treat them as you would a pagan or tax collector. (TNIV)

First step? Go directly to the person who sinned against or offended you. The key words here are "between the two of you." Since avoiders tend not to address things head on, they often feel the need to express their woes to others, safer people who won't get mad at them, reject them or challenge them. Jesus reinforces the importance of keeping the offense where it belongs, between the offender and the offended. No third parties. And if you don't have the courage to go directly to the person, then at least have the chops to keep it to yourself.

I've messed up on this one a thousand times. Jesus' words are so clear and simple that they can't be misinterpreted. We can't rationalize our gossip or venting once we surrender to his authority on the matters of conflict. Bypassing the one person who can do anything about our disappointment in them is so utterly fruitless—it's a wonder we ever do it at all. But just in case we still want to, here's where we listen to God instead of to our sinful, avoider inclinations.

As ministry leaders, if you really want to take this to the next level, when someone starts talking about some conflict they have in their life, kindly interrupt and ask them if they've talked to that person or tried to work it out. It could be a little awkward, but this is one of the best ways I've found to build a conflict-facing culture and minimize gossip and slander too. Point them to the kingdom way. It can help us change the tone and health of our relational cultures.

When you go to the person who hurt you, sinned against you or is even failing you, resist using accusations. Seek to understand them first. Share more about what bothered you, hurt you, disappointed you, and why, rather than framing the conversation around what they did wrong and becoming an accuser or attacker. It's not that you never express what they did wrong, but that's not the best way to enter the conversation, mostly because it immediately puts people on the defense.

The bottom line is, we ought to give the person a chance to apologize and make it right first. Although it's not always easy, if we're fortunate enough and we do everything we know to do it with a wise and tactful approach, the person will often listen and we'll have "won them over."

If they don't listen, and conflict isn't resolved, Jesus commands us to bring one or two others with us. This is hard. That's why most people don't do it. I mean, did Jesus really get the relational nuances here? Did he understand how much someone doesn't like to be ambushed by two or three people, only to be told that they are wrong? This is again where we need to be more concerned with releasing the results to God than with reaching our preferred outcome. Knowing that we're stubborn and have an eternal aversion to any form of critique, Jesus still summons us to proceed. Why? I believe it's because he wants the best for us relationally. I believe it's because he knows that facing conflict is the path toward real unity and love.

If someone has sinned, or is living in sin, they can be incredibly resistant to hearing the truth. Sometimes it takes a good ambush to snap us out of our self-deluded way of living. The more truth (in love) that's given, the more chance someone has to be pulled out of the stubborn darkness they find themselves in. In my ministry experience sometimes I've had to involve other people in the confrontation. It's always difficult when it gets to this point. But sometimes it is necessary to bring others to confront someone who continues to resist reconciliation and repentance.

Bringing one or two witnesses helps not only bring clarity to the person we're confronting, but it somewhat protects us from someone telling a misconstrued story to tarnish our reputation. These things can quickly spin out of control. The more people you bring in to restore the relationship, and to support the authority of Scripture, the more you're protected against potential slander and relational warfare. It's an ugly reality, but it exists nonetheless. Don't shrink back from bringing other trustworthy and respected Christ followers into the interaction when appropriate. We must not fear the outcome. Remember, Jesus knows what he's talking about.

If the person still refuses to listen to *even the church*, "treat them as you would a pagan or a tax collector." In other words, if they won't listen to three respected and godly Christ followers who base their definition of righteous living in the Scriptures, then treat them as if they work for the IRS. Finally, the avoider can avoid! Jesus actually commands it.

It's actually incredibly sad when situations reach this point, but I've seen it. Truth is, nothing more can be done. Jesus knows this too. Ultimately a person can choose whatever way they desire. But that doesn't mean there aren't consequences to that choice. If they refuse to repent or reconcile, there's a different way we ought to relate to them—never with cruelty or complete exclusion, but certainly not as if nothing happened.

At times we have to part ways relationally from someone who only wants to fight the truth, rather than receive it. That's the whole point. There can be no true relationship where there's no truth. Engaging conflict is one of the most essential paths toward discovering the merit of your relationships, and toward helping people grow.

We must find the courage to love others, even when they may not like it. Jesus did it all the time. And his main purpose is to reconcile humanity to himself. We may be surprised at how much relational growth awaits us when we courageously face rather than sheepishly avoid, lean in rather than shrink back, and love rather than ignore. When we see relationships restored, forgiveness given, transformation happen and courage arise, our regrets dissolve. The unknown is scary, but missing out on what God has in store for our relationships is scarier. After all, we serve a mighty and powerful God. And he will help us overcome our fears as we engage the fight worth fighting, the one for love that endures and overcomes. He is with us every step of the way. So avoiders, go and avoid no more.

THE CONFLICT EVOKER

"Conflict is inevitable, but combat is optional."[2] There are those who avoid conflict. And luckily for so many of us, there are those who evoke it. In fact, they seem to thrive on it. If you're not an evoker, I bet you know one.

Again, let me begin with a positive. What are the attributes of an evoker? Well, they like a good fight and they don't allow fear to stop them from jumping in the ring. They make great activists, preachers and boxers. In a world racked with fear and insidious anxiety, these kinds of leaders are refreshing. In truth, they're often inspiring. We respect people who don't back down, no matter the cost. And we're drawn to leaders who plow ahead like a bull into a stadium, ready to take on anything and anyone. They have courage and a willingness to fight, until that courage turns into domination, and that willingness turns into absolute stubbornness.

Conflict evokers often take pride in confronting, and even boast about how good they are at it. They can't wait to tell someone what they said to someone that everyone else was afraid to say. On the positive side, they are usually bold and often serious about helping others change. On the other hand, they haven't always embraced the art of speaking the truth *in love* (Ephesians 4:15), or doing it with gentleness and respect as the Scriptures teach. Their empathy quotient tends to be low. They sometimes inflict truth on people in a graceless manner. Although they're good at standing up and speaking up for what's right and true, they may forget about ensuring they communicate in a spirit of tender love.

I once worked with a guy I admired. He had that kind of fire in his eyes that made you want to join whatever he was doing. It didn't matter if you were cleaning toilets; he'd make it seem like you were taking down the man. I spent time with him here and there, and always took notice of his strength of presence. He actually kind of scared me. He didn't seem like the kind of guy you'd want to cross. But he was such a force to be reckoned with that you had to respect him.

We crossed that invisible line from cordial to combative when we went on a mission trip together. We partnered to lead a team overseas. He gave me quite a run for my money. While I tend to lean more toward the conflict *avoider* side of things, he most definitely leaned toward the conflict *evoker* side. I couldn't believe how much tension flew through the air right from the start. When we corralled our team, you would've thought he was leading the cavalry into war. When we disagreed on something, you would've thought I'd just insulted his mother. Things were tense. I felt like I do with my kids when I have to remove all sharp objects within reach. I had no idea what I was in for when we embarked on this journey. We were only a few days in and this guy had already exhausted my avoider capabilities. I was forced to face him head on.

I'm happy to report that all went well. As volatile as he seemed, it was surprisingly easy to resolve this conflict with him when I faced it head on. I pulled him to the side and addressed the tension between us in straightforward fashion. He was quick to acknowledge his aversion to sharing power with someone else, and to admit he had let himself get carried away in his need to control everything. We both apologized and tried as best we could to adjust to each other's personality. It turns out that as much as he loves a good fight, he also loves people. Avoiders sometimes assume evokers don't. Mostly, avoiders and evokers simply have different ways of handling conflict.

Where avoiders almost have laser-like sensitivity to tension, evokers don't usually project sensitivity at all. Sometimes they are more comfortable in tension than out of it. If emotions aren't roaring, then the environment is boring. Passion and courage are often great strengths of a conflict evoker. But like any strengths, if not harnessed, they morph into an uglier version of themselves—in this case being dogmatic and domineering. They might rush to conclusions, become angry quickly, feel threatened easily and attack prematurely. Conflict and drama follow them wherever they go. They don't mind if you fight back, but you better be prepared for their fury. Most people aren't. And these evokers are further empowered to dominate and dictate.

If you're a leader who tends to evoke conflict, you may not even be aware of it. If you consider your fierce ability to command others with uncanny efficiency, perhaps you'd also be able to see your tendency to inflame tension. Often it's leaders with a high ability to get things done, and to impassion others to do the same, who also struggle with thriving off of war. If you're not fighting for something, you feel useless. So you make sure there's always a fight to engage in.

Here are some signs that you or someone you know may be an evoker:

- You have a hard time understanding why you seem to be the only one who expresses their anger and discontentment. Or you can't grasp why others don't seem like they're being honest and communicative with their frustrations.

- You're quicker to speak and slower to listen.

- You feel misunderstood quite often, and people might assume you're on a power trip. In reality, you perceive yourself as more intense and passionate than the average leader.

- You find yourself easily offended and struggle not to retaliate when your ego gets bruised.

- You find it difficult to share power and control with others. You're more comfortable when you're in charge and calling the shots.

- You've noticed that conflict seems to follow you, and you're not sure why.

- You've been affirmed for your tough-mindedness; however, you've also been told that you can be insensitive and unsympathetic to what people are going through or how they absorb your communication style.

- You're easily frustrated with how things are being handled, led or executed—more specifically, about what's not being addressed.

- You're often more concerned with hashing it out or debating than restoring the relationship.

- You struggle with discerning between appropriate boldness and borderline cruelty.

- You've been complimented on your courage and your aptitude for shooting straight with people. Although a strength, it lends itself to evoking conflict.

- Your fears are usually more about letting things go than actually addressing things head on. That's not hard for you.

In summary, if you feel like you're easily frustrated, angered, offended or misunderstood, you may unintentionally fall into the evoker category. Or if you feel the need to be in control and find it difficult to share power with others, you probably evoke more conflict than you realize. You may have even been accused of being abrasive or harsh. Where avoiders shy away from a fight, you find it hard not to confront someone who has offended you and say what you think.

FIERCE LEADERS

If you're a more confrontational leader, or evoker of conflict, here are a few ways it could affect your relationships in a negative way. When you give feedback to others, they may feel more beat up than they do invested in, more harmed than helped. When you engage conflict, people may feel as though their side wasn't heard or understood because they felt bullied. When people disagree with you, they may feel as if they've personally insulted you because of how strongly you respond, leaving them far less likely to ever verbally disagree with you again. When people feel hurt by you, they may never bring it up for fear that you will reject or alienate them. This hinders healthy community and biblical unity.

When an evoker injects this dynamic into their relational worlds, the same dynamic ripples throughout all circles of influence under them. It can create an atmosphere of fear, even terror. Most people don't have either the courage or the patience to engage so much relational tension. So we, especially as those in leadership, have a responsibility to love others in the way we approach conflict with them. I believe the fiercest kind of leaders create an atmosphere of love, trust and approachability, rather than tension, fear and inaccessibility.

The apostle Paul strikes me as a fierce leader, always ready for a fight. He fought against Jesus before he was converted. He fought for Christ after. All of the character flaws that accompanied that kind of unbridled passion didn't magically disappear when he became a Christian. I imagine he found it difficult to infuse kindness and gentleness into his fierce approach to truth-telling. He was an unstoppable force wherever he went as he engaged people with intensity and bold assurance. How did such a passionate, intense and brave man temper his character with love, grace and acceptance? He held on to one extreme without letting go of the other.

In addition to Paul's fierce nature, he had another side. We see it in a few of the Scriptures Paul penned on how to treat others.

> Be completely humble and gentle; be patient, bearing with one another in love. Make every effort to keep the unity of the Spirit through the bond of peace. (Ephesians 4:2-3)

> Instead, speaking the truth in love, we will grow to become in every respect the mature body of him who is the head, that is, Christ. (Ephesians 4:15 NIV 2011)

> Therefore, as God's chosen people, holy and dearly loved, clothe yourself with compassion, kindness, humility, gentleness and patience. Bear with each other and forgive one another if any of you has a grievance with someone. Forgive as the Lord forgave you. And over all these virtues, put on love, which binds them all together in perfect unity. (Colossians 3:12-14 NIV 2011)

> Brothers and sisters, if someone is caught in a sin, you who live by the Spirit should restore that person gently. But watch yourselves, or you also may be tempted. (Galatians 6:1 TNIV)

> And the Lord's servant must not be quarrelsome but must be kind to everyone, able to teach, not resentful. Opponents must be gently instructed, in the hope that God will grant them repentance leading them to a knowledge of the truth. (2 Timothy 2:24-25 TNIV)

Paul is an inspiring figure because he seemed to hold on to the value of grace without compromising the value of truth. He was merciful, but fought for justice. He was radical, focused, bold and direct. He was also kind, gentle, tenderhearted and humble. If you're one of those leaders who are more comfortable in war than in peace, you may need to soak yourself in these commands. You may find your greatest impact comes when you strike the balance of the warrior poet—brave and kind, fierce and gentle, confident and humble—a description that I believe beautifully captures the image of our Savior, and one I envision could one day describe those who are entrusted to lead in the movement of Christ.

Jesus was a warrior poet, stopping at nothing to expose the truth, while exhibiting all the beauty of that truth through the tender grace of his love. If you're going to be an evoker, create relationships where those you love will "be led to a knowledge of the truth," and where patience, humility and kindness cover everyone you touch. Be a warrior poet. Not just a warrior.

IDEAS FOR MENTORS

1. **Mentoring the conflict avoider.** Invite protégés to take inventory of what relational tensions they're avoiding. Perhaps there's unresolved conflict in their life, or maybe there's someone to whom they simply need to apologize and ask for forgiveness. Whatever and whoever they're avoiding, challenge them to face their fears and engage that conflict to the best of their ability. Make sure you dialogue with them about how to approach the situation, what to say, what not to say, and what fair expectations to have. This can be hugely developmental. Coach them. Instruct them. Guide them. And make sure you follow up with a conversation for accountability purposes, and to debrief and learn from the experience. This is real-life "training" in facing conflict head on, and many of us have much room for growth in this arena.

2. **Mentoring the conflict evoker.** Do a Bible study on conflict resolution. Use verses from Scripture from this chapter, and utilize other resources if you'd like (options you could use are *Boundaries Face to Face* by Henry Cloud and Dr. John Townsend or *Emotionally Healthy Spirituality* by Peter Scazzero). Examine how people approach conflict differently. Perhaps reflect on how people's families growing up dealt with conflict and how that shaped who they are today. Assess what tendencies exist, and help protégés gain clarity about any unhealthy relational patterns that cause

unnecessary conflict. Identify action steps for growth and formulate a "growth plan" together with goals in it. Help evokers understand how others may perceive them when they evoke conflict or engage it with such confrontation and intensity.

MENTOR TIP:
CLARIFY EXPECTATIONS. ENGAGE CONFLICT.

In a mentor/protégé relationship, always make sure the expectations are clear on both sides—the frequency of meeting times, what the mentor and the protégé each desire, etc. And if you have a conflict, make sure you clarify the issue and then resolve it. This may be one of the best relationships in which to teach someone healthy ways to engage conflict.

8 • The Tension of Attachment

OVERATTACHERS AND DETACHERS

WE ALL HAVE A CERTAIN COMFORT LEVEL, even desire, regarding how close we want to relate to the people in our lives. Most of us have a tri-sphere of closeness. There's the first sphere where we give the most of ourselves. Examples of this are the best friend, trusted confidant or even intimate spouse. These people are in what I call the "deep need" category.

The second sphere, where we give a good amount of ourselves, includes fun friends, ministry partners, coworkers whom we find an affinity with, people in our small group at church, or people we really like to hang out with in social or casual settings. These are people we have a mild to moderate need for.

Then there's the third sphere who are the people we keep a safe distance from, even though they're somehow intertwined with our lives.

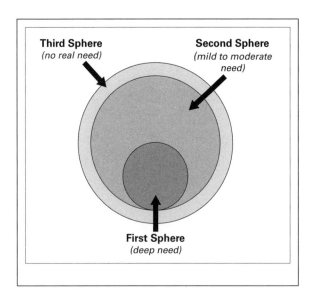

Third Sphere
(no real need)

Second Sphere
(mild to moderate need)

First Sphere
(deep need)

This might be family we don't get along with, coworkers we don't mesh with, or people who want to be our friends but whom we don't feel the same about, for whatever reason.

What I mean by "giving ourselves" is attaching to them in some way that draws out that indefinable dimension of who we are, and longing for the same in them. We have some unforced chemistry, affinity and commonality with them, or we don't. The amount we have, or don't have, determines the closeness we share with them in a monumental way.

This is just a simple breakdown of how most of us function relationally. The thing that varies greatly among us is what type of people and how many people are in each of these spheres. Some have only one person in the first sphere. Some have several. Some have only one in the third sphere. Some have more than is sustainable to have, and the opposite is true as well.

Since most people don't have x-ray vision and can't see into your three spheres, no one really knows who makes the cut into those sacred circles and who doesn't. But who you choose to let in, and how much, has everything to do with the texture, depth and health of your relationships. Those circles indicate how open or closed you are to others, how discerning you are when it comes to the character of those you allow into your trust, how interested you are in knowing people, how disinterested you are in knowing people, how much you depend on others, how much you depend only on yourself, and so much more.

Only you and God can truly know the content and texture of those spheres. And if you're anything like me, you can put on a pretty good show for others. You can come off as more relational than you really are, or you could come off more emotionally disengaged than you really are. People in your life may think they're in a circle they are actually nowhere near. Or they may think they are far outside of your heart, but they mean everything to you. As a result, you may begin to believe you're healthier than you are. Although this tri-sphere concept is rather simple to understand, its incredibly hard to diagnose accurately and see with utter clarity.

We all have a rare opportunity here to take inventory of our relational worlds. Who do we allow in and why? Who do we push out and why?

How close do we really want to be with others? And how much do we want to bring others into our most sacred of journeys, the one inside our very selves? We range from overly attached to others, to overly detached. Another way of saying this would be overdependent versus overly independent, or invasive versus aloof. As we scan the spectrum from overattacher to detacher, consider where you fall and why.

We have so much room for growth when it comes to healthy intimacy with the people God has placed in our lives. Some people in those spheres may need to relocate, and we may have to rethink how we engage with people in our personal and ministry life. As leaders, we set the tone in our relational environments, so it is all the more important to set the right tone. People are looking to us to help define what it looks like to love others in a way that honors God, others and even ourselves.

THE OVERATTACHER

I was talking with one of my friend's daughters not too long ago. It was one of those rare moments where she was helping me in the kitchen and just happened to open up about some things she was going through. She is only ten years old, but relational troubles were already well underway. Moriah told me about a friend of hers who wasn't acting very friendly. Moriah really valued this girl's friendship, but was finding it hard to know how to relate to her. This friend was all over the place. One day she acted like her best friend, the next she acted like she didn't even know Moriah. One moment they were sharing their secrets. The next moment her friend was exposing those secrets with other girls and making fun of her.

My heart went out to Moriah because I could see in her eyes how much she cared for her. She was welling up with tears as she shared how hurt she was every time her friend betrayed her, wasn't there for her or misled her. Well, this was a stumper for me. What do you say to a ten-year-old girl on how to have healthy friendships with a catty, volatile preadolescent? I couldn't simply say, "Be done with her. She is dead to you." And I couldn't say, "Just keep loving her. Everyone deserves to be loved." That would be completely unhelpful.

I suddenly visualized an image that could possibly help her. It was one I knew helped me. I told her to look at the path toward her heart like a series of doors, each one leading a step deeper into her trust. Everyone deserves to go through that first door. Everyone deserves a chance to be known, loved and seen.

Then I told her to continue opening the doors as people exhibited good character and showed that they could be trusted with her heart. If her friends were showing signs that they didn't truly value her, then she needed to close the door. We went on to discuss how she could do all this while at the same time treating them with respect and dignity.

I was amazed at how quickly Moriah got it. She repeated it back to me just to make sure she understood. As she did, I couldn't help but think how many times I have messed this up myself. It sounds so simple, but it's often very difficult to keep relationships in their proper place.

We're not ten-year-old kids trying to figure out how to make it through the wretched territory of elementary school. However, we can certainly relate to the struggle around who we should allow into our inner spheres, and how to remove those who should not be there. For the overattacher, the problem is not that of allowing others close. The problem is allowing people *too* close. Overattachers perpetually pack people into the "need" spheres. The doors toward their heart rarely close, because in their minds, everyone deserves a chance, and everyone deserves their love.

Well, that's true, but to what degree?

SYMPTOMS OF OVERATTACHERS

If you're an overattacher, you may recognize the following symptoms in your life:

- You feel as though you can't keep up with everyone and their demands for your emotional and physical energy.

- You can't remember the last time you've been by yourself for an extended period of time. And you can't remember even wanting to.

- You like feeling needed, and find it disconcerting if you are not being called upon socially on a continual basis.

- You often get hurt by others. And you rarely see it coming.

- You are quick to forgive others for not doing their part in the relationship, and easily let them right back in without addressing the issue(s) at hand.

- You have extremely high expectations for yourself relationally, but low expectations for others.

- You find yourself wondering why you're always running yourself dry for others, while no one seems to want to do anything for you.

- You may also pride yourself in being loyal, invested, devoted and giving. But you may be unable to see how you are benefiting from being needed, and how some of your motivation may be based in softening the ache of loneliness in your life.

Overattachers struggle with deriving life from the right places. They sometimes cling to relationships like fleas cling to a host. They feel like they cannot survive if their lives are not packed full with people, social engagements and service. They are constantly aware of the unpredictability and transient nature of relationships, so they never say no to a new friend. Their loneliness can be almost palpable, so they rarely close the door to their heart—not solely because they are so caring, as they may believe to be the main reason, but because they are so in need of companionship and love.

You may be thinking, *This isn't me. Just because I have a lot of friends and like to be social does not mean that I am lonely or "needy." I just happen to be an extrovert who likes to keep busy.* That may be true, but I would still challenge you to look deeper beneath the surface of your busy social calendar and open-heartedness toward others. We have reasons and intentions for everything we do, and for every person we let into our lives, even if we aren't aware of it.

We are the architects of our lives, designing them the way we want, the way we feel our needs (healthy or unhealthy) are being met. What may look like endless relational giving on the surface could be endless relational and emotional neediness underneath. And what is wrong with that? At face value, nothing. We all have an endless need for intimacy, love and companionship. We never have enough. There is no moment we top it off and say, "Well, that's about all I need or ever will.

So the door to my heart is closed." Where overattachers go astray is not in their need for love, but in the way they go about obtaining it.

There is no schedule busy enough, no relationship rap sheet long enough, no friendship big enough, to fill the loneliness or to satisfy the desire for intimacy that inhabits our souls. When we strive to fill our needs by being needed, or our wants by being wanted, we come up short—very short. And if you have any overattachment tendencies, you already know this to be true.

FIND YOUR CENTER

So, how does the overattacher attach in healthy ways? How do we fill the spheres of our relational worlds in a way that leads to fulfillment rather than endless disappointment? How do we hold on to the one extreme, loving others no matter who they are or where they come from, while also holding on to the value of appropriate attachment and genuinely healthy intimacy? How do we hold on to the extreme of deep human neediness without letting go of the other extreme of dependence on God alone?

I think a good place to start is to ask God (or if you're a mentor, you can use these questions with your protégés), "Who is the *first* person in my *first* sphere? Is it You? Or is it a mere mortal, trying to fill an immortal need?" Is God your most intimate friend, most trustworthy confidante and closest love? Or are you politely pushing him back further and further behind human flesh rather than at the very closest doorway to your heart? Who can love you like he? Who knows you like he? Who can comfort, guide and encourage you like he? Who can be trusted like he? Who will never abandon you or forsake you, even in your greatest hour of need? Who can fill the endless void of darkness you are so desperately afraid of like he?

To the measure you are not attached to God, you will attach yourself to an endless line of relationships in order to find your center, your peace and your absolute acceptance. There is no point in giving advice to an overattacher if they are not first committed to cultivating intimacy with the only One who knows them, *truly* knows them. It would be like telling an orphan child to beg for food on the dark, cold streets

while his long-lost parents were beckoning him to join them for a feast
in their palace. There is no relationship that could fill the hunger of a
fatherless existence. We need to heed the call to our Father's banqueting
table. And once we arrive in that place of knowing and being known,
we can begin to attach ourselves to others in a way that is not only personally fulfilling, but life-giving to those we are attached to.

Psalm 139 tells us,

You have searched me, LORD,
    and you know me.
You know when I sit and when I rise;
    you perceive my thoughts from afar.
You discern my going out and my lying down;
    you are familiar with all my ways.
Before a word is on my tongue
    you, LORD, know it completely.

For you created my inmost being;
    you knit me together in my mother's womb.
I praise you because I am fearfully and wonderfully made;
    your works are wonderful,
    I know that full well. (vv. 1-4, 13-14 TNIV)

If you are living out of this centeredness, this core dimension of intimacy with God, then you will find the temptation to overattach much
more resistible. Your reasons for engaging in relationships will shift
from desperation to desire. The pace of your relational life will shift
from frantic to sustainable, chaotic to centered.

It's much like a marathon runner who instead of sprinting and
burning out in the first couple miles, paces himself so he can finish the
race. Rather than cramming an innumerable amount of meaningless
relationships into your life, you make the ones you have count. And
instead of always giving without receiving (another version of unre-
quited love), you grasp the truth that you are worthy of appropriate
reciprocity. Healthy expectations of others will emerge, and you will
have more awareness of those doors that are always either opening or
shutting within yourself. You will find yourself leaving that scared

child behind (like Moriah), afraid she must accept any kind of behavior because she isn't worthy of anything more. You will set the tone for the kind of mutual respect and trust that genuine love embodies.

Will you still get hurt? Of course. Will you still be tempted to fill the void of emptiness and loneliness with people and busyness? Absolutely. Will you still be without hope of a kind of life that is rich with immortal love and unimaginable depth? No. It is that hope, once experienced, that will propel you forward as you face the despair of the human condition and all its imposter loves. You will remember that overattaching is nothing short of an immortal desire trying to meet its need in a mortal way. And when you remember that, you will also remember the One who has been there the whole time waiting for you to realize it.

MARGINS

Time to take inventory of your relationships. God longs for you to be loved, to love, and for that love to be the kind that spurs others on toward being more like him. If you are currently close to people who treat you poorly or without respect, who take way more than they give and who make demanding their favorite hobby, then it may be time to move them out of the "need" sphere. And if you have a million people in your second sphere, it may be time to focus more deeply on the relationships that are ripe for growth, filled with potential and emulate that aroma of divine friendship.

I love the concept of creating margins in our lives, so as to avoid being maxed out. We so often live with no room for anything to go wrong, or no room to add one more thing to our lives. I learned this the hard way. As a ministry leader, my days were so packed that if one single thing came up unexpectedly (which inevitably happens), like a friend needed to meet and talk, or a volunteer had an issue she needed to work through, or a couple was having urgent marital problems, I simply could not fit them in. I was maxed . . . all the time. This made me irritable and impatient. It even tempted me to disengage emotionally. I didn't have margins in my life so that there was room for the unexpected or the unplanned. As a result I'd find myself almost unable to cope with all the demands in front of me. This is not the way we are supposed to live in the kingdom— maxed out, topped off, pushed to our limits.

But this is what we often do in our relational worlds. Instead of creating healthy margins, we cram our schedules, and even our hearts, with so much that it becomes a crushing burden rather than a lifegiving force. It may be time to create some space, as uncomfortable as it may be. In doing so, we create an opportunity to enjoy the purity that a healthy rhythm of life and friendship offers us.

Overattachers tend to inadvertently dilute their relationships, rather than honing in on the more meaningful ones that challenge and encourage them, as well as being open to us challenging and encouraging them. If your social calendar is so full that the president wouldn't be able to pin you down for an appointment, then consider the possibility that this is a red flag. It is a warning signal that you are stuffing your life with the equivalent of relational junk food rather than nourishing yourself with the substance of God's presence. Scratch a few things off the calendar. Live in the discomfort of silence and solitude. Allow God to invest in you, shape you, encourage and change you. How can you have healthy relationships when you aren't carving time out to be still in the One who makes you a healthy human being? It just doesn't work that way—no matter how badly you wish it did.

THE ROAD TO RELATIONAL HEALTH

As you forge a new relational path in the future, remember that each time you allow another person into *your* personhood, you are opening a door to your heart. Be conscious of whom you are cultivating a need for, and whom you are depending on. Be attentive to what's going on in your interior world and remain responsive to what God is saying about it. Being dependent on others can and should be a wonderful thing, but it is a painful and destructive thing if it is on the wrong kind of person. You are responsible for who has the deepest kind of hold on you, who influences you, who determines where you spend your time and your self, and who is able to really grow from your presence in their life. No one else holds the key to your heart except you. Make sure you use it wisely. Emotional and relational health will follow.

I'm not endorsing locking others out. I'm simply reminding all of us of the responsibility we have to allow the right people in. As an overattacher, you will be tempted to hand the key to many people who cross your path. But if you are to do the most good in the world, you must first protect your heart and ensure that it is in the right hands. Everything flows from that place. Attach yourself to what is noble, what is good, what is excellent, what is lovely, what is pure. When you do, you will find you are free to do what you have been longing to do—give yourself away in all the right ways.

> Above all else, guard your heart,
>> for it is the wellspring of life. (Proverbs 4:23)

THE DETACHER

The detacher sounds kind of like some product that should be sold on an infomercial—like a device that dissolves glue or something. But of course it is not. A detacher could be defined as a person who is under attached, or overly independent. If an overattacher has too many people in their relational spheres, the detacher doesn't have enough. The interesting part of it is that many people in the detacher's life don't even know how detached they are. The detacher may exhibit his or her under-dependence by being emotionally removed, aloof or relationally distant. On the other hand, they may seem just the opposite—engaged, popular, charismatic, charming, fun and sociable. It may appear that the detacher has many attachments, but in reality, they "need" very few people, if any.

There are indeed healthy versions of detachment. In fact, sometimes it's a necessity to detach, like when a toxic relationship needs to end, or when a person becomes overextended and needs to pull back. And there also are unhealthy versions of detachment, like the person who can't bring themselves to trust a beloved friend who has earned the right to be trusted, or like the ministry leader who serves others while never allowing anyone to serve and love them. It is the unhealthy version that I'm going to address here.

It's more difficult to paint a picture of a detacher because many are able to live harmoniously with others, possessing many external relationships, without possessing internal dependence. They are able to safely hide their true self and its needs where no one would even be able to recognize it if they saw it.

I once worked with a leader of a certain ministry, named Austin. On the outside, Austin's life looked very similar to an overattacher. He was very busy, insanely busy in fact. He had a monstrous amount of friends. He was socially skilled and a highly influential person. I thought we were pretty good friends—*at first*. We seemed to have a great connection, and we spent a lot of time together. In my estimation, our friendship was progressing. As time went on, we should've been getting closer but I began noticing the opposite. It was as if the relationship were moving backwards, even regressing. Most true friendships evolve, beginning with a small spark of commonality or affinity, and developing more deeply as time passes. But with Austin, although our friendship started with a bang, over time it practically fizzled into nothingness.

At first, I thought I might have been the one to blame. Then I began to notice the rest of Austin's relational world. Although it looked like he was solid friends with all these people, it became clear that he was keeping everyone at a safe distance. I discovered that the people he called his closest friends barely even interacted with him at least in any vulnerable way. I also noticed an unusually high turnover rate in his friendship circles. When someone got too close, he would start distancing himself, and at times even just go emotionally cold on them. I remember thinking how strange it was for such a seemingly relational person to, in essence, have no lasting, deep or truly meaningful friendships.

Austin never shared his reasons for keeping people at a distance with me. And although nothing obvious had gone wrong on the outside between him and me, it was still really difficult to have a serious or transparent conversation with him. As a result of his internal and emotional detachment, I realized our friendship lacked real substance. I started to observe more keenly that there wasn't much substance in any of his relationships.

Austin seemed to be like a rock skipping across the breadth of water, while never actually submerging. He was jumping from place to place, thing to thing, relationship to relationship, but never dwelling, being or needing. He sticks out in my mind because that was the first time I really personally experienced a high-level leader who was so detached from the people in his life, yet maintained a veneer of authentic connection. I found it strange, mostly because he made relationships look so easy. After seeing and experiencing Austin's aversion to closeness with others, I've been able to more easily spot it in people through the years. Sadly enough, I've seen far too much of it in ministry leaders. On the outside, they appear to relationally attach, but on the inside they're emotionally and relationally detached.

Detachers tend to be uncomfortable with long-term commitments, extended time alone with someone, genuine vulnerability, transparency and especially invasion of their private space. They like to remain detached, being able to enjoy the view of the water without jumping in. They may recognize the value in people and relationships, but they prefer to remain as spectators rather than players.

Detachers may embody proximity but not intimacy. Detachers like to appear close, while not being close. And if you try to get close to a detacher, you'll find it to be bizarrely difficult and awkward. If you are a detacher, you find the project of intimacy almost too much to take on. You know in your mind it's good to need people, but your heart will have none of it—so you compromise. You surround yourself with people without ever allowing them to actually know you, or allow yourself to actually need them.

At times, you may want to give into the temptation of being aloof or distant, but that would make people think poorly of you. Even worse, they may become suspicious of how terrified you are of them coming too close. In your estimation it's better to be warm yet almost entirely removed. That way people will feel connected to you while you are safely disconnected from them. This is your genius strategy because no one suspects your absolute distaste for your inner privacy being breeched, and you can go on with business as usual without upsetting your ministry plans.

The problem remains. Your first and central sphere is closed off. People may need you, but you choose to need no one. You could pick up and leave and never look back. Sure it would be a shame to say goodbye to some good folks you've grown fond of. And the familiarity was nice.

But overall it's better not to get too deep in. Life is unpredictable, and you never know when you'll have to say goodbye. As long as you're helping people, what does it matter if they *know* you or if you *need* them? After all, dependence is for wimps, isn't it? Self-sufficiency is a mark of the strong, right? The question is, does a detacher really buy all that? It's what gets them to accept the reality of proximity without intimacy, but it does not get them to believe in its inherent lie: that detachment is the only real security there is.

THE DETACHER'S FEAR

The detacher wrestles with an insidious fear of being loved only to lose it in the end. They disagree with the famous quote by Alfred Lord Tennyson, "'Tis better to have loved and lost than never to have loved at all." At least on some level, they believe that it's better to not love and to not lose. It's simple math. They're convinced that much more harm can come from attachment than detachment. To them, a removed heart is better off than a damaged one.

Beyond the fear of loss, the detacher struggles with the fear of being vulnerable. The gap between their sacred inner world and the profane outer world is too wide to cross. There are too many things that could go wrong. Too much that could be misunderstood, misinterpreted and mishandled. Often, the detacher would rather emulate what seems to be vulnerable than actually *be* vulnerable. They tend to be more comfortable with the image they project than with revealing the person they really are.

Brennan Manning refers to this projected image as the false self, or *the imposter.*

> He (the imposter) is the master of disguise, he can easily slip into feigned humility, the attentive listener, the witty raconteur, the intellectual heavy, or the urbane inhabitant of the global village. The false self is skilled at the controlled openness that scrupulously avoids any significant self-disclosure.[1]

The moment the detacher exposes his or her true self, the fear of either losing that precious moment of intimacy, or the fear of being rejected or misunderstood, flares up. The only way of controlling this disturbing undercurrent of fear is to create a new way of relating to others. If you can control the image you're projecting, you have a better chance of controlling the outcome. Even if people reject you, it isn't the *real* you. So you have now safely eliminated being hurt on the deeper level. And if you are so unfortunate as to lose a friend, they weren't as needed as they believed themselves to be. You can still move on with only an emotional scrape or two, not an amputation of a limb or a break in the heart like so many other more attached people suffer.

THE FIGHT FOR INTIMACY

It all sounds convincing. Pure logic would endorse the mentality of a detacher. But where does this belief go wrong? If it is protecting them from suffering, what is it in turn keeping out? The rationalizations of the detacher keep them insulated not only from pain, but from love. This is the great tragedy of the detacher's life. As long as they don't need, they don't receive. If they don't receive, they don't inhabit all the gifts the Father longs for them to possess, not only from people who love them, but from God himself. Grace never fully reaches the corners of their souls. Mercy never touches the real pain of their regrets. Light never completely shines on the beauty of who they are. Freedom is never attained. They never allow God's goodness to transform their feelings of incurable unworthiness.

If detachers continue to keep everyone at a distance, even Jesus, they will live only a fraction of the life they were meant to live. By allowing their needs to go unmet, their desire for intimacy turns to atrophy. Their ability to show their true selves dissolves. They forfeit the greatest joys a person can experience on this side of heaven. To love and be loved. To need and be needed. To know and be known. In the light of this possibility, how can detachers allow a fraction of their humanity to barely breathe rather than the wholeness of who they are to thrive?

There are no easy answers to the deeply complicated realities of pain, loss and rejection. There are no guarantees as to how much suffering individuals will face if they open themselves up to closeness with others in community. The presence of pain is too real to minimize. But the power of love is too great to cast aside.

The only choice is not a logical one, but a spiritual one. The detacher must go against their instincts and learn to trust that God is good enough to bless them with people to love and be loved by, trustworthy enough to send the right people into their lives, and strong enough to comfort them when suffering inevitably comes. The choice is spiritual because our spirits recognize what our rational minds cannot—that we are compelled to engage the volatile fight for intimacy, no matter the cost.

I think of Jesus, giving his life to those who were actively rejecting him (see Isaiah 53:3; John 1:11; 1 Peter 2:4). It makes no sense at all, yet it makes perfect sense at the same time. Our hearts recognize what he was doing, even if our minds struggle to absorb the incomprehensible meaning behind such a monumental act of love. How did he face such suffering? How did he give himself away when he knew so many would reject him at the deepest level?

> [Let us fix] our eyes on Jesus, the pioneer and perfecter of faith. For the joy set before him he endured the cross, scorning its shame, and sat down at the right hand of the throne of God. Consider him who endured such opposition from sinners, so that you will not grow weary and lose heart. (Hebrews 12:2-3 TNIV)

"For the joy set before him." That's how Jesus endured such grotesque, unspeakable suffering. So how do we endure it? It starts with fixing our eyes on him. He embodied the essence of sacrifice and love. If we lose heart, if we grow weary, it is him we must look to. If we draw from our own ability to love, we will fail. If we lean on our own bravery in our fear, we will lose courage. If we dwell on what we could lose instead of on what there is to gain, we will grow weary. If we push people out of our hearts, we will lose part of ourselves in the process.

God designed this life in such a way that we need each other. It's full of pain and heartbreak. But it's also full of joy and healing. As spiritual leaders, we must always look to our heavenly leader for courage to abandon the false self and allow our true selves to emerge, for the strength to love beyond our human abilities and to be loved in spite of our deepest fears. It is only then that we can take hold of the privilege of leading and serving others. It is only when we allow God to disrupt our perfectly controlled inner worlds, and inject them with his radically invasive love, that we can begin to show others what he is capable of doing with a human life.

Standing on the outside of love will only keep us outside of our truest selves, and outside of knowing the One who truly sees us and loves us for who we really are. That would not be living. That would only be pretending to live. It all comes down to accepting our need for God, for others, and knowing that we're accepted by God— every part of us. That's what fuels the kind of community each one of us must live in if we desire to create and cultivate kingdom cultures of relational and emotional health. We must find the courage to come out of hiding, to remove the mask, and allow ourselves at last to be seen, known and loved.

> She gave this name to the LORD who spoke to her: "You are the God who sees me," for she said, "I have now seen the One who sees me." (Genesis 16:13)

IDEAS FOR MENTORS

1. **Mentoring the overattacher.** Encourage protégés who over-attach to practice discretion. Have them examine where they have felt hurt or betrayed in life. Reflect on what signs may have been there that warned them not to entrust that person as much as they did. Some people see these danger signs more intuitively, while others have to almost go out of their way to look for them. Being more aware of relational red flags is not an excuse to be cynical or mistrusting; rather it can be a healthy process of discernment when choosing how much, and to whom, to open our hearts.

2. **Mentoring the detacher.** Encourage protégés who detach to reflect on three questions: (1) Ask them to identify reasons why they keep putting people at a distance. What's really going on at a deeper level? This may take some extensive in-

trospection. (2) Ask them what they think they need God to change and heal in their life so they can minimize how often they detach from others. If their awareness level is low, perhaps you can suggest reading *Changes That Heal* by Henry Cloud. For people who cannot afford counseling, this is the book I always recommend to engage them in deeper conversations about how their past affects them. *Emotionally Healthy Spirituality* by Peter Scazzero is another fantastic book that can be a guide in this arena. (3) Ask what people they can identify in their life who have actually earned their trust, but they haven't given it to them. Challenge protégés to demonstrate vulnerability and transparency by sharing their need for friendship, and perhaps by confessing their failure to cultivate a closer, healthier friendship.

MENTOR TIP:
KNOW THE LIMITS OF YOUR EXPERTISE

Don't try to mentor protégés in areas where you're not equipped to do so. In effort to still help protégés grow, connect them to others who are equipped and willing. Take time to think of people you know who could help your protégé in areas of needed growth or required leadership skills. For example, if your protégé feels a call to plant a church, connect him or her to one or two church planters you know who you feel could offer unique insight and guidance in that specific skill set. If they need more significant levels of counseling, help resource them and be a networker for them.

Communication

THE CONNECTIVITY OF THE POET

PART 3

My message and my preaching were not with wise and persuasive words, but with a demonstration of the Spirit's power, so that your faith might not rest on human wisdom, but on God's power.

1 CORINTHIANS 2:4-5 TNIV

The tragedy of our times is that while many Christians have confidence in the power of the Lord to return and change the world, many of us do not have confidence in the power of the gospel to transform society now.

VISHAL MANGALWADI

THE WORDS WE USE AND THE WAY WE SPEAK not only set the tone of our conversations, but they are the difference between being effective and ineffective both as leaders and communicators. One of the largest growth-need areas for emerging leaders is in the arena of communication. I'm convinced that the current deficit of communication skills in the church is reflected in their deficit of influence in our culture and even amongst ourselves. We often falsely assume that we as human beings all speak the same language, and therefore we all hear the same thing. We also assume that if the language we use makes sense to us and is good enough for us, then it must be good enough for others as well. This longing and belief couldn't be more misguided.

A poet may not be the first person that comes to mind when you think of incredible communication skills. One of my favorite things to do in Los Angeles is to attend Da Poetry Lounge in Hollywood. This weekly event became a regular hobby for a season of life, and it put poetry (and communication) in a whole new light. The participants break all stereotypes of poets being too flowery pink, or even removed in their language. They stand on that stage and command the attention of every single person in the room as they stare into their eyes and speak from the depths of their being. It's electric, compelling and dynamic.

I couldn't help but compare this experience to the church. I was actually saddened as I sat there, because I was consumed with the reality that so much more passion, life and vibrancy inhabited that room than I've seen in a lot of church services. I wondered, *Why is it that these poets can engage others in a way that we rarely see in the church?*

Great poets, I've observed, possess a gift that so many church leaders do not strive to obtain—the ability to connect to the depths of the human spirit. Poets do not speak primarily from a vantage point of logic, information or intellect, as we often overemphasize as Christian preachers. Instead, they speak in heart, soul and emotion—all that makes up the deeper layers of our humanity. This kind of poetic, evocative, even prophetic communication reminds me of the Old Testament prophets and also wisdom literature. Poets (and prophets) speak vulnerably about their brokenness, pain and anger. In the church, we tend to hide our weaknesses, fears, insecurities and "negative emotions."

Poets aren't afraid to swallow the beauty they see around them without shame or inhibition. And at the same time, they aren't afraid to plunge into the darkness of their own hearts. Leaders in the church often try to find a safe middle ground, somewhere between light and darkness. As a result, they end up preaching and speaking in the gray, which represents predictability, safety and containability. This often translates to the world around us as apathy, naivety and a kind of separateness that isolates the church rather than connects us to the world at a deeply human level.

In essence, poets speak in human language while we sometimes speak in a foreign tongue only recognizable by a small sect of people. I'm convinced that there's a universal language that touches, reaches and moves people. I believe the poet understands the necessity of connection through communication. Communication is about connecting to the human experience with language that speaks to the heart, the mind, the soul.

THE POWER OF THE GOSPEL

Teaching and training protégés to develop their communication skills is not elevating a superficial value of smooth talk or eloquent speaking, thus diminishing the true power of the message of Christ. It is indeed the opposite. Encouraging our leaders to improve their ability to communicate reveals the power of the message rather than diminishing it. It gives us on-ramps to people's hearts in a way that can only be done through words. Only when people's hearts are opened can true influence occur.

I'm convinced that the deficit of influence we see in our churches and culture will not be optimized until we adapt the way we communicate as ministry leaders. As long as we hold on to predictable, safe and even sterile language, we will keep ourselves separate from the world, and as a result dampen our impact. I often see preachers' attempts at connecting with others as feeble at best, awkward and inauthentic at worst. But things could be different if we grasped the communication insights of great poets. That's why I challenge protégés to read and even write poetry. We cannot underestimate the profound impact words and language have on reaching humanity.

9 • Developing the Gift of Communication

THE WHOLE IDEA OF PROTÉGÉS CENTERS around the belief that we learn best from others, particularly those who are masters of their trade and mavens of their craft. Emerging ministry leaders, like every generation before them, and like poets, must work diligently to develop their ability to be good stewards with their language. One of the most powerful agents of change in reaching people is our *words*.

The New Testament reminds us that we must hold this whole communication gift in highest regard. James 3:1 cautions us with utter clarity, "Not many of you should become teachers, my fellow believers, because you know that we who teach will be judged more strictly" (NIV 2011). The ten verses that follow are powerful descriptions of the eternal weight that our words have on people—for better or worse, for blessing or cursing (James 3:2-11).

I must clarify one thing before further discussing how to improve our ability to communicate in a more effective and creative way. In no way am I promoting some kind of over-inflated value on words while neglecting the priceless value of the gospel itself or the power of the Holy Spirit. I'm fully aware of what the New Testament tells us,

> For Christ did not send me to baptize, but to preach the gospel—not with wisdom and eloquence, lest the cross of Christ be emptied of its power. (1 Corinthians 1:17 TNIV)

> My message and my preaching were not with wise and persuasive words, but with a demonstration of the Spirit's power, so that your faith might not rest on human wisdom, but on God's power. (1 Corinthians 2:4-5 TNIV)

It would be worse to diminish the power of the gospel and speak with brilliance than to know the profound truth of Christ from the bottom of our heart and speak it poorly. These verses remind us that our technique and abilities alone are not the most important dimension of communication compared to God's ability to reach the human spirit. There in the gospel is the true power of the Spirit behind every word we preach, teach and speak forth. Words are merely vehicles to transport this gospel. And there's no doubt that God sometimes does what he needs to do in spite of our precision (or imprecision) with words. At the same time, the Scriptures clearly articulate that we must not neglect our responsibility to steward our communication gifts. In one instance, Romans 12:7 commands those of us with the spiritual gift of teaching and preaching to use it to serve and bless others. And the message of Jesus Christ is far too important to be lost in translation, or ignored because of the way it's delivered. So remember that God will do his part. We must do ours.

LEARNING LABS

One of the environments I use to develop protégés is what I call learning labs. These are informal and interactive environments for groups of leaders to participate in executing a leadership skill in real time that stretches and challenges them. For instance, to help others grow in communication, we create learning labs where protégés practice story-telling, preach a mini-sermon, perform spoken word or participate in improv comedy activities. These environments are different from a typical formal classroom setting that is focused on gathering information or knowledge. Learning labs focus on the application of a skill in front of others while the pressure is on. With heightened pressure to perform, protégés prepare more diligently and face the real-life challenging dynamics of execution. The primary goal of course is to cultivate and accelerate growth through real-time experience and true pressure, and to enhance our "practice" to improve our "game-time performance." We even film this at times and analyze it together.

In this chapter, I want to offer practical ideas that you can utilize in learning-lab-type settings to develop your own communication gift, as well as that of others. If you're a mentor or more experienced ministry leader, you can help protégés more than you realize. If you're a protégé, ask a mentor to help teach and guide you more intentionally. Or just implement some of the following exercises on your own until you find a more seasoned leader to help facilitate this process.

My suggestion is for you, as a protégé or as a mentor, to begin a group that meets monthly, bimonthly or even every week for a short window of time. Then, you can implement the following developmental learning experiences. This process can lead and guide a group of protégés to create a much-needed space for communication skills to emerge and flourish as young leaders strive toward increased effectiveness. These experiences stretch young communicators to learn how to carefully craft language and use their words most effectively and creatively. They also challenge protégés to develop new dimensions of their communication craft.

LEARNING LAB #1: FIVE GOOD MINUTES

Unfortunately so many young leaders learn in a trial-by-fire style. Often the first time they preach is in front of the entire church. They're so inexperienced and nervous that every person can see the sweat beads dripping down their forehead, even in the dead of winter. I've been there. Many protégés end up learning how to preach through public failure and humiliation—sure, some good can come from this, but aren't there other (better) options?

In addition, protégés rarely receive concrete feedback and instead are forced to rely on nonverbal cues and on frequency of opportunites to speak in order to determine how they're measuring up. The more talented speakers rise to the top faster while the faithful (although perhaps not as naturally gifted speakers) fall to the bottom, or continually struggle to keep up. We do a disservice to such devoted women and men who are eager to learn but are forced to figure this out largely on their own. The culture in our churches doesn't have to be this way. Mentors can help protégés make significant progress in a more intentionally guided context. Progress can also happen in peer-to-peer learning groups.

The first exercise that I want to suggest implementing parallels an athlete's routine. Athletes do warm-ups before the big game, attend practices in between and even scrimmage. Otherwise they'd be more apt to flop when it really counted. By warming up and practicing communication skills, protégés can likewise minimize falling flat on their faces when it really counts, decreasing their chance of giving up all together. Such exercises help set them up to succeed rather than fail, and to build confidence rather than spiral downward emotionally from feeling they looked foolish.

One of my favorite sports shows, *PTI*, has a segment called "Five Good Minutes." The hosts interview a guest for five minutes, while striving to foster an interesting interview for their audience. I'm always amazed at how much can be said in such a short period of time. This is also true in preaching. If we can help protégés learn how to steward five minutes, it'll move them that much closer to preaching life-changing sermons that last thirty or forty-five minutes. That's why I ask protégés to give five-minute talks, which in many respects can be even harder than giving a 30-minute talk. Here are some concrete steps to take.

1. Make an invite list of your select group. Choose when, where and how often you'll meet.

2. At group meetings, provide each protégé with five minutes to give their talk (set this up in advance so they have time to prepare). Use a timer, if desired, to keep people as close to the time limit as possible. Decide how many talks you can fit in the given time period, accounting for feedback time.

3. After each talk, facilitate feedback for approximately twelve to fifteen minutes for each speaker. I suggest wrapping that time up by ending on a positive note or with a genuinely encouraging word. This is a vulnerable, challenging experience for most.

4. Then move on to the next protégé to do the same until the group time is over. Sometimes I even record protégés on video and send them the video to watch or listen to (or I do that with them).

5. I almost always have each protégé prepare another talk with the goal to improve on what feedback was given. This usually comes weeks, even months later, but it's a good way to create a concrete action step to help motivate them to keep thinking about what they just learned and take action to apply it.

6. Remember to ensure that you are cultivating an environment of growth as you encourage people to practice their skill and sharpen their craft. People ought not to walk away feeling totally discouraged or beaten up. Make sure you set the tone to be inspiring, uplifting and challenging.

AFFIRMATIVE FEEDBACK

The feedback (from mentors as well as from peers) is the most catalytic component of the five-minute-talk experience. There are two basic kinds of feedback—affirmative and constructive. I suggest that you always offer some affirmative feedback first. As anxious as the protégé may be to hear what they did wrong, it's crucial to first communicate collectively what they did right. Affirm where they shine as a communicator and where they show natural gifting. If it's five good minutes, they need to know what was good so they can replicate it and continue to develop their already existing strengths. Maybe it's their ability to tell a story, be emotionally present and authentic, connect relationally or speak with clarity of thought. It could be any number of things, and we as peers or mentors can facilitate pointing those out, through our own input and fostering the input of others who are present.

Research confirms that people improve more quickly when they're affirmed for what they do well. The best athletes, musicians, artists, coaches and doctors all understand this reality well. They know affirmation contributes to building confidence and future success. Affirmation helps point with precision to areas of greatness so that they can be repeated over and over.

In addition, studies also show that more often than not, people aren't able to recognize their strengths with specificity. In other words, they aren't able to point to the reason(s) why they're able to achieve success in their craft. It almost feels accidental, and therefore nearly impossible to replicate. When we help each other see our strengths and how we use them to be effective, we empower one another to develop that which we're naturally good at but may not know how to replicate.

With affirmative feedback, it is important to be very specific about what makes the talk and the communicator different and unique. Generic feedback is a mindless filler, and not really helpful or meaningful to the person receiving it. The overwhelming majority of feedback that we give and receive in churches falls into this category (e.g., "Great sermon, Pastor!"). It's kind of like saying to your spouse, "You are such a good person," instead of, "You always notice when I'm feeling down and you say the right thing." We want more than broad-sweeping statements when we are being told why we offer something unique and valuable. And we know people are seeing our value when they offer insightful, specific, genuine, honest and heartfelt feedback.

Being recognized for our strengths and weaknesses is a really vulnerable experience. When someone allows us to be part of that, we owe them more than generic feedback. So, be thoughtful, engaged and attentive as you hear others' talks. This way you will be able to give more substantive and affirmative feedback, which in turn will have great impact in helping others grow as communicators. After all, we're speaking into more than the way they communicate. We are speaking into the value they have to offer as a person.

CONSTRUCTIVE FEEDBACK

Now that you have set the tone with a safe and affirming environment, it is more conducive to implementing the more challenging piece of this exercise. We gain trust when a person believes that we recognize their value and treat them with respect. And that trust component is desperately needed when it comes to receiving constructive feedback.

This kind of feedback involves pointing out areas of weakness, and doing so with sensitivity and respect as well as candor and clarity. The guideline of being specific versus generic applies here as well. If the speaker doesn't know exactly where they went wrong in their talk, how will they know they need to fix it? For example, I've heard people say things like this in constructive feedback time: "I just didn't feel moved," or "I found it difficult to stay engaged," or "The talk just felt too formal." How are these kind of statements helpful? All they accomplish is making the protégé feel self-conscious, confused and perhaps undeservingly discouraged.

Instead, ensure more specific comments are offered like, "As you were sharing deeply emotional things, you seemed rigid and removed. You would connect with your audience better if you relaxed a little and were more expressive." Or, "It was difficult to stay engaged because you were jumping too quickly from point to point and I found it hard to keep up. Maybe if you slowed down, or concentrated more on depth than breadth of content, that would help your listeners engage more." Another example of specific and constructive feedback is, "Your talk felt a bit too formal, overly polished and information-driven. You didn't share anything personal. It was more informational than impactful because we didn't get to know you at all through it. Next time, perhaps you could be more intentional about sharing something about yourself too." The best constructive feedback is specific and solution oriented. These insights put flesh on principles that can otherwise seem so intangible to the person trying to grow.

Imagine if six or eight people in the group all had things like that to say. Each protégé could walk away with concrete feedback that they could use to improve their weak spots in communication. And if during the discussions, someone else in the group took notes on a white board, flip chart, computer or piece of paper, protégés would even leave with written down, concrete advice given to them. Through group feedback, protégés can improve at a more rapid pace than if left to figure it all out on their own.

Group environments are conducive to rapid learning. Being in the presence of others who are intentionally studying strengths and weaknesses of our communication abilities can be daunting. Whenever we know we are being judged, we tend to be more nervous and self-conscious (think *American Idol*). But the experience of being evaluated is so critical to development that almost nothing can take the place of it. As a result of knowing we're being assessed, we tend to try harder, reach deeper and, hopefully, give our best. That's the upside of the intensity of this type of learning environment.

Although this kind of feedback is incredibly valuable, it can be extremely difficult to receive. The more challenging part for the speaker is that it is an incredibly vulnerable position to put oneself in, and that feels threatening and exposing. As difficult as those emotions are, they can be the primers for intense growth because we have something to lose. When we have something to lose (e.g., our credibility, our image, our desire for approval, etc.), we tend to put more effort into being the best we can be. Without knowing we're going to be evaluated, we have less incentive to push ourselves as far as we can. It's the difference between your coach being at practice watching and evaluating you, or him being absent that day. And if we don't stretch ourselves, we'll never know how far we can go. Growth often comes when we're exposed to doing or being something different that we already are.

It is so important for the mentor, as well as peers, to have not only the insight for constructive feedback, but the courage to communicate it. I've been on both sides of the feedback experience. Both can be tough. Receiving it is nerve-racking and vulnerable. Giving it can almost be harder. It's kind of like ending a relationship. Wouldn't you almost rather be the one broken up with than the one doing the breaking up? Well, that's what we all say, but let's be honest, no one wants to be the one who is broken up with. It's a similar struggle here. We really don't want to be rejected nor be the rejecter. We don't want to hear what we feel is negative feedback. And we don't want to be the ones giving it (unless you are the rare type who enjoys it—maybe you should sit this part out if that's the case!).

It takes guts to say what someone doesn't want to hear, even if they're inviting you to do so. It can be scary. But what is the alternative? In the church especially, we're often so supportive and friendly that no one ever changes, grows or stretches themselves like they could. So, if you're scared to death to say unpleasant or uncomfortable things, do it anyway—maybe you'll grow in courage. Even if you are anxious or fearful, you can still show courage because it is the right thing to do to serve others. And that has to be enough reason for all of us.

If you, the mentor, or you, the protégé, notice that someone in the group is being unnecessarily negative or unhelpfully generic, step in and guide the discussion to a more constructive place. I've stepped in many times, as others have done for me, when it almost seems like a feedback-giver is just pulling criticism out of the air that makes no sense at all. Or they're just being harsh, or unnecessarily critical.

We need to foster environments where people are healthily challenged, not unfairly beaten up or made to feel inadequate. And we all play a part in that, whoever we are in the group dynamic. Remember, the key word here is *constructive*. We give this feedback to build others into more of who they can be and the full design God has in store for them. Being constructive isn't easy, but it is essential to growth. So, let's help each other develop our craft of communication, one brick at a time.

LEARNING LAB #2: PRACTICE IMPROVISATION

Not only do our learning labs (which are informal and relational) involve giving five-minute talks, we also incorporate improvisation comedy. In improv comedy, beginners often avoid playing off of an awkward moment or the bizarre words of a fellow actor. Naturally, they bubble up with anxiety because they don't think they'll be able to build on what was just said, and as a result will look foolish. In contrast, the best improv actors actually seek out, look for and engage in the most bizarre and wacky situations. They realize this is where an opportunity for genius lies.

When most of us hear the word *improv*, we cringe inside—that is, if you're normal like me. I think of bad skits on *Saturday Night Live*, or the worst of *Whose Line Is It Anyway?* Or even worse, some ice-breaker activity at a church event. The good news is this next communication exercise has nothing to do with any of those things. You won't have to act. Relax. None of us wants to see you pretend you're a rock star trying to travel west.

Improv can be done in groups led by a peer, a mentor or even by someone more experienced in improv. I took part in a group led by a friend of mine, Andrew, one of the best communicators I know. There were about twenty people in it. All were people from our church who were being invested in because they had potential communication gifts. Andrew personally invited this list of people who he saw had the desire to grow in communication, and who were serving faithfully at our church. I, for one, was really excited about being a part of this—very nervous, but very excited. Nervous because I knew I'd have to speak in front of a bunch of people who would be evaluating my every word.

Excited because I'd be learning from one of the best, and I'd be growing much faster than I ever could on my own.

One of the first exercises Andrew led was improv. He broke us up into groups of five, threw a huge stack of magazines in front of us, and told us we had three minutes to look through them, pick something we wanted to talk about, and then give our little two-minute speech in front of our group. The group would give quick feedback to each speaker, then pick the best talk and vote for the champion of magazine improv. The champion of each subgroup would get a second chance to speak in front of the whole room, along with the other subgroup champions. I already wanted to lose.

I remember flipping furiously through a bunch of magazines, trying to find some hidden gem of an article or image that would inspire me toward greatness. I felt sick to my stomach—you would've thought I was giving a speech at the inaugural ball. You'll be happy to know that I did find something and I did manage to give the talk.

I wanted to get my talk over with, so I volunteered to go first. That seemed like the safest bet to me seeing as I couldn't really do worse than the person before me. The hardest part was ending strongly. I've seen too many young speakers not even know how they're going to end at all, meaning they basically wing it in their conclusion. As I saw that my time was almost up, I started to panic. I actually needed to bring closure to this disaster. I didn't want to be one of those people who just kept rambling until they were forced by the facilitator to quit talking. As terrifying as it is to give a spontaneous two-minute talk in front of people about something random (somehow trying to make it meaningful), it stretched me beyond what I even thought it would. And I have to say, I felt pretty good afterward. It was kind of thrilling actually. Doing something out of our comfort zone, and that we can't really prepare for, always provides an adrenaline rush. More importantly, it moves us one step closer in our journey toward becoming a better communicator.

Improv makes you think on your feet, draw meaning from your immediate context and communicate it in a way that stays engaged with that context. It forces you to become relevant and present in the moment, not just when you feel prepared or when it is convenient for you. It can also teach you the value of humor and timing. What is most surprising about it all is that developing these dimensions of communication is possible. And this development is more within your reach than you probably realize. We just don't tap into these skills often enough to know that we have a greater capacity for them.

As the facilitator, you can be creative with how you execute the improv element of your group. You can be like one of my evil mentors who threw a stack of magazines at me. Or you can be nicer and hand each protégé a card with a subject to talk about. In the Protégé Program, we've even invited improv comedians to come do half-day workshops to help us develop in speaking on our feet. Not only do we grow, but the fun factor is off the charts.

Another improv-related learning lab that I do involves pointing to an object in the room or having people randomly shout out an object. Put someone on the hot seat and have them connect that object mentioned to some truth about God or life. After the object is identified, we'll tell them to give a one-minute talk right then and there about that random object. Just for fun, I sometimes challenge protégés to share the gospel using the selected object as their metaphor. Another version of this involves giving a verse of Scripture to each person and instructing them to give a two-minute "sermon" on that verse right then and there. No prep. Think on your feet.

I've led many kinds of improv groups, and used various creative structures for them. You can vary the props and the time limits, and come up with your own fresh ideas. But the purpose is to help protégés learn to communicate well in the present moment, on their feet, and to do so with meaning, humor, relevance and insight. That doesn't sound too hard, does it? Ok, yes it does. But like I said, it's more within your reach than you realize. And it provides pressure situations that can be immensely valuable in the communication development process. I am convinced that young communicators must develop their own improv skill set; and the more they develop this, the better prepared they'll be to preach and communicate as a leader.

LEARNING LAB #3: PRACTICE THE ART OF RELIVING A STORY

In Los Angeles, there's an event that happens monthly called The Story-SLAM competition. It's hosted by The Moth, which is a community of storytellers (see www.themoth.org). Their tagline is "True Stories Told Live." In different moments throughout the night, attendees may laugh hysterically, be moved to tears, be challenged, get compelled to change something about their life, or they may just feel awkward or depressed—depends on the storyteller. After these competitions, I walk away inspired to create environments like these in the church where storytellers practice and execute the art of storytelling, even compete to improve performance. The heat of competition challenges people to step up their game. The basic goal is to sharpen our storytelling abilities. The best storytellers are people who really relive their story—that is, *story relivers.* And why shouldn't we help emerging and potential communicators develop this craft with greater diligence, practice and intentionality? Start your version of a story slam, perhaps in your own backyard or home. Keep it informal and relational, as well as instructional, developmental and intentional. Have fun too. And remember, the best storytellers capture the culture.

LEARNING LAB #4: FACILITATE RIGHT-BRAIN THINKING

There are various ways I try to develop right-brain thinking and imagination in young communicators. One way I do this is by asking protégés to find a three-to-five-minute scene from a movie that captures a significant part of their life story or faith journey. They then share it at a retreat or team meeting. I invite them to take a couple minutes to introduce the scene and a couple minutes afterward to discuss it. This exercise challenges them to think creatively to find a scene that communicates something they desire to communicate. It also gives them an opportunity to integrate a film clip inside a "talk," which forces them to think about transitioning in and then out of the film clip. This is also a great exercise for team building.

IDEAS FOR MENTORS

1. **Five good minutes.** Create an environment for developing communicators to give five-minute talks, engage in improvisation, practice story reliving, use a film clip to communicate or even write a spoken-word poetry piece to share.

2. **Establish a pre-talk feedback loop.** Ask a protégé to bring you their notes for a sermon they are going to give. Review it. Offer them input and feedback. It's a wide-open door to mentor them and teach them how to improve their communication in concrete fashion.

MENTOR TIP:
EMPHASIS MATTERS

Make sure you apply the right pressure to the right issues. In other words, don't get derailed by overemphasizing peripheral matters or minor issues. Be aware of what you emphasize, what you talk about most and how hard you are pushing on something, whether that's in communication, character, leadership or whatever. What you choose to focus your energy on most will be translated as what you care about most.

10 • Communicating with a Missional Lens

IF WE ARE TRANSFORMED BY THE GOSPEL, the gospel will flow in and through our life, which includes through our actions and words. The explanation or action of the gospel was never intended to stay at our worship services, or in our homes. And the meaning, in breadth and depth, was never meant to be solely discussed in conversations with the already convinced. The transforming message of the gospel was always intended to spread to outsiders and ignite a spiritual movement in the backdrop of culture.

In our day, there are a plethora of obstacles to bringing the life-changing, eternity-altering message of the gospel to almost anyone without facing hostility, animosity and resistance. We live in what many call a "post-Christian culture." In other words, we live in a period of time following the decline of the importance of Christianity in our society or region.[1] The resistance to Christianity is strong. As leaders and communicators of the gospel in the context of our culture, we face many challenges:

- How do we effectively communicate the truth of the Scriptures to people who don't believe the Scriptures are true, or don't even believe in the idea of "truth"?

- How do we translate the gospel of Jesus Christ to a world that assumes they already know who Jesus is, and in many cases even that they already "believe" in him?

- How do we help people find God when they appear satisfied with the "God" they've already found?

- How does the church translate the love of Christ to people who don't believe in or trust his church?

- To what degree is it even our responsibility to convince people who maintain a disdain for the church and Christianity that Jesus cares about them, wants to establish a relationship with them and "save them"?

- How do we tell the biblical story in a cultural language without compromising the message?

- How do we move forward and *advance the kingdom of God* when everything in culture seems to be going against us?

These are complex issues, ones that emerging ministry leaders must face head on with wisdom, discernment and intention. I'm convinced that we can break through the mind-numbing resistance, hostility and spiritual strongholds that have gripped the minds and hearts of our pluralistic, post-Christian society.

MIRRORING THE MARS HILL CULTURE

After being conquered by Rome, Athens had become the cultural and intellectual center of the Roman Empire and the literary capital of the ancient world. In the middle of this city was the *agora*, which is usually translated "marketplace." However, *agora* has a much more extensive meaning when we explore it more deeply.

The *agora* was the seat of philosophy and a place where intellect was celebrated, and where people were enthralled with discussing the latest cultural ideas. It was the center for media, art, entertainment and culture, as well as the financial district of Greece. It was the home of philosophers, orators, sculptors, painters and poets. It was also the great university where thousands of strangers gathered for study. In that day, where did people get the news? Where did artists display their work and perform? Where were financial transactions made between investors and businesspeople? Where were philosophical ideas debated and discussed? You guessed it, the *agora*.

In addition, the *agora* was the backdrop where the apostle Paul sought to effectively communicate the life-changing message of the gospel. When he was invited to speak at Mars Hill, his cultural context wasn't all that different than ours. He stood in Athens, the most cultured city on earth and the chief city of Greece in the first century, and boldly communicated the gospel while being enmeshed in a pluralistic, anti-Christian society full of skeptics, cynics and agnostics. Paul knew Athens was a place where many thought of themselves as "enlightened" and "open-minded" because they didn't want to limit themselves to believing in just one God. In the minds of many, all paths led to the same place, all gods were worthy of worship and whatever spirituality someone believed in was essentially validated. Isn't it hard to imagine a culture like that? Paul took the gospel to this cultural hot spot and proclaimed it strategically, boldly, humbly and compassionately. He did it with great tact, clarity, intention and relevance.

Our culture today mirrors the culture of Mars Hill. In Paul's day, it was every bit as difficult to share the gospel in a way that compelled people to change the trajectory of their lives and see the present and eternal value of the kingdom. But we cannot overlook the fact that, as we read in Acts, the case for Christianity is made so powerfully that outrageous numbers of skeptics, cynics, pluralists, agnostics and even atheists believed and were transformed by the gospel. In fact, history reveals the unmistakable reality that the gospel changed the very culture of the entire Roman Empire.

Acts 17:16-34 offers a poignant example from which we can learn about communicating with a missional lens. (Although I'm aware of various nuances of terms, in this chapter I will use the term *communication* synonymously with *preaching* and *teaching*.) I will extract five significant frameworks that can be applied to our communication process. So, let's take a guided tour through these verses, looking through Paul's eyes and sensing his heart, as we examine his unique communication frameworks. In the process, we'll gain solutions and insights into how we can interact with the current culture with greater impact, through the power of the gospel and the transformational gift of communication.

THE LIFEBLOOD OF MISSIONAL COMMUNICATION

Framework 1: Communication must always be rooted in mission.

I'm gripped by the way this passage begins, and then evolves. It speaks pointedly and prophetically into many of the challenges we face today in missional communication. From the outset of this passage, we discover the core of Paul's motivation.

> While Paul was waiting for them in Athens, he was greatly *distressed* to see that the city was full of idols. So he reasoned in the synagogue with both Jews and God-fearing Greeks, as well as in the marketplace day by day with those who happened to be there. (Acts 17:16-17 TNIV, emphasis mine)

The Greek word *parōxuneto* often gets translated "distressed." This verse tells us that Paul "was greatly distressed to see that the city was full of idols" (17:16). In other translations we read, "his spirit was being provoked" (NASB); "his spirit was stirred" (KJV); he was "deeply troubled by all the idols he saw everywhere in the city" (NLT). An ancient proverb claimed that there were more gods in Athens than men.

Here we see the lifeblood of missional communication revealed in Paul's interior world. We see what elevates his urgency and reminds us why we do what we do. As communicators of the gospel in culture, we must monitor our internal motivation, paying close attention to what stirs us, troubles us, even provokes and distresses us.

When we ponder the people who worship an array of idols, are we distressed at the destructive effects their way of life causes? Is our heart attuned to outsiders, and is our spirit stirred as a result? Is this distress more compassionate or judgmental? If we are not *distressed, stirred or troubled* that people without God desperately need him and that they are looking in all the wrong places, we will never communicate effectively in the culture we live in. And if *distress (parōxuneto)* is not engrafted into our motivation, perhaps something inside us is disconnected from the heart of God.

Embedded in the meaning of the word *parōxuneto* are connotations of someone being "ripped with contradictory feelings." *Parōxuneto* is the complex feeling that is, first and foremost, fully embodied in Jesus Christ. It describes a complex emotion that God himself experiences when he sees human beings committing spiritual adultery. Paul has a dose of this complex emotion, one that involves love and anger. He maintains a feeling of love of the deepest kind for people. But because he sees them destroying their lives, he's also angry. This is an anger that flows from love, and then helps motivate action. It gives us a glimpse not only into Paul's heart and motivation, but into God's heart for humanity.

God looks and sees human beings worshiping idols, building their lives on everything else but himself. He knows these things enslave people, even destroy them. And he says, "I love you too much to let you destroy yourself. Therefore, I'm coming to get you, to win your affection back." That's what drove Jesus to the cross.

Jesus didn't come to condemn the world, but to bear the condemnation and offer life (John 3:17). The cross reveals that Jesus was so angry with sin that he came to die—he had to die—so we could come to life. He so loved you and me that it even brought him joy to die for our sake (Hebrews 12:2). When we see this reality clearly and embrace it deeply, it changes us. What develops is a heart and motivation like Paul's.

Paul's complex emotion for the people in the Roman Empire was the feeling and passion that fueled his urgency to communicate the truth of Jesus to people who believed in a plurality of gods, to people who claimed to know God but didn't really *know him*. Paul desires to introduce these women and men to the Way and the Truth, to people who already have a way, and to people who act like they already know the truth. This took tenacity, wisdom, tact, humility and dependence on God. Ultimately, it was all fueled by Paul's *parōxuneto* (his core motivation).

Paul wasn't paralyzed or depressed by his "distress." He was spurred to action, moved to do something about it. Communicating the Scriptures to people who didn't believe the Scriptures to be true was a driving motivation, passion and focus of his life. As kingdom leaders, we can cultivate this same essence. Our burden for people can become the fuel that drives us to effectively communicate the gospel with persuasive power and to have a potent and authentic effect on people's lives.

THE DISGUISE OF RESISTANCE

Framework 2: Resistance isn't always resistance.

The apostle Paul initially debates with the Epicureans and Stoics, the two leading schools of philosophy in that day—the cultural and intellectual elites. Both of them rejected traditional religion, meaning they didn't make religious sacrifices, they didn't go to temples to worship and they didn't openly pray. The Epicureans believed the gods were a long way off, were very happy and didn't care much for what was going on in the world. The Stoics believed God and the world were one (pantheism). However, they were also both still intrigued by Paul when he shared how the resurrection of Jesus Christ had changed his life and eternity. And as we travel through this passage, we notice Paul's firm but gentle approach in addressing what the Epicureans and Stoics would have believed (for example, he argues God and the world aren't the same, God is not far off, heaven and earth are overlapping).

> A group of Epicurean and Stoic philosophers began to debate with him [Paul]. Some of them asked, "What is this babbler trying to say?" Others remarked, "He seems to be advocating foreign gods." They said this because Paul was preaching the good news about Jesus and the resurrection. (Acts 17:18 TNIV)

Paul is accused here of being a "babbler." His God was called "foreign." Don't you think those accusations could have frustrated Paul? Maybe he wondered why it wasn't all making sense to them? Why were these philosophers resisting his message that was supposed to be filled with hope and life?

Have you ever preached a sermon and been so certain that you were hitting the bull's eye that you secretly concluded that the people who weren't responding were hardhearted and resistant to God? I have. But could it be that these people are actually interested, although cautious and deliberative? Maybe they're diligently trying to make sense of what they hear and grasp about a God who seems "foreign" but who intrigues them?

At times I've misinterpreted someone's seeming resistance to God, failing to recognize their immense curiosity about God—their cautious, but honest search for truth. There are people who long to know the truth, and the appearance of resistance is their front. Just because they ask skeptical-sounding questions, or doubt things that we don't think should be doubted, let's not discount their search, even hunger for God. Often these people have a genuine desire to understand God and Scripture, but they feel as though they haven't received adequate and sufficient responses to their questions, struggles and doubts. Over-simplistic answers, or no answers at all, have kept them at a distance or even pushed them away. Affirming their courage, authenticity and honesty can pull them in.

My friend Doug always asked skeptical questions. Initially, I thought his questions revealed his resistance to Jesus. They were almost always framed in the negative. In other words, "You don't really think Jesus is the only path to get to heaven, do you?" Or, "How can you believe the Bible is inspired by God and didn't accumulate errors in translation over the years?" I often got frustrated because it seemed he was purposefully being antagonistic. In the end, I discovered that he was genuinely pursuing God, and was even intrigued by Scripture. He was partly trying to make sense of his spiritual background. In a sense, he was testing my beliefs so that he could discover what *he* really believed.

I had been in countless conversations with him, and hardly felt he was making progress, but I finally saw his openness when his search culminated. He told me, "Okay, I'm ready to follow Jesus." I was shocked. But at least I knew he had counted the cost and thoroughly wrestled with what he believed about life, God, the Scriptures and faith.

Whether it's in one-on-one conversations or one-on-many, we as ministry leaders have a responsibility to steward people's questions, skepticism and doubts. If we have a hard time drawing those kinds of people to our churches, perhaps we need to rethink and reevaluate what we're doing. If we have a hard time drawing those people into our lives, perhaps we need to rethink how we're living. Many times, we're doing or saying things (even unintentionally) to communicate that those conversations aren't really welcomed.

We live in a day where one of the primary roles of the communicator is helping people make sense of their many spiritual experiences and bringing clarity to the confused and muddied waters of their ongoing spiritual understanding. Many of those who appear resistant and cautiously skeptical are instinctive doubters, even critics, but they are genuinely searching for truth. Although they may appear hardhearted and rebellious, their resistance, skepticism and doubt are not always signs of rejecting God.

AN INVITATION TO MARS

Framework 3: God is everywhere.

Paul gets invited to a place called the Areopagus, or "Mars Hill." In Roman mythology, Mars was the god of war. The counterpart in Greek mythology was Ares, so "Areopagus" was "the hill of Ares." Mars Hill describes the location that was situated between the Acropolis and the Agora, where the most accomplished and elite of the city were invited.

So when the Epicureans and Stoic philosophers invited Paul to share his story and message in this space where the wisest and most learned philosophers of the day gathered, it was a great honor. This invitation would be something equivalent to being asked to speak to the elite of Princeton, Yale and Harvard all at the same time. The invitation itself was an act of trust and a risk on the part of the philosophers. We're not exactly sure why Paul got invited, but doesn't it make you wonder what Paul chose to say and do in this high-stakes situation?

Then they took him and brought him to a meeting of the Areopagus ["Mars Hill"], where they said to him, "May we know what this new teaching is that you are presenting? You are bringing some strange ideas to our ears, and we would like to know what they mean." (All the Athenians and the foreigners who lived there spent their time doing nothing but talking about and listening to the latest ideas.) Paul then stood up in the meeting of the Areopagus and said: "People of Athens! I see that in every way you are very religious. For as I walked around and looked carefully at your objects of worship, I even found an altar with this inscription: TO AN UNKNOWN GOD. So you are ignorant of the very thing you worship—and this is what I am going to proclaim to you.

"The God who made the world and everything in it is the Lord of heaven and earth and does not live in temples built by hands. And he is not served by human hands, as if he needed anything. Rather, he himself gives everyone life and breath and everything else. From one man he made all the nations, that they should inhabit the whole earth; and he marked out their appointed times in history and the boundaries of their lands. God did this so that they would seek him and perhaps reach out for him and find him, though he is not far from any one of us. 'For in him we live and move and have our being.' As some of your own poets have said, 'We are his offspring.' Therefore since we are God's offspring, we should not think that the divine being is like gold or silver or stone—an image made by human design and skill." (Acts 17:19-29 TNIV)

The Epicureans believed that the gods were remote and uninvolved in their lives, simply looking on from a distance. To a large degree, the Stoics didn't believe in God at all because God and the world were identical. It's interesting that Paul doesn't begin his discourse by denouncing his audience, nor does he suppose that they'd be convinced by mere dogmatic assertion. Instead, Paul starts by building on common ground, finding agreement and acknowledging the already existing spiritual activity in their lives. Paul comes along and essentially says, "I'm not trying to introduce you to a God who hasn't been involved in your life, or to a God you've never seen or encountered."

In essence, Paul challenged them on what it meant to *really know God*. He zeroed in on the idea that they know about this *unknown God* and even attempt to worship this *unknown God,* but they don't *really know him*. They may see this *God* present in their lives but they don't know his name.

There are many people in our day who are every bit as spiritually minded as those at Mars Hill. One of our challenges is that we as Christ-following communicators often don't enable people to feel dissonance in their *knowing about God* versus actually *knowing God personally* and *experientially*. There are people who talk about God and may even proclaim to worship or follow him, but in reality they don't really know the living presence of Christ. They haven't been transformed by the power of the gospel, even if they know what the gospel is. This isn't the case only outside the church—it's an all-pervasive reality inside the church.

Paul laces different forms of the Greek term *ginosko* ("knowing through personal experience") through his discourse at Mars Hill to emphasize this idea of, "you know God but you don't really know him the way he wants you to *know him*." Paul's essentially trying to connect to the familiar spirituality in their world as a bridge to help them connect to an unfamiliar reality of knowing the one true God through Jesus Christ. We can trust that God is already at work in people's lives.

Then, we can draw on people's spiritual familiarity to help them fulfill their intrinsic desire to connect to *the unknown God.*

Building on common ground and affirming the already existing activity of God in people's lives steers us away from an us-*versus*-them approach, and steers us toward an us-*for*-them approach. God is *for us,* so why shouldn't we be *for others?* Unfortunately, many who stand outside the walls of the church perceive us to be against them rather than for them. In my experience, most people are open to dialoguing about God if they feel embraced, validated or valued—if they feel we are truly *for* them.

It's interesting that Paul is invited to speak at Mars Hill. The philosophers seem to not only trust him, but be intrigued by the transformation in his life. When people see that the power of the gospel has changed a life, they often become intrigued. People lean in and listen more deeply because ultimately they're looking to us in hopes that we can help them make sense of this *unknown god* that they are intrinsically compelled to seek after. People everywhere are wondering, Can God really be known?

Once people realize they won't be condemned or inappropriately criticized for their thoughts, opinions or beliefs, they tend to open their hearts a little wider to us, and more importantly to the *unknown God.* What often causes them to shut down, or disengage, is the posture in which we enter or frame the dialogue, or whether we treat their opinions with value, dignity and respect (from the stage or in person).

As Colossians 4:4-5 points out,

• Are we "being wise in the way we act toward outsiders"?

• Are we "making the most of every opportunity"?

• Are our conversations "always full of grace, seasoned with salt"?

Paul is essentially declaring, "I know this unknown God who dwells among you and I have been changed by the power of the gospel. I want to communicate to you who God is and help you discover and encounter his living and transforming presence." One of our primary roles as communicators in the emerging world is to facilitate dialogue where people can have an unmistakable revelation and undeniable experience of God. In other words, we can cultivate environments through our sermons that provoke a desire for *ginosko* to happen. In those environments, individuals are then given the opportunity to respond to the presence and conviction of the Holy Spirit.

DOGMATIC CONFRONTATION VS. BOLD INVITATION

Framework 4: Decipher the difference between boldness and dogmatism.

There are always complex, deeply spiritual dynamics going on when someone is deciding whether they will choose Christ, whether they will turn from their way of living and turn to God.

In Acts 17:30-31 we read,

> In the past God overlooked such ignorance, but now he commands all people everywhere to repent. For he has set a day when he will judge the world with justice by the man he has appointed. He has given proof of this to everyone by raising him from the dead. (TNIV)

Calling others to repentance is a nonnegotiable and necessary part our preaching. It is a critical part of communicating with a missional lens. In some Christian circles this is a lost art and forgotten value. In other circles, I think the idea and application of calling a person to repentance gets overcharged and misconstrued.

In addition, repentance isn't something that applies only to non-Christ followers. It's not a term just to be used when a non–Christ follower becomes a Christ follower. Repentance must always be part of the ongoing way of life for a follower of Jesus. As communicators of the gospel, we're responsible to call sin what sin is and boldly communicate a picture of a new redemptive reality that we are inviting people into, followers and non-followers. Spiritual leaders must never stop calling people to change the direction of their lives, to turn from idols that are destroying them and turn to God.

One of the biggest mistakes I've observed in preachers has to do with their application of what it means to call someone to repentance. I think we sometimes use dogmatic confrontation and call it boldness. But calling people to repentance doesn't mean being dogmatic, nor does it mean we have to awkwardly confront people and force something on them.

The apostle Paul did not engage the Athenians with dogmatic confrontation, rather with a bold invitation rooted in the convincing communication of the resurrection. By dogmatism, I'm primarily referring to an assertion of views that is so straightforward that it ignores the complexity of the human experience. When enormous ideas are presented without recognizing the genuinely difficult process people go through as they attempt to absorb such life-altering realities, it can feel aloof, flat and even arrogant.

Our preaching must emerge from a humble posture and yet never to be void of passion and deep, strong convictions. We must trust the Holy Spirit and allow him to do his job, while we do ours. Ultimately, it is the Holy Spirit who convicts of sin, righteousness and judgment, not us (see John 16).

We aren't responsible to convert or convict. Like Paul, we're called to be witnesses of the good news through the power of the Holy Spirit (Acts 1:8). We're called to be gospel messengers who share God's message of love, truth, forgiveness and grace to the world. If we keep to this, perhaps a movement of Jesus will happen in our midst.

A FOLLOWER OF WHOM?

Framework 5: You are the fifth gospel.

Acts 17:32-34 states, "When they heard about the resurrection of the dead, some of them sneered, but others said, 'We want to hear you again on this subject.' At that, Paul left the Council." We then read that some of the people "*became followers of Paul* and believed. Among them was Dionysius, a member of the Areopagus, also a woman named Damaris, and a number of others." Did you catch that? Dionysius, Damaris and a number of others *became followers of Paul* on their way to becoming followers of Christ. Doesn't this make him a cult leader or false prophet? Shouldn't Paul have stopped them from following *him*? Not exactly.

As a spiritual leader, many people will choose to follow you on their way to beginning their journey of following Christ. They'll learn what it means to follow Christ by following how you follow him and even how you project what it means to follow him. This reminds me of another time when Paul said, "Follow my example, as I follow the example of Christ" (1 Corinthians 11:1). As people turn to follow us, we become conduits who usher them into experiencing the one true God in Jesus Christ. This is what sparked the movement of Jesus in the first century. This is what can spark a movement of Jesus in this century.

In the emerging world, the spiritual lives of ministry leaders are often what help others make sense of the gospel. We are representatives of Christ, not just with our words, but with every move we make. The gospel is always first about living it before it is about speaking it. Many people are desperately looking for someone who has been changed by God because they're desperately looking to be changed by God. People's desire to know the God we know will be sparked when the God we know seems real, compelling and good. They want to listen to the conversations we're having with him and learn how to live the life we're living as we follow him. They want to see into our soul by looking closely at our life. That's when they'll decide if they want what we have.

The church needs spiritual leaders who don't solely have knowledge about God and Scripture (although that's critically important). More important, we need spiritual leaders who have authentically and deeply experienced the transcendent God and the transforming power of the Scriptures. We need to be deeply and relationally connected to the One in whom we "live and move and have our being." The emerging world is desperate to hear from leaders who hear the voice of the Divine and encounter his visceral, transcendent presence in their lives.

People are eavesdropping on the conversations we're having with God. They want to know what he's saying to us, and how we're experiencing him. There's no doubt that this generation is seeking transcendence. They want to hear what we're contemplating and about our spiritual encounters.

Interestingly, the classic definition of preaching is *contemplare et contemplata aliis trader*, which means, "to contemplate and to hand onto others the fruits of your own contemplation." Preaching cannot be reduced to simply transferring information or knowledge. We create problems when we reduce the mystery of God to what we can learn in a classroom or from our studies. We must hold on to knowledge without letting go of the mystery of Christ in us (Colossians 1:27). Hold the value for knowledge and learning. Hold the awareness of God's unending mystery and unquantifiable dimensions. Outsiders want to see how God's power, truth and grace are transforming our life so they can begin believing that he will transform theirs.

For us to effectively communicate, people must conclude that we're honest women and men who reveal evidence that we really know God. In Jesus' case, even his enemies were forced to acknowledge his integrity: "We know that you are an honest man, that you are not afraid of anyone, because human rank means nothing to you, and that you teach the way of God in all honesty" (Mark 12:14 njb).

Sharing personal stories of real and current transformation in our lives can illuminate the truth we are teaching from Scripture. At times, it can even become the most powerful part of our preaching because it captures emotion and engages the human spirit in a deeply spiritual way. Stories of personal life change are our testimony. They can build trust and enhance our credibility. Where there is established trust and earned credibility between a communicator and the listener, that's where a culture of deep transformation is cultivated.

We need more women and men to share the story of God through the lens of how the Scriptures are molding them, rather than solely transferring information about God in cognitive form. As public spiritual communicators, we should be the best examples of people who are continually being transformed by the presence of the living God. Whether we like it or not, we are the face and essence of Jesus to the masses.

Paul certainly experienced this. I love how he shared his life, and even allowed others to learn from him in very personal ways as he followed Christ with such clarity and resolve. It was as if his life were not his own, on loan so the world could see God through his walk and testimony. But Paul was also very aware of the danger linked to following a follower rather than God himself. Sometimes admiration of leaders in the Christian movement can almost border on hero worship. Everything starts to revolve around their gifting, charisma and personality. And sadly, this can inhibit followers from experiencing Christ, because all the praise and glory is going to a mere human being.

Paul speaks directly to this issue:

What, after all, is Apollos? And what is Paul? Only servants, through whom you came to believe—as the Lord has assigned to each his task. I planted the seed, Apollos watered it, but God has been making it grow. So neither the one who plants nor the one who waters is anything, but only God who makes things grow. . . .

So then, no more boasting about human leaders! (1 Corinthians 3:5-7, 21 TNIV)

It's as if Paul is admonishing them to not lose sight of the One we are all striving to serve; not to get lost in great human leadership at the cost of not finding the eternal leader. This can be a big problem in the church. As women and men in ministry, we must remind people that although it is good to "follow us as we follow Christ," we pay too big a price if we channel our worship toward mere human leaders rather than our Creator who deserves every single ounce of it.

With an understanding of Paul's warnings, continue to allow your life to be a living example of God's lifeblood running through your own. God is pleased with servants who invite others to walk this sacred journey with them. It is for this reason that we have regularly invited people into our home, and in some cases even to live with us. As you see profound results come from opening your life, remember the temptation that is always lingering to make it about you, and remind those who are inspired by you that it is Christ they are ultimately called to follow. We are all followers when it comes to Jesus . . . no exceptions, no matter how great of a spiritual leader we may be.

REFLECTING ON THE MARS HILL EXPERIENCE

- How do we look at what Paul did in his culture and do the same in our culture?

- What are the "temples" in our culture that have the unknown God in their midst? How can we engage in deeper dialogue in these contexts?

- What can we do as church leaders to become more equipped in our understanding of other worldviews, and as a result expand our capacity to unmask half-truths?

- Which poets will you quote in effort to connect to our post-Christian, pluralistic world?

- What doesn't our culture know about spirituality that we, as communicators, can teach and guide them in? How can we stretch ourselves to do this more effectively?

IDEAS FOR MENTORS

1. **Create a metaphor log.** One personal discipline of mine is keeping a metaphor log. When I come across a metaphor or have a life experience that could be retold as a story, I try to write it down and file it away, especially if it connects to an eternal or biblical truth. I use a small notebook (and random Post-it Notes), later organizing it all on my computer. Compelling, intriguing metaphors and great stories are two of the primary methods Jesus used to communicate, so why shouldn't we use them? Keeping a log of metaphors can also help cultivate our imagination, which includes our overall right-brain thinking. Most preachers preach in left-brain orientated ways, which isn't bad, just sometimes limited. I do try to find metaphors that people outside the faith can relate to, and sometimes I even find ones that help them make sense of what's going on inside their soul. My favorite book on right-brain thinking is *A Whole New Mind* by Daniel Kirk.

2. **Increase story usage.** Encourage developing and aspiring communicators to practice sharing stories from their life in various contexts. Stories can be tools to connect to people. Encourage protégés to develop their storytelling abilities by telling stories, refining those stories and then retelling them (to different people of course). Making storytelling a life rhythm and habit can increase one's ability to communicate effectively and creatively.

3. **Simple. Unexpected. Concrete. Credible. Emotional. Stories.**

My favorite book on communication that I integrate in protégé development is *Made to Stick*, by Dan and Chip Heath. It's actually a book on marketing, but has brilliant insights into communication that revolves around the acronym SUCCES. Steve Martin's autobiography, *Born Standing Up*, Seth Godin's book *Purple Cow*, Ken Bain's *What the Best College Teachers Do*, Neil Postman's *Teaching as a Subversive Activity* and Andy Stanley's *Communicating for a Change* are all good reads on communication as well. Read through one of these with a protégé or group of protégés. Discuss, debate and dialogue about what makes communication effective and what doesn't. Remind people that it's not just about information transfer.

MENTOR TIP:
LEAN INTO MOMENTS

Crisis often creates the greatest opportunity for growth. Pay attention to when someone is going through a crisis (circumstantial, emotional, psychological, spiritual, etc.). Recognize when someone gets triggered deeply by something. Moments like these are when protégés need mentors the most. Coming alongside them can help foster substantial growth. Engage them deeply with care and honesty, with grace and truth, with presence and availability. Help draw out what can be learned and what God may be saying or doing.

PART 4

Mission

THE MOVEMENT OF THE GOSPEL

I see a future for you. In fact, I can envision you becoming something that even you cannot imagine. And so from now on, I'm going to call you Rock, and it's on you I will build my church. And the forces of hell will not prevail against it!

JESUS TO PETER (MATTHEW 16:18, PARAPHRASE)

Someday the church is going to be like a city on a hill that cannot be hidden.[1]

JESUS (MATTHEW 5:14, PARAPHRASE)

Christianity is not a message which has to be believed, but an experience of faith that becomes a message.

EDWARD SCHILLEBEECKX[2]

THE DRIVE TO MAKE A MARK IN THIS WORLD is inseparably connected to the idea of mission. There's no doubt that followers of Jesus believe in mission. As a tribe of Christ followers, we know that we cannot make a difference if we are not taking action. We spend lots of time thinking about mission. We may even feel guilty for not doing it well enough, if we even do it at all. The reality is the church is more known for mission statements than for doing the mission. There's a huge gap between believing and doing. Unfortunately, many outsiders slip through the cracks of our inaction.

The essence of the movement that Jesus Christ admonished all his followers to be part of as he departed from earth is: "Go and make disciples of all nations." In other words, God is sending his followers out into the world to help others to find and know God as they seek after him and become more like him themselves. But let's face it, we're really good at writing these sentiments in our mission statements, even talking about them in our ministries, but how well are we carrying out this mission?

Mission is a call to action. Protégés are often more attuned to this call to action, simply because their calling to ministry is often in its early stages, and leaders young in age or in experience have the advantage of a fresh and unstoppable passion. But all leaders in the church need to be reminded of the call to action that is required, the marching orders that challenge us to leave the safety of our church walls and bring God to the borderless world around us. The church exists to equip and mobilize Christ followers to embody Christ's mission. The church must never lose sight of being a sending base for the mission of Christ—which ought not be limited to sharing *the message* of the gospel, although that's eternally significant. It must also encompass *being the gospel*, which flows from a life being transformed by the gospel.

Mission can happen in countless ways. God's heart to see his kingdom take shape in this world involves us doing our part to extend compassion, justice, wisdom, grace, truth and love to everyone we can (being the gospel). In the Protégé Program, we focus heavily on developing a twofold mission: one aspect being evangelism, the other being social justice. I've heard it said that mission is like two blades of scissors. If both are not moving together, there will be incomplete impact. In this book I chose to focus primarily on the blade of evangelism as I unfold the layers of mission. But that is not a reflection on the indispensable value of social justice from God's perspective. Other authors have written about social justice in very compelling, biblically grounded and practical ways. One of my favorite books on this topic is called *Generous Justice* by Tim Keller. I recommend it to every protégé I mentor because of its profoundly important message and insight on the interconnectedness of the gospel. Often we read through it together.

As we consider the missional values we believe in, we must remember that they are not attributes to be displayed like trophies in glass cases in our church buildings. Rather, these are to be the extensions of the essence of God reaching into all dimensions of humanity. Mission is the difference between having an emotion and actually doing something about it. It is putting our money where our mouth is, adding works to our faith, sending ourselves out to the front lines when no one else will go.

The idea of the missional church, or even the use of the term *missional theology*, has had a resurgence of interest in recent years. It begins with the Latin phrase *missio Dei*, which means "mission of God." Ultimately, the mission of God starts with God himself. He is a God on mission. As spiritual leaders, we must always be reminded (and remind others) that mission was embedded into the essence of God before it ever became an activity of the church. Missiologist David Bosch articulates this intersecting truth: "The classical doctrine on the *missio Dei* as God the Father sending the Son, and God the Father and the Son sending the Spirit was expanded to include yet another 'movement': Father, Son, and Holy Spirit sending the Church into the world."[3]

From that foundation, it is through our relationship with this God that we must find our motivation to join him in doing his mission. The mission of God is intended to be formed inside the human heart, embedded into the essence of our character and flow from a life of worship. In other words, before we can become a missional community, we must become a worshiping community. That's the place from which we receive our marching orders, to continue bringing restoration of life to this world as God intended it. That's the kind of mission that our churches ought to be organized around.

Alan Hirsch defines what a missional church is in *The Forgotten Ways: Reactivating the Missional Church:*

> Missional church is a community of God's people that defines itself by, and organizes its life around, its real purpose of being an agent of God's mission to the world. In other words, the church's true and organizing principle is mission.[4]

One of the primary reasons I decided to move from Chicago to Los Angeles to join forces with Mosaic Church in 2003 relates to Mosaic's first core value: *Mission is why the church exists.* And Mosaic didn't just value mission on paper; they lived it out. I am disheartened when I look around and see the lack of mission at the core of many churches. Research shows that very few pastors (and even everyday Christians) carve out time and energy to develop friendships with people outside our faith. We often neglect our responsibility to establish relationships in our communities that enable us to meet real needs involving poverty, injustice, violence and despair—that's all part of the mission of Christ.

So many ministry leaders relinquish the responsibility to use their gifts and talents to reach people who would never step inside a church building. Taking care of our own is important, but when we do so at the expense of loving others on the outside, and translating this love into missional action, we are like a puzzle that's missing pieces essential for completing God's design for our world.

We're not only called to build up the church, we're also called to reach and serve our city, as well as the nations, for God. Jeremiah 29:7 says, "Work for the success of the city I have sent you to. Pray to the Lord for that city. If it succeeds, you too will enjoy success" (NIRV). We're called to be ambassadors of Christ, people through whom God makes his appeal (see 2 Corinthians 5:17-21). This is a high calling and a difficult mission. There's no doubt it requires great sacrifice and devotion. But, it is the only way to live according to the words of Jesus. And remember, God has not left us to do it on our own.

Jesus said to his disciples *and to us*, "As the Father sent me, I now send you" (John 20:21 NCV). Quite often, we try to hold on to our ways of doing things, our agendas and our priority lists. Jesus reminds us that it's when we lose our lives that we can finally find them. It's when we set aside our perfectly well-thought-out plans for the trajectory of our lives that we instead discover the plans Jesus has for us, which he reveals through the Spirit.

I've seen many protégés embody, sometimes in uncomfortable and risky ways, getting off the sidelines and getting in the game. As a result, I continue to see protégés become game-changers for the future direction and current impact of the church. They take mission seriously. At times, protégés can even evoke a hunger that was once strong in those of us who have been in the game a bit longer and may be a bit more exhausted, even disillusioned.

Truth is, living a missional life is far too easy to drift away from because if we're honest, it's hard. But mission is not optional for followers of Jesus. We must find ways to stay on course. And I'm convinced that it's time for a new generation of leaders to lead the church into being what it's intended to be—a powerful, transforming movement that holds the gospel at the center of life itself. It's time to get out there and take action to do our part in advancing the mission of God. Share Christ. Be Christ. Live Christ. When we do this, we'll create a kingdom culture of mission in and through our churches.

Now, let's turn to learning how we can live on mission more effectively in the context of our culture.

11 • Gospel Momentum

I MET MICHAEL THROUGH MUTUAL FRIENDS and didn't antic-ipate what I would eventually learn from him about the way the movement of Christ works. At first, our paths crossing seemed to be a random encounter. But when we clicked, a friendship began.

Michael was an impressive guy. He was a young entrepreneur who ran an athletic training business. He worked with clients from all over the city. Because his expertise was in such demand, the cost to hire him kept increasing. People continued to pay for his services because what he offered was exceptional. And not only that, he had a sharp mind, relational intelligence, and was someone who turned everything he touched to gold. He was successful and wealthy. He seemed incredibly happy and optimistic about life. He even had a way with the ladies. Don't you hate people like this? It's just not fair.

As our friendship grew, I began listening more closely to Michael's story. I soon learned that underneath the exterior was an undisclosed struggle. I discovered that everything wasn't going quite as well as it seemed. Michael was an alcoholic. We began talking about his struggles and fears that not only drove him to this place, but often kept him there. As our friendship grew, he told me how his AA meetings were helping him, even changing his belief system. He also expressed his sense that there was something more. His spiritual curiosity emerged.

As months passed, his spiritual search intensified. He began exter-nalizing his internal questions about who God was and what it meant to relate to him. He was searching for meaning. He was ultimately trying to find God. I recognized that these same fears and struggles were driving him closer to the God who created him.

After many spiritual conversations, I started inviting Michael to church. He loved the services initially because they "spoke to him." He was also intrigued by the acts of compassion and service that our church participated in. He was compelled by a church that was on mission. Michael's spiritual search continued to intensify.

One day, he told me, "I feel like I've been searching, and that I'm trying to give God a central place in my life, but how exactly do I meet the God I think I'm looking for?" Opportunities to share about Christ certainly don't happen like this every day. But on that day, I explained what it meant to become a follower of Christ in the clearest and simplest way I ever had. I told him that it would involve a passionate, focused commitment, and that that the journey would take courage and perseverance. I also told him that giving God the leadership reins in his life would be the most critical decision he'd ever make. That day, he counted the cost and decided to trust and follow Christ.

Then, within a couple weeks, he asked me if he could start a small group with his friends from AA. I was surprised, but said, "Sure." He asked if I'd help. "Of course, I'd be happy to." I was shocked to see twelve people show up a week later, all from AA—I was the odd man out. I later found out that all of their spiritual lives were really in an ambiguous state. Some were in complete shambles.

After we socialized a bit, we all gathered in the living room. I had coached Michael a little on how to lead a group discussion. He seemed like he knew what to do. I was ready to watch Michael lead these people in a lively spiritual discussion when he looked at me and said, "All right, Steve, you can start now." I was totally caught off guard. Are you kidding me?

It was time to think on my feet. The first question that came to my mind was, "So where do you guys see God at work in your life lately?" I was really just trying to buy some time. I never expected what happened next. Over the next hour, these women and men poured out their hearts. They honestly expressed their fears, personal struggles and doubts about God. I listened in amazement as these people who were searching so desperately for God expressed that they didn't know where to turn to talk about it more thoroughly than in their AA meetings.

This group continued for weeks, engaging in deep, transforming conversations. I was blown away. At some point I realized I was up close and personal to a little movement of Christ happening right before my eyes. The Holy Spirit was active. Spiritual momentum abounded. Their newfound faith search became viral.

A few weeks later, I was hanging out with Michael. I had been so inspired with how he used his influence to affect those around him. So I began curiously probing as to how he got that many people to come to his group. I wanted to know if he had a secret that I didn't know about. He told me three distinct things he thought were the core reasons for why they all came that night. They are simple, but I'll never forget them.

First, he was motivated by compassion. He told me, "I know for certain that my friends are still so broken, even with how far they've come. I was, and I know they are. My heart goes out to them. I simply want to help them explore God the way I have, and perhaps they will find what I've found." This reminded me of the heart of Jesus: "When he saw the crowds, he had compassion on them, because they were harassed and helpless, like sheep without a shepherd" (Matthew 9:36). It also reminded me of Jesus' statement in Luke 5:31-32: "It is not the healthy who need a doctor, but the sick. I have not come to call the righteous, but sinners to repentance."

Second, Michael shared his faith story naturally, respectfully and humbly. He later expounded, saying, "I also made sure I didn't talk down to them, demean them or undermine what God was already doing in their life. I made sure I respected their journey and process." Michael's story reminded me of the important task every one of us has to make faith and spirituality part of our natural way of relating to people. Notice, Michael didn't pressure anyone to believe what he believed; he simply shared his life story in an authentic way in an effort to help his friends. That's a powerful and personal way of living on mission in our day. That's a brilliant example of what the Scriptures call being a *witness:* one who shares what he or she has heard, has seen or knows. It also reminds me of Peter's words to always share the gospel "with gentleness and respect" (1 Peter 3:15).

Third, Michael's friends recognized the changes in his life. Even the most skeptical ones couldn't help but admit that something was changing. In other words, it wasn't just that Michael talked about his newfound faith; it was that they saw him changing before their eyes. They saw him changing in how he related to people. They noticed his newly formed contentment and peace in his life. They commented that he had a different strength and joy that exuded from him. His generosity, compassion and humility were evident.

Michael essentially revealed what it looks like to live as a witness to God's work in his life. He was on mission without ever using that language. He had compassion for his friends who didn't know Christ, and the transformation in his life was recognizable and inspirational.

After Michael shared his three reasons for why he thought his friends came that night, I couldn't stop thinking about what he said. I had heard it before, but something was different. He was fueled by compassion, and as a result, he lovingly created a space where his friends could authentically engage in substantial spiritual conversations. Along the way, they were compelled by his naturally genuine way of dialogue, and his openness about how important Jesus was becoming to him. His life became consistent with what they were hearing. His real-life story about real life change gripped their hearts.

As I reflected on Michael's insights, I thought to myself, *If only Christians understood what he just articulated and could do evangelism in that way. What if we were fueled with compassion and invited others to explore who God is, and can be, in their life in an urgent, yet unforceful way? What if talking about Jesus became a natural part of our conversations—including sharing our struggles, fears, doubts and all the ways we're changing? What if we didn't try to hide everything that doesn't look like we think it's supposed to look, and simply lived with transparency? What if we let our life story speak?*

Spiritual momentum follows authentic life change. We see it through Michael. And we can see it in our lives. This is the kind of momentum the next generation of ministry leaders can cultivate if we capture how to help others live this out. What if the people we were helping in their search for God became the people God used to create momentum for the gospel?

And what if the changes in who we were becoming were so evident that others were compelled to come to a group we were facilitating to discuss spiritual things?

A CULTURE OF HOSTILITY AND RESISTANCE

Perhaps you're still a little hesitant to believe evangelism can look like this. To be honest, so am I at times. You may not have seen it happen quite like it did through Michael, where multiple people became Christ followers all through one person's catalyzing conversion experience. In your world, perhaps you question whether people are really that open. While it's certainly true that there are different levels of spiritual openness, and even resistance, we must not lose hope. We can actively contribute to cultivating this kind of spiritual momentum.

In the first century, the movement of Christianity was birthed in a hostile and resistant culture, not all that different than what you may experience today. In spite of that, explosive growth and expansion of the church happened as women and men took the responsibility of listening to and obeying the Holy Spirit seriously. These women and men sought to align their hearts and lives with God. And no matter what resistance pressed up against them, they were ready for the challenge. The culture of Christianity gained momentum because their lives were being unequivocally and undeniably changed by the power of the gospel and through the work of the Spirit.

Throughout Acts, we have an ongoing series of episodes that unveil conversion after conversion. In some cases, we see explosive growth where thousands come to faith. A dynamic spiritual awakening emerged. We see ordinary people beginning to live extraordinarily missional lives, many becoming passionate evangelists and guiding thousands who were searching for a newfound faith to the foot of the cross. History reveals that this movement radically changed the existing first-century society.

Indeed, God's mission sprung forth and created a momentum of missional formation through his followers. Leaders paid attention to spiritual openness and receptivity. And they navigated through the resistance and hostility.

Enter the twenty-first century. Sometimes I wonder if we fully understand the movement that we're part of. Sometimes I wonder how deeply we believe in the promises of God from years ago. And sometimes I wonder what emerging leaders are going to do to advance the movement of Christ in the world that is yet to come.

To do our part, I'm convinced that we must rethink how we as missional leaders *do evangelism,* and train others to *do evangelism.* As fundamental as evangelism is, many leaders have lost sight of how to carry it out in the context of our culture and have even shrunk the gospel. Our church leaders need to strengthen and reestablish a missional theology that's rooted in the New Testament.

DEVELOPING A MISSIONAL THEOLOGY

How was evangelism actually done in the first century? In 1 Corinthians 3:9 we're called to be God's *coworkers,* or *ambassadors.* But what does that mean for our responsibility as Christ followers? And what about as current and future leaders in the church? What is God's role if our role is to be his partner, or coworker, or ambassador? If all Christians are called to *do evangelism,* then why do so many relinquish that responsibility, or worse, do it poorly and distastefully? Many ponder whether evangelism should even be done at all in our post-Christian, pluralistic world of "tolerance." So how are we supposed to engage with the outside world in a way that advances the movement of Christianity? Are there things we can do to produce explosive growth? The questions go on.

There's no doubt that the waters have been muddied when it comes to how we must *do evangelism* in our day and how we must lead others in our churches to do the same. As a result, if leaders want to create healthy missional cultures and once again see something like the movement in the book of Acts emerge among us, we need clarity in our understanding of what "missional" means. In an effort to cultivate a deepening theology of mission in the lives of protégés, I often take them through a Bible study on the book of Acts. Perhaps you can begin a new journey through Acts yourself?

WHAT DOES IT MEAN TO BE MISSIONAL?

To be missional means more than just to evangelize.

We see ourselves as missionaries right where we live.

We see ourselves as "sent ones" who represent Jesus to our neighbors, communities and circles of influence.

We, the church, seek to align all that we do with the *missio Dei.*

We see the church not as a location we go to on Sundays but as who we are throughout the week.

We realize Jesus is active in culture and we join in to participate in what he's already doing in people's lives.

We are engaged in the culture and world we live in but aren't conforming to the world.

We serve our surrounding community, build relationships with people among them instead of seeing people as our evangelistic projects.

We remain attentive and responsive to God's promptings to step where he says step, and do what he says do.[1]

IDEAS FOR MENTORS

Prayerful evangelism. Carve out time and space to bring some of your protégés together to pray for their friends, family, neighbors and others who don't know and follow Christ. I know people have different theology that informs how they pray for nonbelievers but whatever that looks like, cultivate a prayer-focused environment. You may even want to discuss the role of the Holy Spirit in evangelism. My three key goals in doing this involve helping protégés cultivate a more compassionate heart, reminding them how important intentional personal evangelism is and challenging them to pay closer attention to the Holy Spirit in the process.

MENTOR TIP:
CANDID CONVERSATIONS

From a humble and respectful posture, mentors must be willing to have hard, frank conversations with protégés if they desire to optimize their growth. Doing this wisely, tactfully and humbly ought to be a regular part of one's mentoring process.

12 • The Spirit of the Gospel

ONE OF MY PHILOSOPHICAL APPROACHES to developing young leaders is rooted in creating novel learning experiences. Research reveals that novel experiences stimulate our brains and jolt our imaginations—which can result in effective learning and change. Without getting into neurological specifics, our brains are fundamentally lazy. They take shortcuts in their thinking processes. In other words, they don't want to waste energy, so they take the path of least resistance. But when our brain is forced to work harder and think differently, we become more likely to change a pattern of behaving, believing, thinking, or even to change an attitude. So when we deliberately confront our brain's shortcutting tendencies, we're able to expand our capacity to learn new things and, perhaps most importantly, unlearn old things.[1]

One experience that I facilitate to guide protégés in missional formation involves taking them on a tour through the Church of Scientology in Hollywood. My goal is not for them to be converted, nor do I want them to start submitting to the spiritual authority of Tom Cruise or John Travolta. I'm going for something a little more significant.

Before the tour, I direct the protégés' focus to three main things. First, I challenge them to maintain a humble, learning posture. They're free to ask genuine questions to gain understanding about Scientology, but no debates or arguments. Second, they must be respectful about the beliefs that are articulated, which includes staying engaged and visibly interested. Third and most importantly, they must closely observe how it feels to be on the other side of conversion. In other words, when the Scientologists attempt to convert them, they pay close attention not only to the external process of what's being said, but also to their internal, emotional response.

After the tour, we debrief the experience. Usually none of the protégés have ever participated in something like this, which makes it a novel experience, which enhances learning. Plus, most of them don't know much about Scientology going into it, nor have most of them ever had someone try to convert them.

When we debrief, I see my role as a facilitator who seeks to draw out those things that I perceive need to be *unlearned* about their theology and practice of evangelism. I listen closely and steer conversation where applicable. I encourage them to pay attention to what their emotional responses were when a belief system was forced upon them. I highlight what it feels like when someone we just met assumes that we should be convinced and converted on the spot.

Then we analyze how we could and should alter our approach with others. They share what they just learned and what applications to their own approach to evangelism they'll make. Most importantly, this whole experience sensitizes their hearts toward outsiders and helps them realize what someone else may be thinking when we share Christ with them in a forceful or invasive way. The message of the gospel is essential, but we must not stop there. In the emerging world in particular, our method matters too.

When debriefing with the protégés, I always hear comments like:

- "I felt violated when they pressured me to become a Scientologist right then and there."

- "It made me feel so awkward, uncomfortable, even trapped. It's as if they wanted me to make a life decision right on the spot."

- "It seemed like some of their questions were intended to set me up."

- "It felt like they were cornering us into telling them we wanted to know more. For instance, they asked, 'Have you ever been sick and wanted to be healed?' Of course the answer is yes. And once we say yes, then they tell us how Scientology will do that for us. They usually follow with a question like, 'So, what is stopping you then from becoming a Scientologist?'"

Through this experience, we mostly learn about what not to do when it comes to living on mission. We discover things to *unlearn* related to what we've been taught in terms of evangelism. Education (and development of leaders) is often more about unlearning than new learning. Perhaps that's one of the main reasons why the church is stuck in not knowing how to live out personal evangelism more gracefully and effectively—we have a hard time unlearning our theology and practices of evangelism.

There are certainly moments to be intentional, even urgent, when it comes to sharing the message of Christ with others. And to some degree, discomfort is an inevitable part of evangelism, for the Christian as well as the non–Christ follower. But we must not grow complacent simply because discomfort is inevitable or because the message is true. It is easy to forget how being challenged on what you believe can feel demeaning, even insulting. Being aware of those feelings while engaging these meaningful interactions around evangelism will help soften your approach with love and humility, and will therefore expand the possibility of others opening up their hearts to you, and ultimately to the God you're trying to share with them.

Although there are many episodes we could look at in Scripture, there's one in particular that I want to focus on. Embedded in this passage are critical insights for living more effectively on mission and cultivating the context for a dynamic spiritual movement in the twenty-first century. Acts 8:26-40 suggests five shifts in evangelism that I believe can guide us in how we think and live as coworkers with God and ambassadors for his kingdom, as we join with him in doing his mission. I strive to live these shifts out in my own life, as well as to teach and train others, because I'm persuaded that these are the core heartbeat of New Testament evangelism. I'm convinced that we must use these insights to guide how we train, equip and develop others in creating missional cultures in our churches and our ministries.

In that context, let's look at the five significant shifts that may not only change the way we do evangelism, but also increase our effectiveness in it. This chapter will address the first of the five.

SHIFT 1: THE SPIRIT: FROM INATTENTIVE TO ATTENTIVE

The first critical shift in evangelism from Acts 8 involves the role of the Holy Spirit.

Now an angel of the Lord said to Philip, "Go south to the road—the desert road—that goes down from Jerusalem to Gaza." So he started out, and on his way he met an Ethiopian eunuch, an important official in charge of all the treasury of the Kandake (which means "queen of the Ethiopians"). This man had gone to Jerusalem to worship, and on his way home was sitting in his chariot reading the book of Isaiah the prophet. The Spirit told Philip, "Go to that chariot and stay near it." Then Philip ran up to the chariot and heard the man reading Isaiah the prophet. (Acts 8:26-30 TNIV)

Notice the detailed instructions of the Spirit. First, the angel tells Philip to "go south to . . . the desert road." The Spirit follows that current with, "Go to the chariot and stay near it." The specificity of the Spirit causes me to reflect on my frequent inattentiveness to potential divine intersections that come through the whispers of the Spirit. Or to put it even more bluntly—too often, I care more about my own life than being a participant in the mission of God. And I don't think I'm alone in this. In our day, far too many disciples of Jesus live inattentive to the Holy Spirit.

Next, Philip runs to the chariot. I use to wonder why he ran until I realized that chariots move and that Philip was probably running to keep it in sight. After all, he was eagerly anticipating his role in God's next move. If the next generation of leaders wants to see explosive growth through conversions like we see in Acts, we must listen more attentively the specific, detailed guidance of the Holy Spirit. We must be ready to go south when he says, "Go south," and wait when he says, "Wait." We must learn to care more about the mission of God than our own lives.

God is in the business of giving specific directions to his followers (and his leaders). Some of us may feel we are being obedient but still aren't experiencing this specific kind of guidance. But instead of feeling discouraged, be inspired. That is one reason why the stories in Scripture are given to us: to inspire us toward what seems to be impossible but is within our reach. In this case, to receive specific guidance from God that results in Spirit-led evangelism.

God is on mission and he's intentionally inviting us to participate in reaching those who don't yet know him. No matter what generation we live in, this will always be God's mission. This is why it ought to be ours as well. And no matter where we land on the theological spectrum of evangelism, God's desire is that all would come to repentance and to the experiential and intimate knowledge of him (see 2 Peter 3:9). And for reasons I don't fully understand, he chooses to use his followers who are most attentive to his voice and responsive in obedience. Philip was. And we can be too. Will you be a leader who listens attentively, participates fully and responds obediently?

WORLDS BETWEEN US

It was Wednesday when I was invited to a dinner party that my neighbor Sunny was throwing on the upcoming Friday night. At first, I wasn't interested in going, mostly because I only knew one person who would be there. Plus, I figured some friends might be doing something better so I said "maybe"—we all know what that means.

Friday night came, and no "better plans" took shape. Then, I got one of those inner nudges that I wasn't sure was from God. I thought to myself, "Nah, that's just me." But even after casually ignoring it, the nudge kept returning—that's usually when I get a little nervous because it's probably God stirring me to do something that demands risk and courage. This quiet but strong prompting persuaded me to go to the dinner party. That night I met Sagar, whom I probably wouldn't have met if I ignored that prompting.

Sagar was a graduate student in Los Angeles, from India, and a devout Hindu. That night, we began a friendship that continued for months to come. Along the way, I learned about Indian culture, Hinduism, Sagar's favorite foods and hobbies, his family background, his dreams and passions, and so much more. In addition, one of the things I quickly discovered about Sagar was his spiritual curiosity. Since moving to LA, he had attended numerous Hindu temples, none to his liking.

One night, our mutual friend Sunny invited him to Mosaic. I later found out that Sagar wasn't really interested in attending, but he came anyway—mostly out of respect for Sunny, and not wanting her to feel rejected. That Sunday afternoon, I went to a barbecue with Sagar. I asked him what he thought of Mosaic. He said, "I like the Mosaic God." The next week he returned, which, to my surprise, soon became his weekly ritual. When I found out he had been taking the bus to church, I offered to pick him up. For months, every Sunday was filled with meaningful car conversations. Plus, since I had to come to church early, I even invited him to join our connection team to help new people connect in community.

Sagar asked me many different questions about the "Mosaic God." For instance, does he answer prayer, what do healthy spirituality and faith look like, what are the secrets to dating a Christian girl? (I had no answers for that one.) One day he had an epiphany that the name of the "Mosaic God" was Jesus. And he expressed his desire to make Jesus one of his gods—knowing enough about Hinduism informed me that this was a big step of progress for him.

At some point I was struck by how God was using me in Sagar's life to offer him spiritual guidance. He felt I was a safe person to ask his deepest questions and discuss his doubts and fears. I remember wondering how people from different sides of the world with completely different cultural and religious backgrounds crossed paths. Must be God. I was reminded how deeply God cares for the nations, how common it was for Jesus to express his desire for the gospel to permeate all cultures and religions, and how God wants to direct me in how I can participate in this mission. It's local. It's global. It's personal. It's communal.

All this to me paralleled why God brought together this middle-aged Jewish man named Philip and this accomplished, wealthy, Ethiopian eunuch. Clearly, we don't have the script of where and whom God may bump us into in a seemingly ordinary, coincidental way. That's why attentiveness and responsiveness to his Spirit is so critical.

We see in Scripture that God wants to use his followers to reach people who are different from us, even to reach the nations (see Acts 1:8 and Matthew 28:18-20). This was happening in Acts, it's happening in my life and it is what God desires to happen through his church today. That's the current and flow of God's Spirit. He desires that we'd be open and willing to go and do what he wants us to go and do. That's how his mission advances. And if we desire to care more about his mission than our own, here's where it begins.

Biblical scholar N. T. Wright articulates this same reality in a unique way:

> Matthew's Jesus instructs his disciples to make disciples and baptize in all the world. Luke's Jesus commissions his followers to go to Jerusalem, Judea, and the ends of the earth. And John's Jesus says, "as the Father sent me, so I send you." The story of Acts *is* the story, or rather a story, of early Christian mission. And . . . the letters (of Paul) confirm that not only he but a good many other Christians . . . believed it their business to travel around the known world, telling people that there was "another king, this Jesus."[2]

Despite how easily we drift toward people just like us, God still orchestrates divine encounters where we're called to help others be reconciled to him and even to help us be reconciled to one another. Acts poignantly reminds us that even though we can be starkly different from each other, we have universal human longings that bind us together—longings for purpose, transcendence, beauty, intimacy, meaning and truth. The Spirit still invites us to go places where we may never have gone or expected to go. To live on mission requires a willingness to listen attentively and obey responsively. It's only by remaining attentive to the *specific guidance* of the Spirit that we'll discover how we can play a significant part in the spontaneous movement of Jesus Christ—both locally and globally, both personally and communally.

IDEAS FOR MENTORS

1. **Scientology tour.** If possible, plan a tour at a local Church of Scientology. If there's not one near you, contact a Hindu temple, Muslim mosque or Mormon temple. Participate with a group of protégés in an experience similar to the one described in this chapter—with the same intentions and goals.

2. **Virtual evangelism.** To foster a missional culture in the Protégé Program, we simulate evangelistic dialogue by posing questions that nonbelievers and skeptics may ask. Then we offer our top-of-the-mind responses. Everyone gets

numerous opportunities to respond. From there we take time to give feedback on what we think are helpful insights and questions that equip us to serve outsiders well. In an effort to learn, we also share stories of recent spiritual conversations that went well, and ones that didn't.

MENTOR TIP:
UNFORCED GROWTH

Rather than forcing growth in areas you may find personally beneficial, pay attention to God's activity in a protégé's life and where he or she is struggling. Lean into that. Guide them to be attentive and responsive to God's voice. Ask directly, "What do you sense God saying to you right now?" or "When is the last time you really sensed God nudging you to take an evangelistic risk?"

13 • Gospel Conversations

IF THE FIRST CRITICAL SHIFT IN EVANGELISM revolves around the divine conversation, the second revolves around the role of human conversations.

SHIFT 2: THE CONVERSATION: FROM MONOLOGUE TO DIALOGUE

As Philip hears this eunuch reading Isaiah the prophet, he initiates conversation with a question: "'Do you understand what you are reading?' . . . 'How can I,' he said, 'unless someone explains it to me?' So he invited Philip to come up and sit with him" (Acts 8:30-31). Philip postures himself to listen as this African man explains his search to know the God of the Scriptures. Before he ever offers the Ethiopian his expert advice, gives well prepared answers or presents a preplanned gospel presentation, he does one very simple thing. He asks a question. Then he listens. This doesn't imply that we never provide answers but it does remind us of the critical nature of questions in living on mission. It's quite interesting to me that in Luke's Gospel, Jesus asks 129 questions. In Matthew's Gospel he asks 87. What follows is listening.

Listening is one of the great manifestations of love. When we ask questions and then listen before assuming and asserting our views, it translates as love. Spiritual leaders ought to become mavens in how to ask thoughtful questions and then listen to the deeper subtext beneath people's words. Mentors ought to spend time training protégés in this skill set. It is this kind of genuine approach that will communicate that we care more about being in a dialogue than we do about dominating with a monologue. Anytime we can show our love through listening, we ought not hesitate to do so. It is through love that people like this Ethiopian, and people all around us, will know that we are Jesus' disciples.

QUESTIONS THAT LEAD TO FAITH

In my own journey of faith, the most significant conversations that I remember in helping me decide whether I wanted to follow Jesus came through two people in my life, David and Kevin. These men consistently asked inquisitive questions that challenged me to reflect and then articulate my deeper longings and real needs. Their questions revolved around where I found my worth and purpose, and what my beliefs were about life, the Bible, God and faith. At times, they offered solid, grounded answers that served me well, but it was always in line with them paying attention to what God was really doing inside of me. It never felt like rote responses that were disconnected from their perceived reality of me. I always knew they were listening with great care.

David and Kevin had an authentic desire to understand my perspective, even when my beliefs weren't rooted in anything credible, even when I remained resistant to God and even when we disagreed on all fronts.

David and Kevin were like *Philip* to me. Their greatest contribution in my life was not what they said specifically but that they cared. They didn't have to tell me they cared; they simply did. They were available to me. They didn't get anxious when I asked skeptical questions. And they didn't oversimplify "the right answers." Looking back, giving me "the right answers" every time I asked a question would have stunted my spiritual process. At the end of the day, their questions, and then willingness to listen, were ultimately what advanced our dialogue, because their interest communicated to me that they were invested in me as a person and didn't simply have an agenda for me. Their willingness to dialogue instead of just monologue moved our conversations deeper, ultimately leading me to trust in Jesus Christ as Savior and Lord. Having felt listened to, known, accepted and heard—that was the kind of love that compelled me toward them, and then to Christ. In theory this sounds quite simple. But my experience tells me how rare it is to find Christ followers who are known for this way of relating.

HOW TO BE A PHILIP

I've been honored to have a few Philips in my life to guide me, including Kevin and David. I've also had the privilege and opportunity to be a Philip for others who were searching for God but weren't quite sure how to find him. When I first met Rich, I sensed a prompting from God to invite him to lunch—so I did. At lunch a few days later, as I listened to Rich in our initial conversation, I discerned spiritual receptivity and genuine curiosity about God. Although by his own admission he is "a British skeptic who believes in God but isn't sure I want to follow him," I began asking him questions about his spiritual background and interest level in God. I don't always do this the first time I meet someone, but in this case, I sensed God leading me to engage in a dialogue about spirituality.

I initiated our conversations by asking questions. Inspired by people like Kevin and David, I resisted offering pre-packaged responses or oversimplified answers to his complex and curious questions, and I listened attentively. Trust grew. I refrained from preaching at him, as so many evangelism approaches do (and which is rarely effective in interpersonal relationships). I wanted to get to know where God was specifically working in Rich's life so I could authentically serve him in his quest for truth. I listened and cared what he thought, believed and desired without trying to control what he thought, believed or desired. Although at times it was tempting to rush the process by doing less listening and more talking, I chose not to take the shortcut. Rooted in the conviction that God was at work in this man's life, and that I was being used as a fellow truth seeker, I chose to take the longer route—the one that was sure to lead us to the right destination. Offering my genuine friendship, along with allowing the Holy Spirit to guide my way, seemed to be the keys that were unlocking spiritual doors in Rich's life, right before my eyes.

Rich's search for truth was growing, yet he still had questions. At one point, Rich mentioned that he was reading the Bible recently, and that he didn't understand certain passages. Welcome to the club. I'm not sure why Christians pretend to understand everything in the Bible, because I certainly don't. I think we falsely believe that if we don't understand it all, that it loses its credibility, or we lose ours. Engaging honest conversations about the Bible can be a vulnerable path to embark on with a non-Christian person. Who do you know who has *all* the answers to *all* the hard questions about the Bible? Okay, maybe the Bible Answer Man. But I'm a pastor who graduated from seminary who's been in ministry for more than fifteen years, and I certainly have passages that stump me.

I think it's okay to be honest about this with people. As we offer what *is* clear to us, I believe we actually gain credibility because we don't pretend to know or understand it all. Unfortunately, what we may consider to be certainty can be perceived as arrogance to others. We need to join them in acknowledging that our humanity has its limitations, and that means that we are all plagued with questions that we may never find the answers to.

I continued to offer the insight I could, along with validating that some things remain a mystery. Along the way, I tried to gauge where Rich wanted my input. At one point, I simply asked, "Rich, what have you been reading recently that you don't understand? Maybe I can help you make sense of it." This was my initial attempt to be a Philip. His response? "Oh, I'd love that!" Obviously this told me that he wanted me to go deeper with him. Off we went.

A SOUND-BITE GENERATION

One of Rich's questions was, "Why did Jesus have to die?" Not exactly a lightweight question. I knew these weren't just intellectual questions. Rather, he was on a search to discover whether Jesus Christ was someone he wanted to follow. I took a deep breath and gave it my best shot. I started by giving him a few succinct, but thoughtful answers. Sometimes this is all people want—short, quick and to the point instead of long, drawn out and overly theological answers.

It's not that there aren't times for longer responses, but we live in a sound-bite generation. If we want to increase our effectiveness in reaching people, we must improve our ability to give solid answers in brief but potent form. This is one application in our day of the verse: "Always be prepared to give an answer to everyone who asks you to give the reason for the hope that you have. But do this with gentleness and respect" (1 Peter 3:15). One of our responsibilities is discerning what people are looking for in a moment and pondering how we can best serve them in that moment. Remember, dialogue, not monologue.

After a couple sound-bite answers that seemed to pique Rich's curiosity, I could tell he wanted more. So I continued to elaborate. Sometimes our 140-characters-or-less-type answers are what engage people's curiosity to learn more. I believe Jesus used this strategy at times. In fact, as we read through the Gospels we find many occasions where Jesus asks a question or makes a statement and allows people to walk away pondering and wrestling with it. Novel idea, eh? We don't seem to be comfortable with that. Instead of forcing more information on someone, what if we learned to trust that God will lead the process, and that maybe the question that we ask is the question God will use to move them forward in their faith journey.

Gauging someone's desire and interest level is one aspect of developing the art of listening. Not only can we develop this art in our personal life, but in our ministry life as well. To create a missional culture in our churches, we as leaders need to not only grow our own ability to have quick but meaningful responses, but also equip others to do the same. The church has far too many people whose approach to evangelism focuses on giving all the answers—mostly long ones.

Just a few weeks later, after a handful of lunches, Rich revisited our conversation about the need for Jesus' death. "Remember that day you explained why Jesus had to die? I was a bit skeptical when I heard you explain it, but for reasons that are a bit beyond me I came to not only believe it, but to put my faith in it. I'm ready to trust and follow him with my life and for the life to come." Wow! It was a good day . . . on earth and in heaven.

CELEBRATE CONVERSATIONS, NOT JUST CONVERSIONS

Our questions can reveal what answers people are really looking for, and how much we ought to elaborate in that moment to serve them in their process of coming to faith. And just because we don't walk away seeing someone converted, it doesn't mean we haven't served him or her in making spiritual progress. Loving someone does not always mean fixating on an exact conversion moment, or with leading them across the line. A lot of us need to celebrate spiritual conversations that help others make progress just as much as we need to celebrate spiritual conversions.

We must trust God's Spirit to work in a person's life and relieve ourselves of the guilt and pressure to convert people. Effective evangelism in and through our churches ought not only to be evaluated by conversions, but also by how frequently we foster dialogue that serves people well in their search and helps them progress no matter where they are in their spiritual quest and no matter what the outcome is. Remember, the outcome isn't up to us. God is the one who does the converting, not us. We simply need to play our part and let him play his. After all, some plant seeds, some water, but ultimately God is who makes it grow (1 Corinthians 3:6-7). This leads us to the third shift.

SHIFT 3: THE RELATIONSHIP: FROM INVASION TO INVITATION

A third critical shift in learning how to navigate our way through conversations about God and spirituality involves a relational dynamic I refer to as *invited vs. invaded*. We must pay attention to it. We see a snapshot of this in Acts 8:31: The Ethiopian eunuch "*invited* Philip to come up and sit with him."

In my conversations with both Sagar and Rich, I tried to pay close attention to the clues and cues they sent me—some verbal and some nonverbal. In both cases they were *inviting* me to "come up and sit with him." I observed when they were simply expressing their own opinion and not interested or open to mine. Rather than being "pushy," I respected their relational space because I know that when I don't do that, trust can quickly dissolve.

Others times, I recognized when they were struggling and searching for a solid, reasonable answer, and when they genuinely wanted my guidance for that answer. They revealed this in their body language, indirect verbal cues and sometimes directly through their words. There were distinct moments when I knew they were inviting me into a dialogue because I didn't sense any resistance or notice closed-off body language.

Discerning this relational dynamic isn't always easy, or even concrete, but it's critically important to develop in order to have great missional impact. Those of us in leadership also have to help others know how to navigate these dynamics in conversation so they don't short-circuit their ability to live on mission and even push people further from Christ. Much damage has been done because Christians have "forced God" on people, or pushed God on them in inappropriate ways. Unfortunately, many have confused the virtue of boldness with dogmatism.

There has been damage, but there has also been great good that has come from missional men and women who lace their relationships with grace and truth, side by side, working in perfect harmony. We need to acknowledge where we as a church have failed those outside our faith. But we also need to celebrate where we have served them. I know many fellow believers who embody the missional spirit and have played an integral role in the lost being found. One of the traits I've observed in them is a commitment to being invited rather than invading. And when they are invited, they are ready to engage with boldness, grace and love.

THE SPACE BETWEEN US

To develop true spiritual influence, we must learn the difference between being invited into someone's "relational space" and invading their relational space. By "relational space," I mean that invisible dynamic where people either open themselves to someone else's advice and guidance—or they resist it. In other words, if someone refuses to allow us into his or her "relational space," it means they are resisting our guidance and input.

In evangelism, we often don't adhere to this interpersonal dynamic. In the process, we become the *invader* of someone's space. As a result, we break trust, lose credibility and diminish our capacity to influence those outside our faith. If we want to increase our effectiveness in living on mission, we must learn to recognize the tone and openness of this relational space.

Think about this dynamic in a different way. Imagine hiring a personal trainer at a local gym to help you get in shape. By hiring him, you give him permission to coach you, guide you and even push you to exercise with greater effort and focus. You are inviting him into your "space."

On the contrary, imagine seeing a friend at the mall. After saying hello, he verbally assesses your physical health, explains to you how much exercise you need, how the extra fifteen pounds you are carrying is bad for your health, and then commands you to do fifty pushups. I don't know about you, but I'd be looking for the hidden camera.

Even if our motives are sincere in wanting to make a positive impact, and even if what we are advising is good advice, it will fall on deaf ears if we are not welcomed first. When we force our way into a person's relational space, they sense our relational invasion . . . and will almost always resist it. They resist because they feel we're barging in without knocking. They haven't opened the door and welcomed us in.

IS THE DOOR OPEN OR CLOSED?

Let me offer two contrasting examples to explain this one step further. I was at lunch with a USC student named Chris who was not a follower of Christ. For reasons I don't fully understand, he liked to ask for my advice on issues in his life, especially when he was going through a tough time. This day was different. He told me he had something vulnerable to share with me. I could tell by his body language that he was nervous. He was about to confess something and wasn't sure how I would respond. "I don't know if you know this, but I'm bisexual."

He seemed relieved to get it off his chest but remained curious how I would respond (knowing I was a Christian). My initial response was to thank him for having courage to share what he did. I affirmed how difficult it must be because he didn't know whether I would judge or reject him. In addition, I knew he was looking to dialogue. So I first explained that my view of him didn't change. As the conversation evolved, I asked a question: "Is your sexuality something you are settled with, or is it a struggle and at times a confusing aspect of your life?"

He responded by describing his struggle to make sense of his sexuality, explaining that for years he has been confused about it. As he elaborated, I discerned that he did want my input and guidance. He wanted help to try to make sense of it all. Not that I had easy answers;

they never are with issues of sexuality. One thing was clear—he was inviting me into a sacred conversation, into a deeper spiritual dialogue. He was saying something similar to what this Ethiopian was saying: "How can I understand unless someone helps me make sense of it all?" A profound conversation began, one that continues taking shape today.

In contrasting fashion and on a different occasion, I sat at a local café with Brian, who expressed interest in having me become his "spiritual mentor." He told me: "I want you to know that I consider myself a 'gay Christian.' I'm totally convinced that this lifestyle is okay to God and I'm not interested in changing my view. I just want you to know that."

This set the tone for how we were going to relate to each other. It was a fair boundary for him to set, but it also informed me about how I ought to approach the relationship going further. Needless to say, I knew this wasn't going to be a wide-open kind of mentoring relationship. I believe a certain level of openness is necessary for progress and growth, and Brian was not inviting me into that deeper conversation that would require entering his relational space.

In case you're wondering what I did, I talked to him with compassion and candor about how I respect that he's given thorough thought to this issue, but that it would be difficult to mentor him if he's is already telling me he doesn't want to open certain aspects of his life to me, and ultimately to God. At the core, "spiritual mentoring" is really about paying attention to how and where God is working in someone's life and guiding them to lean into God's activity no matter where it takes them. That would be true no matter what issues were on the table, not just because the issue was sexuality.

I assured him that I didn't think it was my responsibility to change his sexual orientation—because that was his underlying assumption of what I would do. However, I did tell him that God might be interested in doing a deeper transformational work in his life in the arena of sexuality, not to mention in other arenas. That's what the spiritual journey with Christ is all about. And if you shut off one dimension of your life to God, the truth is, you hinder growth in other dimensions as well. Sexuality is just one issue of many that all of us have to bring before God and invite him to do a deeper work in us. And if we're mentoring someone who resists going deeper in some arena of their life, they are essentially telling us we aren't invited into that arena, and really that God isn't either.

Brian understood where I was coming from, but stood his ground about not wanting to put this issue on the table, which affected the tone of our relationship. This wasn't about trying to exclude or alienate him. I was simply being up front about the relational and spiritual dynamics that are necessary for a healthy mentoring relationship to exist. Brian and I remained friends, of course; we just didn't engage in the "spiritual mentoring"–type relationship that he initially wanted. To this day, we don't really discuss his sexuality much, but perhaps one day down the road this conversation will surface if he allows God's Spirit to work freely in his life.

My main point here is not about how we ought to handle conversations about homosexuality, but rather that we must pay attention to what dimension of people's lives they are inviting us into—and what dimensions of life they're keeping us out of. That doesn't mean we don't push or challenge people at times. But if we want to cultivate healthier, God-honoring relationships that don't short-circuit the spiritual process, it does mean we need to respect the boundaries of others, whether we agree or disagree. These boundaries may be given directly and verbally, or indirectly and nonverbally.

The reality is, some people invite us to come sit next to them to have a sacred conversation . . . and some people don't. We aren't in control of that. When it comes to evangelism, I know we often want to be in the driver's seat, but in actuality, we don't always get that right or privilege. To reach people with greater effectiveness, we must surrender control of the driver's seat, whether we like it or not. God has not asked us to drive, but rather to be available to guide those who are looking to be guided, those who invite us in. As ministry leaders, part of us equipping the saints must involve us teaching this dynamic to others. When we do, we will improve their relational intelligence and ability to effectively build relational trust and credibility as they seek to share the gospel with those who desperately need to hear it.

The spiritual openness and receptivity of the nonbeliever determines the pace, direction and to large degree the substance of the spiritual dimensions to our conversations—for better or worse. Ultimately we must embrace this relational and spiritual reality as we learn to trust in the activity of God in someone's life, and release the results of conversion and transformation to God. This is an act of surrendering control and trusting Christ in our relationships, something we Christians often think we're better at than we really are—myself included. This is the wise path that helps us release the undue pressure that we put on ourselves, and guides us to trust in God's work and movement.

We can trust what the apostle Paul wrote about God's role:

> For it is God who works in you [and others] to will and to act in order to fill his good purpose. (Philippians 2:13)

Paul also articulates our role:

> Be wise in the way you act toward outsiders; make the most of every opportunity. Let your conversation be always full of grace, seasoned with salt, so that you may know how to answer everyone. (Colossians 4:5-6)

We are called to be gentle and grace-giving conversationalists with those outside our faith. But let me make one thing absolutely clear. I'm not advocating relational passivity, nor is Paul. And, this doesn't mean there aren't moments when we push through resistance and challenge people to grow and change. It's just that in many circles, we rarely acknowledge the relational dynamic of inviting versus invading. Many of us continually overlook both nonverbal and verbal cues, often forcing our agenda upon someone and eroding trust and influence in the process. This isn't our calling from the Scriptures. Emerging ministry leaders must teach, train and envision their churches and ministries to engage relationally in ways that don't break down trust, but build it. Relational trust always precedes the creation and progression of missional cultures.

When we undermine the process through relational invasion, it can do great damage to people's perception of Christianity, even of Jesus himself. Since Jesus doesn't force himself on people, neither should we (see Matthew 11:28; John 7:17, 37). His posture is always bent toward serving others, as well as offering people a choice according to their free will. He's a model we can emulate in our relationships as we respect and honor the sacred soul of others.

IDEAS FOR MENTORS

1. **Debate theology.** Create two or more groups of protégés. Decide on a theological topic that is debatable or controversial. Give each group an assignment: read, reflect on and study the theological issue. Then, bring both groups back to debate and dialogue about that topic. As a mentor, you may need to serve as facilitator, and perhaps you even need to provide appropriate coaching, which may have to wait until after the debate. Doing an activity like this can challenge people to really dialogue instead of just telling others what to think and not conversing about it. This will not only stretch their theological understanding; it will hopefully teach them how to better interact with people about sensitive issues that inevitably evoke disagreement. You could refer to the books *Across the Spectrum* by Paul Eddy and Gregory Boyd or *Adventures in Missing the Point* by Brian McLaren and Tony Campolo to identify key theological issues to debate.

2. **How to spark spiritual dialogue.** Here are a few examples of questions you can ask nonbelievers to spark spiritual conversations, or samples of questions you can equip protégés with. Create a group discussion with some young leaders and have them bring three to five questions they've used in spiritual conversations. Have a brainstorming session where you provide each other with ideas for questions that you can use in evangelism.

   • What have your experiences been with what you perceive as the religion of Christianity, or church in general?

   • What are your views about Jesus? How have Christians or churches shaped your views?

   • When you've encountered the dilemma of finding meaning and purpose in life, how have you resolved where to find that in your life?

MENTOR TIP:
PRE-THOUGHT QUESTIONS

Be intentional and thoughtful about what questions you ask protégés. The questions you ask communicate what you value. I suggest preparing a few intentional questions that you plan to ask before sitting down with a protégé. Great questions can help foster significant personal discoveries and guide protégés into the right conversations for their development. Always enter a mentoring session with two or more intentional questions that are designed to facilitate growth.

14 • Gospel Community

IN ACTS 8, THE ETHIOPIAN EUNUCH WAS EQUIVALENT to a modern-day CFO. He was literate and educated, which in that day was a novelty. In addition, he owned an Isaiah scroll, which was rare for anyone and extremely expensive. Scrolls like these were usually kept in public places like synagogues.

Along comes Philip, who asks this accomplished, brilliant, wealthy African if he needs any help. The natural thing would be to say, "No thanks. I don't really need anyone. I can handle it on my own." However, this Ethiopian asks for help through a series of three questions, all of which point to the importance of community as the optimal context for transformation.

The first question: *"How can I (understand) unless someone explains it to me?"* (8:31). At that moment, this is the part of the Hebrew Scriptures the eunuch was reading (from Isaiah):

> He was led like a sheep to the slaughter, and as a lamb before its shearer is silent, so he did not open his mouth. In his humiliation he was deprived of justice. Who can speak of his descendants? For his life was taken from the earth. (Acts 8:32-33)

The second question: "'Tell me please, who is the prophet talking about, himself or someone else?' Then Philip began with that very passage of Scripture and told him the good news about Jesus" (8:34-35).

As they traveled along the road, they came to some water and the eunuch asked the third question: *"What can stand in the way of my being baptized?"* (8:36-37 NIV 2011).

We know that the eunuch heard the gospel and chose to enter the kingdom of God. Maybe he even prayed a private salvation prayer. Have you ever noticed when people pray a private prayer, they still sort of wonder internally if their faith is real, and if their eternal destiny is forever changed because of that moment? They may wonder, "Is that all it takes?"

I've heard this nervous murmuring on numerous occasions as people wonder if it all took root. It's not that they're making a timid, wavering or uncertain decision. It's just that people, especially those without a religious background, look to others to see if we'll validate this for them, maybe even wondering if we'll baptize them to somehow confirm that their faith is real and that their eternal destiny is forever changed.

We aren't certain of all the details here, so we have to speculate a little. This Ethiopian seems to be looking for Philip to affirm his newfound faith. And sure enough, Philip baptizes him. That day, the eunuch joins the community of Jesus followers (8:37-38). This leads us into seeing the fourth key shift in effective evangelism: *understanding the role of a gospel community*.

SHIFT 4: THE COMMUNITY: FROM INDIVIDUAL CONVERSION TO COMMUNAL CONVERSION

I remember the day I had the privilege of baptizing my good friend Sagar. It had taken him a number of weeks to really prepare for it because there were many complex dynamics he had to navigate with his family as he moved from Hinduism to Christianity. That day, he welled up in tears as he shared the names of people who played significant roles in his conversion process. He recounted specific moments and conversations. He thanked several people for their patience, compassion and accessibility.

Then he said, "The greatest gift to me was the presence and availability of a community of people like you. This life transformation for me would have never happened without the love and inclusivity of this church community." We were the names and faces that helped Sagar make sense of the gospel. I'll never forget the spiritual electricity that existed in that backyard environment as dozens surrounded Sagar while I baptized him. There was an indescribable joy, overwhelming gratitude and heartfelt worship. It was a profound picture of life change, the very reason why I entered vocational ministry in the first place.

Baptism is often the culmination moment that reminds us that conversion is not just an individual act, but a communal one. Not only do we celebrate people's personal decision to follow Christ; we also ask others to sign off on a commitment and choose to live as interconnected, interdependent followers of Jesus (see Ephesians 4:11-16). When someone is converted, it is a conversion of more than an individual, but an individual into a community. This ought to change the way many of us see salvation, do church and execute baptism celebrations.

Moving forward, it is always community that shapes the ongoing discipleship process, usually having more effect than most realize. To large degree, people become a product of whatever communal context they're in when converted—for better or worse. Salvation is a communal way of life, not just a one-time individual moment in our rearview mirror.[1] Therefore, community always shapes us and helps us "work out salvation with fear and trembling." Emerging spiritual leaders must bear the weight of this discipleship responsibility as we strive to cultivate biblical values in our ministries and relationships.

WHAT KIND OF DISCIPLES ARE YOU PRODUCING?

I always take time at baptism parties to ask those being baptized to share with the crowd (both followers and non-followers of Jesus) what people have been instrumental in their journey to find and follow Christ. Inevitably, people share names. They often get choked up as tears fall. Onlookers at the baptism celebration get a window into the power of community in a person's life and how deeply they have affected the transformation process, as well as the discipleship process (which always starts before actual conversion).

How someone comes to faith in Jesus teaches them a methodology or thinking process of how it's supposed to happen. If salvation is reduced to a transaction, the danger is that these new followers will think that's all it is. This is why it's so important to draw out the importance of community in people's faith stories and to communicate that as a value.

Fostering relationships where people are invited into a spiritual and relational process is what ultimately leads to life change and spiritual transformation, followed by a new and ongoing kingdom way of life. This is what Jesus invites people into, not simply to pray a prayer. And the discipleship process always works better when people open their lives to others and ask for help in biblical interdependence so the body of Christ can be built up and strengthened. In this life and the next, salvation is intended to move us toward becoming whole, toward restoring the image of God within us. Is that the intended outcome of our discipleship process? Do we evaluate how it's going? What values exist in your ministry and community that are being transferred to people coming to faith? Which values are good? Which aren't?

REDISCOVERING THE ROLE OF COMMUNITY IN DISCIPLESHIP

My good friend and protégé Ben has become a remarkable story of rediscovering the meaning and role of community. Ben grew up in a toxic and highly dysfunctional family situation, and his parents divorced early in his life. After that, everything in his family situation turned to chaos, for years to come. And due to endless painful experiences he went through growing up, he learned to trust no one. Everything he had experienced taught him that people were all liars. They wanted to hurt him or somehow take advantage of him.

As he moved into adulthood, he began to explore Christianity by attending a traditional church. But something seemed to be wrong with the people who called themselves "Christians." Although he was compelled by the compassion and love aspects of Jesus' story, he rarely saw them lived out. He saw exclusivity, hypocrisy and self-righteousness everywhere he looked. Where was the love that Christians are supposed to embody?

He left the church.

The years that followed were incredibly difficult. Ben once shared with me about those years, "When you trust no one, you have no one. It's a very lonely place to be." When that reality sunk in, Ben knew things had to change. He began a process of relearning how to put faith in people again—which was a huge risk for him.

One day Ben asked his roommate Sean where he went to church, and Sean invited him to Mosaic. It was a big step for Ben to start attending. Fortunately he met some incredible people who became immensely significant in his journey toward faith and finding a healthy community of friends.

Monica and Joe were two of the first people at church to take time to talk with Ben. They later became two of the most important individuals in his process of learning to trust in people again, which ultimately led him to reengage a personal faith journey. As Ben began to serve at his newfound church, they also helped him make progress in his spiritual journey. Several months later Ben realized that he not only needed a new community of friends, but he needed to enter into community with Jesus. That's when he became a follower of Jesus Christ.

When Ben recounted his journey, he expressed, "It's just crazy the difference in the way the world looks from eyes filled with hope. I feel so fortunate to have finally realized I've been invited to a life of redemption and relationship. Life is beautiful and bright, no longer dark and gray."

Ben's story continues to unfold today. After becoming a follower of Jesus Christ, he quickly emerged as a leader within our community, primarily in ministry areas that involved social justice and compassion. His heart to serve remains remarkable to this day. His passion for those in need, for those who don't have a voice, for those who are hurting and for those who are desperate for hope is unprecedented. Because of the kind of people who came alongside him, he now chooses to come alongside others in similar fashion.

FROM COMMUNITY TO LEADERSHIP

Along the way, Ben also decided to enter the Protégé Program because he had a voracious hunger and eagerness to learn and grow. I actually recruited him to be a protégé because of who he was, how much he had to offer, and because I sensed a remarkable openness to grow and learn as a leader. I saw firsthand how his journey of transformation never would have happened without the right kind of community. Today, he strives to create communities that treat others the same way he was treated—with love, compassion and inclusivity. This is a far more significant part of people's salvation process than we often realize.

It's hard to think of a protégé that I'm more proud of in terms of the scope of who they have become since engaging deeper dimensions of their development as a leader. Ben continues leaning into life, waiting for all that God has awaiting him.

The church needs to remember that the gospel intends not simply to make conversions, but to make Christlike people. And Christlike people are formed in the context of Christ-centered community. And Christ-centered community is created by Christ-centered leaders. Whether someone needs to relearn how to trust, how to express their darkest doubts and fears, or is simply lonely and without hope, the role of community is critical. The gospel is intended to permeate every aspect, every dimension and every fabric of a person's life, worldview and core belief system. But again, it rarely does that without a community who helps people heal, change and find traction with what the gospel is and can do in their life. That's why community is so critical to the holistic journey of someone's spiritual life.

When we see the deficit of Christlikeness in our churches, it doesn't reveal that the gospel isn't working. It more likely reveals that we're not allowing the gospel to work in and through us in the way the Scriptures point us to do. It tells us that our community may not be doing discipleship as well as we could be, with interdependence among each other and dependence on God. It could be that we're not being as inclusive, or compassionate, or as open to those outside our faith as we think we are. Maybe this detrimentally affects our attempts to help others become like Christ. Maybe we need to rethink our process of inviting people to follow Jesus and what a more community-oriented, inclusive approach looks like.

We ought never to forget about the critical role different people play in our ongoing journey through life. One of the amazing things about Ben is that he not only humbled himself to learn from others before he was a follower of Jesus, but he continues to do this today as a devoted disciple of Christ. He continues to lean on others as significant players in his growth—that's the body of Christ working right. Whether out of pride, fear or some other inner working, many Christians don't live this way—truly open to allowing others to shape and change us. If this is really happening, it will be revealed by conversations that we can point to that are changing or have changed us.

As leaders, we have responsibility to model the traits required for authentic community to work—humility, trust and interdependence. Leaning on each other for growth and transformation ought to be a way of life for us, and ought to extend to all whom we entrust with the privilege of leading, yet another way we build kingdom cultures.

SHIFT 5: THE GOSPEL: FROM TEMPORAL UNDERSTANDING TO ETERNAL AWAKENING

The fifth shift in evangelistic approach circles us back around to the gospel, which is the core foundation on which we stand as a movement and community of Christ followers. The gospel is central to everything we do and everything we are. So once again, let's look at the centrality of the gospel in the narrative of Philip and the Ethiopian eunuch.

In the Mediterranean world, the Greek word for eunuch is the same word that can be translated "prime minister" or "high court official." Why is this important? Royal officials tended not to trust a male to work with any females unless they castrated him. Extreme, I know. But that's how it worked. So in many cases, for a male commoner to reach a high position in the royal courts, he had to weigh the cost of castration.

It's quite possible that the Ethiopian eunuch chose this path. If in fact this is the case, he paid quite a price to climb the ladder of success and get to the top. As a result, he would've become wealthy, accomplished and powerful as he reached the pinnacle of success.

Some of us know all too well that to reach the top sometimes costs us quite a price. In our day, this often happens at the expense of families, marriages, friendships or our own freedom and life satisfaction level. When people get to the top, what they almost inevitably discover is a lingering emptiness they'd thought would disappear. Similarly, when this eunuch reached the pinnacle of success, he thought he wouldn't still feel spiritually empty.

How do we know this? Remember that he's an Ethiopian, which means he would've lived on the outskirts of the known civilized world. He was on his way home after having gone to Jerusalem to worship (Acts 8:27). Can you imagine when he told the people in Ethiopia that he was going to take a long, dangerous journey to Jerusalem? They would've thought, "Are you kidding? There are temples here, why go there?" He may have responded with something like, "I want to learn about the God of the Hebrews, the God I keep hearing about who changes lives, and through whom a dynamic spiritual awakening is occurring." We know this man is in serious spiritual-search mode because of where he traveled and why.

But what must have made all this a frustrating experience was the fact that when he arrived in Jerusalem, he would've discovered that eunuchs weren't allowed in the temple because they were considered "unclean." Imagine the turmoil as he's returning home—how rejected, humiliated and cast off he would've felt.

MUSINGS OF THE UNBELIEVER

In this context, we peer into the story of the eunuch scouring the Isaiah scroll. On the same page that he's reading, we also discover from the extended context what other musings may have led him to this climactic conversion. In that culture, who your descendants were, and whether you had sons and daughters who carried on your name, was of immense significance, especially in an era when there was not yet confidence of an afterlife. So, Isaiah's prophecy (in Isaiah 56) is given fulfillment in the life and ministry of Jesus Christ, who did not have physical descendants but gave everlasting life and name to all those who followed him, even those who are "eunuchs for the sake of the kingdom" (see Matthew 19:12 NIV 2011).[2]

On the same scroll, the eunuch would have also been reading:

Let no foreigners who have bound themselves to the LORD say,
    "The LORD will surely exclude me from his people."
And let no eunuch complain,
    "I am only a dry tree."

For this is what the LORD says:

"To the eunuchs who keep my Sabbaths,
    who choose what pleases me
    and hold fast to my covenant—
to them I will give within my temple and its walls
    a memorial and a name
    better than sons and daughters;
I will give them an everlasting name
    that will endure forever." (Isaiah 56:3-5 TNIV)

This must have been a powerful and personal moment for him. Because this man was a eunuch and no one was going to carry on his name, he must have been wondering, "Who is this that gives an everlasting name?" Something about that idea seemed to compel him deeply.

And, on the nearby pages of the scroll, he would've just read this extended context (about Jesus):

> Surely he took up our pain and bore our suffering, yet we considered him punished by God, stricken by him, and afflicted. But he was pierced for our transgressions, he was crushed for our iniquities; the punishment that brought us peace was on him, and by his wounds we are healed. We all, like sheep, have gone astray, each of us has turned to our own way; and the LORD has laid on him the iniquity of us all. (Isaiah 53:4-6 TNIV)

The eunuch had to be wondering, "Who is this figure who voluntarily chooses to die on our behalf? Who is the one who was cut off so we could have his eternal name? Did this man go through all this for me? Did he die for me?"

These musings ultimately led him to understanding the gospel and experiencing an eternal awakening. We see the culmination of this when the eunuch asks, "who is [Isaiah] writing about, himself or someone else?" (Acts 8:34 TNIV). And then there's Philip who responds to his soul stirring, eternally minded questions. This is the big moment. And Philip was available to the eunuch—and to God.

PEOPLE ON THE FRINGES

The church was and is always intended to be focused on people on the fringes. I'm convinced that many churches could be filled with (and some are) people on the fringes, people who are furthest from God but are waiting for someone, even a community, to help them enter the kingdom. They're looking for a community that will embrace them where they are and respond to questions they have in a humble, gentle, honest and loving way. I believe there are people being compelled by God's Spirit to read the Scriptures in honest fashion in a community of people postured to guide them. However, the church has just not been the place where many outsiders think to go for guidance in their spiritual exploration. But don't we want it to be?

Changing this reality begins with leadership. The next generation of leaders can be agents of this change. What if churches that we help build in the future had this as a core part of their ethos? What if those outside the church started to think of churches in their city as places that actually embrace wherever they are in their journey, and felt served and loved by Christ followers in the process?

We need to improve the spaces in which we lead. As leaders we need to build an ethos in our churches where people's questions can be asked and where the gospel can be understood in a way that makes sense to them. Are we fostering environments where nonbelieving people can come read Scripture, ask hard questions and interact in a non-threatening way? This is one great way to expose others to the living gospel.

LIFE'S TOUGHEST QUESTIONS

One way to cultivate this in your church's ethos is by offering groups for those who are asking tough questions and searching for God. I've personally led various groups like this that I've used different names for, including Curious Groups and Quest Groups (for people who are *curious* or on a spiritual *quest*). This isn't a new idea, but one that can be effective for serving people on a search for faith and God, as well as for mentoring others in developing a missional life. In essence, I pull a handful of non-believing people together to discuss their biggest, hardest spiritual questions. The discussion can involve as much structure as you see fit. Many churches have done similar things, using models like Spark Groups (www.sparkgood.com), N. T. Wright's *Simply Christian* resources[3] or GIGs (Groups Investigating God, http://intervarsity.org/biblestudies/gigs-index). Whatever route or structure you choose, I simply suggest that every local church seek to create spaces through your community where people have the opportunity to ask and resolve their toughest questions in respectful and dignified ways—where they can flesh out what they don't fully understand.

We are imperfect leaders, so we are an imperfect church. I believe people will continue to show us grace if they know that we are at least giving our best, and attempting to get better at helping people where they are. Let's continue to build on the things we're doing well, like offering a place that provides the truth and a community that cares for all who enter its care. Continue to think of ways to expand the doors of your church so the people who are trying to get in are assured a place. This is one of the great tasks of next generation church leaders.

The wonderful news about engaging this journey with nonbelievers is that we are not in this alone. God doesn't expect us to go on his behalf in the sense that we make him more palatable or acceptable to people. He inhabits all glory and beauty and authority within himself. He certainly doesn't require our very limited selves to represent his very infinite being. We can trust that God is not only capable but incomprehensibly involved in revealing himself to humanity in a way that is individualized for each human being he has made.

The point of writing on and challenging leaders about mission is mostly to remind us what we already believe. That we somehow, in a very mystical and spiritual way, contribute to other's search and discovery of the one true God. When we join him, he gives us the gift of sharing in his joy and pain as he beckons humanity to himself. We get to play a role in the greatest reality a person will ever experience . . . salvation and transformation. When we do not, we in a way unplug ourselves from the lifeblood of God's heart for the world. In doing so, we bring on an unspeakable pain by separation from an essential dimension of the one we are created to dwell in, as well as be a temple that he dwells within.

Ultimately, all of us must remember that sharing the gospel is about helping people connect their temporal story with the eternal story. If they desire intimacy, the gospel offers intimacy of the deepest kind. If they're searching for purpose or freedom or hope, that's what the gospel provides. If seeking meaning and significance in life, the gospel offers eternal perspective and fulfills at the deepest level. If people want emotional, relational and spiritual health, the path to healing is found in the gospel through Jesus Christ. If they need strength to overcome addiction, the gospel is their only hope. On and on it goes.

Just as Philip shared the *euangelion* (the "good news") with the Ethiopian eunuch, may we hear the longings in people's hearts and help them connect the dots of those longings to their only hope—Jesus Christ. That entails walking the journey of life with others. That involves building trust, extending compassion, remaining patient and choosing humility. No one wants to be cornered or coerced. No one wants force applied to him or her unwillingly. No one wants to be a target of someone's agenda who doesn't genuinely care about them or know their world. No one wants to be a project. And the good news for us is, none of that is what Jesus requires us to be.

THE FIFTH GOSPEL

The gospel doesn't just get explained in a moment, but through a life. Perhaps the most powerful way for any of us to share the gospel in our world is by remembering that the story of our lives can be the *fifth gospel* that testifies to the transforming power and grace of Jesus Christ. Or as the apostle Paul told first-century Christ followers, "You yourselves are our letter . . . known and read by everybody" (2 Corinthians 3:2). What story does your life tell when someone reads it?

The emerging generation desires not only to learn about faith, they desire to live the faith they are learning. And in order to live the faith they are learning, they need to see that faith lived out before they are compelled to do the same. 1 Peter 2:12 says it like this: "Live such good lives among the pagans that, though they accuse you of doing wrong, they may see your good deeds and glorify God on the day he visits us." If our faith communities and churches live a missional way of life and cultivate missional cultures in our ministries, not only will we experience some of the deepest joy, gratitude and fulfillment of ministry, we'll become spiritual guides for a world who's desperately searching for a faith that's vibrant and alive. The journey awaits us . . .

IDEAS FOR MENTORS

1. **Story in one image.** One activity I do with protégés involves asking them to find or take a picture of something that communicates God's heart for outsiders, or something that communicates what the gospel is really about or how they understand the role of community in experiencing life transformation. I usually have them bring this to a team meeting or retreat to share. It can be a powerful experience

to be challenged to tell a story through one image. One time, before we did this activity, I even brought a group of protégés whom I was mentoring to a sports photography museum intending to show them how powerful one image can be and how much it can communicate. The main goal here is to deepen our heart of compassion and clarify our missional focus. We just do it in a creative way.

2. **Throw a baptism party.** Find one or more people who have recently become followers of Jesus and organize a baptism party (at a pool, in the ocean, in a river or a lake). Expand your invitation list to nonbelieving friends and family. And you needn't limit the invites to those in close or direct relationship to the person being baptized. Make it a party and a celebration. Also, make sure you talk to each person being baptized and walk through their faith story with them as you guide them in deciding what may be important to share (why they chose to devote their life to Jesus, who was significant in influencing them, how they see God working in their life, etc.). This whole experience is about much more than the baptized. This is a communal celebration and witness of the transforming power of the gospel.

MENTOR TIP:
GENUINE INTEREST CHANGES EVERYTHING

Never make mentoring only about production, tasks and performance. It must be relational, and people must know you care about them as a person. Check in with protégés about personal matters, like asking them how their family life is going or how other things in life that aren't related to their ministry are going. The dynamics of the mentoring relationship will change dramatically.

PART 5

Entrepreneurial Leadership

THE POWER OF POSSIBILITY

From the days of John the Baptist until now, the kingdom of heaven has been forcefully advancing, and forceful men and women lay hold of it.

MATTHEW 11:12 TNIV

The difference between school and life?
In school, you're taught a lesson and then given a test.
In life, you're given a test that teaches you a lesson.

TODD BODETT

Jesus was a real revolutionary, but there doesn't seem to be a whole lot of revolution going on at the moment. There tends to be a whole lot of talk about mission . . . and not a whole lot of direct missional action. . . . This must change.

MICHAEL FROST AND ALAN HIRSCH,
THE SHAPING OF THINGS TO COME

I OFTEN HEAR YOUNG, AMBITIOUS Christ-following leaders speak these words: "I want to change the world." I celebrate their desire to make a difference in the world. In many cases, I even strive to help them discover how they will pursue this endeavor. I know that in its purest form, their drive to change the world isn't about fame, or notoriety, or wealth accumulation. At its core, changing the world for these Christ-following leaders is about helping others live in and live out God's kingdom on earth . . . and then forever. It's about moving the reality of the gospel into people's lives in a way that pervades everything about them—their beliefs, their worldviews, their lifestyle. But then again, we all know that changing the world is no easy task.

The idea of changing the world touches on the dilemma of being *in* the world but not *of* the world (John 15:19; 17:13-16). It also reminds me of the challenge and application in what it means to be *"all things to all people"* (1 Corinthians 9:22). How should we be worldly enough to reach the world we live in without being double-minded or diluted in our faith and purity? How should we be all things to all people while being exactly who we're supposed to be by God's design? It all comes down to this dual calling to remain separate in our commitment to follow Christ, yet united in the way of our commitment to reach people where they are.

One approach I've found that embodies this peculiar yet necessary relationship between separateness and togetherness centers on what I call kingdom entrepreneurship. It is a way of ministry life that keeps spiritual leaders anchored in the person of Jesus, and enables us to branch out to the people he is wooing to himself who are knee-deep in the world and all its darkness.

Many churches haven't yet embraced the critical need for kingdom entrepreneurship. By kingdom entrepreneurship, I don't mean starting new companies, although perhaps that's a part of it. I'm talking about becoming leaders who are discontent with existing ministries that are ineffective and unfruitful. I'm talking about being kingdom-minded leaders who strive to pioneer new kinds of ministry environments because we desperately want to reach new kinds of people.

NEW EXPRESSIONS OF CHURCH

One of the great modern tragedies in the Western world is the regression of the church's influence in culture. One reason for this regression that I've observed involves church leaders allowing themselves to remain passive, ineffective or even outdated in their approach to reaching people far from God. Another reason relates to the ethos of the environments we create, whether intentional or not. This includes how we do small groups, how we execute Sunday services and how we host an array of other events or experiences. We convince ourselves that these environments are compelling for nonbelieving, spiritual people to engage in authentically. However, they often fall quite short. We falsely assume that those who aren't willing to come to our churches, or church functions, are uninterested in God, and we essentially conclude that it's their problem not ours. In an effort to compel outsiders, next-generation leaders need new kinds of church expressions as well as new community-orientated textures for our ministry environments.

When I read the book of Acts, I see the spirit of kingdom entrepreneurship as a pervasive part of the movement of Christ. In our day, I'm convinced that we must embody this same spirit if we want to creatively compel others into the movement of Christ. To accomplish this, we must begin by cultivating a spirit of entrepreneurial leadership in our ministries and in our own lives. We need to create the space for women and men who are willing to step out in courage to do what no one else is doing to reach people no one else is reaching. I'm convinced that making this form of leadership an integral part of our ministry ethos will be the primary vehicle through which we establish new and unique ministry environments that reach the generation lurking outside the walls of the church.

15 • Kingdom Entrepreneurs

LYDIA WAS A PROGRESSIVE ENTREPRENEUR and successful business-woman in a culture that didn't value women (see Acts 16:11-15). She was originally from a city called Thyatira but moved to Philippi, probably because it was the most prominent city in the district of Macedonia (modern-day Greece). There were not many places where one could buy, sell and trade quite like in Philippi. Lydia was much like a fashion CEO in our day. She had an eye for design and a knack for making money. She produced purple cloth, which may not sound that exciting to us, but purple was probably the most expensive dye of the day—it was the color of royalty.

History tells us that Lydia was also the first person to become a Christ follower in Europe. And since she had become a successful leader, a wealthy woman and now a person of faith, she had great potential to reach her unique circles of influence, especially in the city of Philippi. And since her primary home in Philippi was quite large, it soon became part of her ministry. This later became the meeting place of the first church ever planted in Europe. In short, the ministry Lydia began led to an eventual church plant that significantly impacted her circle of influence in Philippi and beyond.

One thing that excites me at the moment is the church planting movement—especially since an increasing number of emerging twenty-something church planters desire to plant unique kinds of churches. In addition, the multi-site movement is a unique movement in the direction of pioneering new church expressions that's driven by a strong degree of entrepreneurial leadership. While these efforts must continue to innovate and expand, we ought not to reduce entrepreneurial leadership in the church to starting new churches or new church sites. That is part of it, but it cannot be all of it.

I'm convinced that entrepreneurial leadership must become part of the skill set of emerging spiritual leaders to effectively build the next and future church. And even more specifically, I believe every Christ-following leader must become a *kingdom entrepreneur* in a way that aligns uniquely with who they are if they desire to reach their full potential of spiritual influence and optimize their kingdom impact. If we want to build kingdom cultures, we must become kingdom entrepreneurs.

WHAT IS A KINGDOM ENTREPRENEUR?

1. *Kingdom entrepreneurs embody the spirit, and have developed the skill set, of a true entrepreneur.* At the core, entrepreneurs are self-motivated and take initiative to start new things. They create what is not yet created, and do what has not yet been done to serve a need that is not yet being served (or serve a need in a more effective way). We normally think of entrepreneurs as being motivated by monetary value, but entrepreneurship in the kingdom context is about eternal value. It begins with courageous decision-making and a willingness to risk, even fail, as part of the process of growth and increased effectiveness. As a mentor, I see a significant part of my role as challenging protégés to take initiative, be risk takers and be willing to fail. That's where kingdom entrepreneurship begins, a journey I believe every protégé should engage.

2. *Kingdom entrepreneurs harness their efforts to help others live in and experience the kingdom of God now and forever in fresh ways.* They long to bring an eternal kingdom life to those whose souls are aimlessly wandering, even suffocating and dying. They understand that the normal way of doing things doesn't always get it done. They know the importance of being "the aroma of Christ among those who are being saved and those who are perishing" (2 Corinthians 2:15). They strive to introduce people to the revolutionary way of the kingdom of God and help them live in that reality in their ordinary life. As a mentor, I remind and envision protégés of what the kingdom of God really is about, both here and now as well as for eternity. The vivid language and vision of Jesus centered around the kingdom of God—and ours ought to as well.

3. *Kingdom entrepreneurs create new ministry mediums to help non-believers experience Christ in a way they wouldn't necessarily experience it in a normal church context.* The world needs kingdom entrepreneurs to take on this task and help make it a normal part of our churches' culture if we want to have broader and deeper impact on those far from God. The emerging world needs spiritual leaders to create environments where religious obstacles get stripped away, so that people searching for God can see him, find him and know him. We must break outside our existing paradigms to reach people who stand outside our walls.

A CULTURE OF CONTROL

In far too many churches, I've observed young ministry leaders who aren't empowered to lead in the ways they were gifted to lead. Leaders are wired to pioneer new things, or at least to change what isn't working. Leaders, by nature, are driven to move things from status quo to increased effectiveness and success. Leaders are built to create new things that cultivate and harness momentum. They are created to cast vision and turn that vision into action. They're created to build teams that focus on a cause and then strategize to pursue the change they desire in the world, or in their church and ministry area.

There are seasoned leaders who have yet to learn how to truly delegate not just responsibility but also authority. In other words, they hesitate to give young leaders "too much authority" or "too much power" or "too much control"—mostly because of fear and a need for control. But for the next generation of spiritual leaders to rise up, churches must become the very place that cultivates trust and allows young entrepreneurial leaders to envision, plan and execute without constantly having to prove themselves, and without having to be micromanaged.

That being said, I know there are pragmatic challenges that accompany this line of thinking. It's wise to have a clear process or system for how senior leaders delegate authority. It's wise for young entrepreneurs to know what the "rules" are and to work within them (in most cases). I live in the Silicon Valley and have become a big fan of how Google allows their employees to spend 20 percent of their day as free time to work on what they're passionate about. So much of Google's innovation has emerged from that habit. Perhaps if church staffs offered similar freedoms, they might reap parallel innovations?

In addition, I think structured accountability as well as performance reviews ought to be a part of this entrepreneurial process. And although there are organizational risks that come with releasing and empowering entrepreneurial leadership, I believe it's essential for the expansion and growth of the local church in our day. And I think it's critical for a leader's own development.

In the hearts of younger leaders lie dreams of what others feel is impossible to do in and through the church. Some older leaders may accuse young leaders of being idealists. Or they may look at their ideas and consider them far-fetched, naive or motivated by cynicism. But so many of these young leaders actually believe in inventing and reinventing ministries that have the potential to change the world. They believe that new and fresh ideas must surface if we're going to reach the culture around us. They see innovation, creativity and risk as essential characteristics of leadership in our new world. But unfortunately, when these younger leaders bring their new ideas to the table, they often get shot down, casually listened to, blown off or, at best, welcomed but never acted on. Perhaps we think what many young leaders are trying to do is impossible when in actuality, it's quite possible, even necessary.

Leadership guru Warren Bennis studied leaders who turned around impossible situations. Patterns of common traits emerged. Almost always, these leaders were thirty-five years or younger. Their energy and passion was high, and they exuded a near delusional confidence. They didn't project their success, because they usually didn't have much to project. They didn't know what was supposed to be impossible. In certain ways, their view of what could be accomplished was unrealistic to the onlooker. But in Bennis's research, all of these factors are what drove these young leaders' success.[1] Is it possible that future *success* in the church could be contingent on whether seasoned leaders create space for young, entrepreneurial leaders to emerge with innovative, culture-shaping ideas? Is there breathing room in your ministry and on your teams for collaboration and idea generation to happen? If not, what could you do to cultivate an environment of risk-taking innovation and kingdom entrepreneurship?

STUNTED GROWTH

Because a lot of young leaders are insulated from real-time leadership risks, their growth and development gets stunted. More seasoned church leaders and more established churches often aren't even thinking about how to create contexts for young leaders to start new things, or to spread their entrepreneurial wings. Often this is because they fear the failure that may come. Their goal, spoken or unspoken, is simply to plug people into what already exists, and try to make what they're already doing work. There's no doubt that this can be an important task, even at times the right move for the organization. But unfortunately the fear of failure and the fear of not having control have stifled many seasoned leaders' ability to delegate authority and offer the right amount of freedom and flexibility to these young idea-making kingdom entrepreneurs.

I once heard a senior pastor of a megachurch tell another seasoned leader that entrepreneurial leaders disrupt where his church is headed. He explained how he'd rather they "fit into the system" than "buck the system" that has worked for years: "If they don't want to do that, they should go find another church." Although I was surprised to hear that come out of his mouth, that's a reality in many churches—whether spoken directly or indirectly. There's usually a structure or hierarchy that stifles the spirit of entrepreneurial leadership that is stirring inside the hearts of young, ambitious, kingdom-minded leaders.

What we often forget, or overlook, is that when emerging leaders are given responsibility to cast a vision, build teams, think creatively, practice innovation and motivate others to make their new ministry a success, their development process accelerates tenfold. They are forced to wrestle with and develop a skill set they may or may not have. They are positioned to see their strengths more clearly and understand their weaknesses more profoundly. As protégés, I'm not telling you to demand all the freedom or flexibility you think you deserve. And I'm certainly not declaring that you're entitled to this. However, I am challenging you to seek a work environment that frees you to exercise your entrepreneurial muscles. And when you do spread your wings and fly, remember to never let the fear of failure stop you.

WHAT IF WE FAIL?

Not that we hope anyone's ministry fails, much less our own, but inevitably some will fail. And frankly, those moments of discouragement or crisis often foster the prime context for transformational learning. That's often where protégés discover their greatest lifelong leadership lessons. In fact, I often hear protégés retell stories of failure two or three years later, commenting on how formative these failures were in the learning process. Embracing our own failure is one of the primary pathways toward accelerating our maturity. Every protégé needs to learn this lesson. *It is possible to embrace failure in a way that motivates us rather than demoralizes us.*

In an April 2011 *Harvard Business Review* article titled "Failing by Design," Rita Gunther McGrath describes the critical nature of failure within organizations: "Failures are more common than successes. And yet, strangely, we don't design organizations to manage, mitigate and learn from failures. When I ask executives how effective their organizations are at learning from failure, on a scale of one to ten, I often get a sheepish, 'Two—or maybe three' in response. As this suggests, most organizations make no systematic effort to study failure. Executives hide mistakes or pretend they were always part of the master plan. Failures become un-discussable, and people grow so afraid of hurting their career prospects that they eventually stop taking risks."

I'm not arguing that failure is a good thing in and of itself. However, when we understand failure as inevitable in uncertain environments, we can see its greater value. If managed well, failure can be a very *useful* thing. Indeed, organizations can't possibly undertake the risks necessary for innovation and growth if they're not comfortable with the idea of failing.

No matter what results an aspiring kingdom entrepreneur produces, I try to always celebrate their diligent, intentional and courageous efforts. I make sure I affirm risk-taking and initiative. And although the conversations about how and why they failed can at times be grueling, these experiences are worth it for all the growth potential that emerges. Future church leaders must learn to create cultures where failure is celebrated and affirmed because the right kind of risks are being taken for the right reasons—most importantly, to reach people far from God.

Author and psychologist Dr. Henry Cloud writes about the importance of failure when it comes to growth:

> People who grow jump in over their head. They try things that they cannot do, then stretch to become able to do what they are attempting. They take on challenges that ask them to become more than they have been or done before. Then the pressures of those demands call for them to become more in order to meet them. The bar is raised, and they have to jump higher. Here is the rule: *You will not grow without attempting things you are unable to do.*
>
> To learn how to skydive, you have to jump out of a plane. To learn how to sell, you have to make some calls. To learn how to develop a better marriage, you have to try to do some things you have never done, such as open up, become vulnerable, and even confront.
>
> We do not grow without some sort of necessary reach. That is why the ones who produce increase nearly always have clear goals and expectations that are written down. Then, they put themselves out there to reach them. Some of those are in areas where they are already capable, such as doing more of the same. But some of those are reaching at things never before attempted.[2]

If we want to maximize leadership development in the church, we must create room for failure and remind people of the cost of not embracing failure as part of the growth process. Even when we fail, we must keep moving forward together with a courageous, risk-taking spirit that doesn't allow the fear of failure to stifle our progress and development. For protégés, we must keep spreading our wings as we attempt to fly. For seasoned leaders, we must seek ways to help free our young kingdom entrepreneurs and ensure they have the flexibility to spread their wings and exercise some of their greatest gifts to the body of Christ and to the world.

Michael was a protégé who decided to be a kingdom entrepreneur. His heart for getting clean water to desperate places was growing, and as a result, he decided to fund and then build a well in Ghana. He did all the research necessary, and then organized a program that would invite twenty-five people to give ten dollars a week for three months (totaling $3,000). He set things up online and off he went. It was a risk and he had to take initiative and apply courage to talk to people about this endeavor. Eventually Michael joined the staff at a nonprofit called Generosity Water. In the first three years of their existence, Generosity Water funded 242 water wells and 8 cisterns in 17 countries, serving over 100,000 people with clean, safe drinking water (www.generositywater.org).

Justin, Smitty and Joe were also kingdom entrepreneurs. They started a grassroots mentoring program at a public junior high school in Los Angeles. The program wasn't "Christian based," but it became a portal of Christ-centered influence on the students and even their families and a few teachers. This effort took courage and a willingness to fail. It also took initiative, passion and character. Great impact followed. David and Bill started a monthly event for twentysomething artists downtown. He leveraged artistic talent of people he knew and created an event where local artists, filmmakers, musicians, poets and more could display their work. The spiritual texture he created was central, but it happened primarily through relationship. We often had more people participate from outside our church than from within. A plethora of new relationships were established with nonbelieving people in the city.

Courage, risk-taking, initiative and a willingness to fail are the lifeblood of kingdom entrepreneurs. As a mentor, this is why I keep pushing protégés to take bigger risks and why I keep challenging them to attempt great things for the sake of the kingdom. I remind them that if they fail, to remember the depth of learning and formation that will emerge. The fear of failure will lose its power. In many ways, failure has the potential to create the fastest path to maturity—*if we learn from it*. Most people don't regret taking too many risks. Many people do regret not having had the courage to risk more simply because they feared failure.

IDEAS FOR MENTORS

1. **Cultivate a risk-taking culture.** Engage in dialogue that challenges protégés to take risks in ministry, in their relational

world, in how they lead others, etc. And when someone takes a risk and "fails," come alongside them and celebrate their courage and initiative and willingness to risk. I often celebrate these kinds of things with public affirmation because it helps communicate that your church or ministry area is a place that welcomes risk and innovative ideas.

2. **Start a risk group.** One of my friends, Jason, decided one day to start a "risk group." Basically, he pulled a group of eight people together (a mix of Christ followers and non–Christ followers), and challenged them to commit to this group for five weeks. During week one, everyone went around and shared one risk they were going to take in the next week. Some were relational risks, others were spiritual risks, and others were the next step in achieving a personal dream. The following week, everyone came back to share how it went. People's risk-taking spirit and behavior was celebrated and affirmed. They did this for five weeks, and then the group didn't want to stop. Over time, Jason changed the name and now calls them "spark groups." Challenge a protégé to start a group like this, and perhaps you could even start a group with them. To get more information on "spark groups," visit www .sparkgood.com.

MENTOR TIP:
CELEBRATE RISK AND INITIATIVE

When a protégé takes a risk, steps out in courage or initiates, make sure you affirm their proactivity. Part of leadership development involves taking personal responsibility for our own growth and pushing ourselves to step out of our comfort zone and face our fears. Protégés need mentors to cheer them on in this pursuit. Celebrate the right kind of risks even if the desired outcome doesn't happen.

16 • The Pre-church Experience

ONE OF THE MOST PRACTICAL WAYS to guide others toward becoming kingdom entrepreneurs is by creating "pre-church experiences." At Mosaic, my friend Jason used to call these environments "pre-Mosaics" (because our church was called Mosaic). Starting a pre-church experience involves starting a group, ministry or ongoing event (weekly, bimonthly, monthly, even annually or semiannually) that's designed for people who aren't yet ready to walk through the doors of a local church on a Sunday, but who desire to engage conversations about God, faith and spirituality.

As part of the Protégé Program, and with other young leaders whom I interface with, I challenge these protégés to start a pre-church experience with a team of people that focuses primarily on reaching non–Christ followers in a unique and new way. I'm essentially asking them to be kingdom entrepreneurs, which is also part of our strategic leadership focus as a church. This is part of what we do to create a culture of kingdom entrepreneurship and to establish an ethos that communicates that we're a place for young leaders to emerge. We want them to step up to this challenge not only to reach people for Christ, but to develop their own leadership skills. And although some people are more natural entrepreneurs than others, I've come to believe that exercising this set of muscles is important for every leader because it pushes them in creativity, strategic thinking, planning, recruiting, team-building, vision-casting, reaching nonbelievers through innovation and much more. These are all critical components of leadership development.

I don't know if you consider yourself an entrepreneur already or whether you've ever started something from nothing, but in this chapter, I want to share three examples of emerging leaders who started pre-church experiences and embraced kingdom entrepreneurialism. These were beginners more than experts—all protégés in their own right. And none of them saw themselves as entrepreneurs before starting their pre-church experience. I want to pass on the lessons I've learned in hopes of helping spark new ideas for you, or to at least give you a more concrete starting point in your own unique development process of becoming a kingdom entrepreneur. These are ideas and/or processes that provide guidance on how to launch *pre-church experiences* and on how you can spark a culture of entrepreneurialism in and through your church.

NATHAN'S STORY: FINDING THE MISSIONAL LIGHTNING ROD

> Wherever you go, whether it is into a town or a village, find out someone who is respected, and stay with him until you leave. As you enter his house give it your blessing. If the house deserves it, the peace of your blessing will come to it. But if it doesn't, your peace will return to you. (Matthew 10:11-13 Phillips)

Nathan Neighbour was a protégé who bought into this idea of becoming a kingdom entrepreneur. He started a brand-new, innovative ministry that has effectively reached non-Christians who were totally disinterested in church. It was birthed because his desire to connect to nonbelieving artists in Los Angeles grew stronger week after week. As a result of our dialogues about being proactive and taking risks to start a pre-church experience, he decided to begin a process despite not knowing exactly where it would take him. At first, he took initiative to start bringing friends to any art function that he could find—it was the only thing he knew to do to spend time with more artists.

As he visited a few intriguing spoken word venues, one of the spoken word poets, Judah, always stood out. He seemed open to faith as Nathan noticed spiritual undertones in his poetry. Nathan wondered what his story was, and if he might be the person of peace (Luke 10:6) who could be the "in" to the poetry community in Los Angeles to help reach these artists with the gospel.

The next thing Nathan thought of doing was to send Judah a Facebook message telling him about Mosaic and what we did with the arts. He didn't think it would go anywhere. However, not only did

Judah respond, he showed up the next Sunday at our church. But he hated it. He felt extremely out of place.

But on that Sunday, as an application from the message, we challenged people to give away their shoes as a gift to homeless people. Nathan worried what in the world Judah might be thinking. He thought, "Oh great! Not only does he look miserable, but now this pastor is asking him to donate his shoes!" To our surprise, Judah was the first person to stand up, go to the stage and place his shoes on the altar. Later, he described how deeply impactful that experience was to him—that we would boldly challenge people to give that sacrificially.

Just so happens, we were also advertising these Quest Groups, where people met at Starbucks and could ask any question they wanted of our campus pastor. Judah showed up that first night. Substantive conversation lasted two hours, and more conversations would follow.

I soon discovered that Judah had always wanted to open a spoken word venue connected to a spiritual community. He had been shot down consistently by a few churches that were initially interested, but only wanted certain people in their doors (or more importantly, didn't want certain people in them). He was skeptical when we told him that we'd been thinking about starting our own spoken word venue and that we were looking for a guy like him to help us—a "person of peace."

That night, a few people went down to the Crash Lounge (a building that we just *happened* to have finished remodeling as a lounge a few days before). We prayed over the place together, and really asked God to use us a hub for the arts community in that area of Los Angeles. Three weeks later, we opened our doors and eighty people experienced opening night of spoken word at Mosaic! We've even have had nationally known HBO poets visit regularly. And, both our youth and adult slam teams were recognized as being among the top twenty in the world, beating out San Diego, San Francisco, Sacramento and other groups in LA. This whole experience emerged from one protégé's heart and decision to be a kingdom entrepreneur, to take initiative and to risk in an effort to reach people who weren't being reached.

Along the way, numerous people from the spoken word venue have asked about and attended Mosaic on a Sunday. Some have even become devoted followers of Christ! Although we don't preach the gospel explicitly at this venue, we are extremely intentional and strategic about how we build relationships and connect with these artists. In the right moments, we invite others to our church, we share the message of Christ with them through our personal story, and we do whatever we sense God's Spirit leading us to do, without putting unnecessary obligations or pressure on them. We trust God's Spirit to work in them and through us. God has done way beyond what we could have even imagined. And God isn't done yet.

ILA'S STORY: REINVENTING EVANGELISM FOR NON-EVANGELISTS

> The Kingdom of Heaven is like the yeast a woman used in making bread. Even though she put only a little yeast in three measures of flour, it permeated every part of the dough. (Matthew 13:33 NLT)

I worked with one college student named Ila at our church who told me one day that she was not an evangelist, and that she never would be. I wanted to understand what she really meant and what informed her thinking on this matter, so I asked lots of curious questions. Come to find out, she was, by her own admission, very timid when it came to discussing spiritual matters with people who didn't believe in God, Jesus or the Bible. Plus she was uncomfortable "pushing anything on anyone, especially religion." She also told me, "I'm just not a confrontational person," and "I don't think it's my calling to convert people." These were all obstacles for her being a steward of her circle of influence—the very one God had given her.

Because Ila was very new on her spiritual journey, I wanted to approach this situation thoughtfully, perhaps helping her to rethink what it meant to share Christ with others. I wanted to set her up for success and show her that personal evangelism could take on a positive form in her life. Deep down, I wanted to help her discover a style that would fit who she was naturally.

I started asking her what she liked to do for fun, what her hobbies and interests were. I think we can often find natural points of relational connection in environments we already enjoy being in that can lead to deeper friendships and conversations, that at some point can lead to others finding faith in Christ in a very natural way.

I discovered that one of Ila's talents was cooking for people. More specifically, she loved making fondue—and she loved hosting. Then I thought, let's throw fondue parties for people, with Ila as the host. If we do it for free, people will come. Ila liked the idea, so that's what we did. And it was even biblical—an application of Romans 12:13.

I helped Ila pull a small team together to help make this happen. We shared our vision to do fondue parties once per month. We discussed how we would be intentional in conversations at the parties. Our strategy wasn't to share the gospel outright, unless it felt natural or if God ushered in the right moment. This was a relational event, which we think of again as a "pre-church experience." Part of our missional strategy was to create environments that were nonthreatening and good on-ramps for people who weren't quite ready to attend church but desired community and belonging. We often say, "once people feel they belong, their belief will soon follow."

Ila had a good-sized studio apartment, maybe eight hundred square feet. At the third party, we had over eighty people in her apartment, which made it a pretty packed house. This became the norm for us as more and more people heard about it. Many from the parties came to our church over time, as a result of the relationships that were built at and through the parties, and because of the intentional invitations we made. When people meet Christians who seem "normal" and likeable, it often helps them get past their pre-existing stereotypes of "church people." This is an important part of personal evangelism—being an enjoyable person to be around, being likeable, being "normal."

Ila's experience was a defining season of her life as a follower of Jesus. I remember her thanking me for believing in her and for helping her discover what she referred to as "a way to do evangelism that just feels like me." This was a beautiful reminder for me of how hospitality, hobbies and natural friendships can reach people for Christ. It also reminds me that young leaders don't need a large and established platform to be remarkably effective at evangelism. And, if we want to help people live missional lives, we have to help them overcome their resistances to "doing evangelism." We have to help them see and discover the unique and natural ways that they can reach their circles of influence. We need to be creative in helping those folks who consider themselves non-evangelists become effective evangelists. I know that Ila didn't consider herself a *kingdom entrepreneur,* but she is. She started a new kind of ministry that began reaching new people in a new way. She took a risk. She practiced innovation. She served a need.

JASON'S STORY: REFRAMING A MINISTRY PARADIGM

> To the weak I became weak, to win the weak. I have become all things to all people so that by all possible means I might save some. I do all this for the sake of the gospel, that I may share in its blessings. (1 Corinthians 9:22-23 TNIV)

They say that when all you have is a hammer everything looks like a nail. Well, when all you have is the traditional ministry model, everything looks like prayer and singing worship songs with a guitar. Not that there's anything wrong with that, but as a protégé and new college pastor, Jason understood the difficulty in inviting college students to their campus ministry who would rather be caught with their pants down than go to an outright Christian event with Christian students singing unfamiliar Christian songs, talking to the Christian God who is invisible to them and hard to believe is real, and then listening to a monologue about an ancient text about Christianity that they're quite skeptical about. Ideally, it'd be great to get them there. Practically, it wasn't going to happen. If Jason wanted to reach these people, he knew he had to rethink the traditional approach to campus ministry.

The group of college students that Jason began to work with was doing a traditional prayer and worship time in a chapel on campus at a private university in Los Angeles, Loyola Marymount. They had gotten a pretty good crowd of around twenty students or so coming. It was a truly meaningful time. But it wasn't having the desired effect on the student population that they were really longing for.

So, under Jason's leadership, they decided as a team to explore together in the Scriptures what characteristics were involved in becoming devoted followers of Christ. One of their main discoveries about what spiritual maturity was related to the ability we each develop *to partner with God to serve humanity on God's behalf.* Long story short, this led them to the conclusion that they should change the way they do their ministry. They believed there was certainly a time and place to spend extended periods of time in prayer and singing songs to God in worship. However, they knew that if they were to reach their campus, they'd have to do some things differently.

As a result, they changed locations to a small centralized concert venue on campus. They created a platform for guest speakers to facilitate discussion on what it means to live an inspiring life. They had original music created by people from all walks of life and faith, which helped draw in nonbelieving bands and their friends. They created opportunities for the group to serve other people together, like making peanut butter sandwiches for homeless people who were looking for a meal, or doing others acts of kindness and generosity on campus to creatively initiate relationships.

At first, attendance dropped in half at this newly designed prechurch experience. But then this ministry (called Late Night because it started at 10 p.m.) started to connect with people who would have never come to their more traditionally designed nights. Sorority girls, Goth kids, artists and even some atheists started attending, performing, connecting and exploring. Because the strategy wasn't to "do evangelism" from the stage (which was banned by the school anyway), they had to rely on the quality of their relationships to invest in people.

Five years later, Late Night is going strong—with no operating budget and led almost entirely by students. Many nights more than one hundred people attend. It has endured a couple leadership successions over the years and continues to win awards on campus for both its leadership and the content of programming. It is widely viewed on campus as a gift to the students. And, most importantly, many students' lives have been transformed because of the changes this team of people made to humbly and courageously follow God as he led them to completely alter their mindset. These were kingdom entrepreneurs who started and led a pre-church experience. They were inventive, creative and passionate for people who were searching for God but wouldn't come to church to find him.

To be clear, my conclusion is not that every campus ministry should be done this exact way. But the reality is, the emerging world needs the next generation of leaders to lead the way in creating new kinds of environments that foster deeper dialogue and build on the already existing activity of God in people's lives. Maybe this is the next step that people need before they'll step through the doors of a church, or more important, the step they need to find God.

THE DEVELOPING ENTREPRENEUR

These are three examples among dozens of stories that I've seen firsthand. One of the most remarkable and rewarding pieces of this whole entrepreneurial process revolves around what leadership skills (and character traits) develop along the way. Of course our growth isn't ever totally predictable, because God is the one who grows us. However, there are six primary leadership skills that I've seen develop in myself and others over and over again throughout the process of starting pre-church experiences. These are the main reasons why I continue to challenge protégés to be kingdom entrepreneurs, and perhaps compelling reasons for you to do the same.

1. *Entrepreneurship.* It forces protégés to think like entrepreneurs in terms of vision, strategy, planning, team building, evaluation, innovation and accountability—usually with little or no budget.

2. *Self-initiative.* It teaches protégés the value of taking risks, being proactive and taking personal responsibility—all essentials for spiritual development and leadership growth.

3. *Team building.* It encourages protégés to cultivate team environments of idea formation, strategic planning and collaborative goal setting.

4. *Failure.* It steers protégés to believe that the fear of failure is a real part of leadership, and reminds them that it doesn't have to hold them back from doing what's necessary to reach new people in new ways. After all, there's much to learn from failure.

5. *Missional innovation.* It reminds protégés of the importance of mission-focused leadership, and how innovation and creativity play an integral role in advancing the kingdom.

6. *Compassion.* It forces protégés to learn and grasp the mindset and emotions of nonbelieving people who are searching, which results in sensitizing their hearts as well as deepening their compassion and empathy for them.

HOW DO I MOVE FORWARD?

Having read these three examples of pre-church experiences, I realize some you already have an idea and you can't start moving forward soon enough. Others have too many ideas, so much that it immobilizes you from choosing just one to act on. Still more of you might be thinking you can't do this because it's just not you. Truth is, you feel incapable or inadequate. Wherever you are on the spectrum, there really are endless ideas to draw upon—and I know there's one for everyone. It all begins with a leader who's willing to risk, even fail. I know plenty of very ordinary people who have started and executed extremely effective pre-church experiences who never thought of themselves as entrepreneurs.

In the Protégé Program, protégés aren't forced to be a point person of a pre-church experience, because that's not the way everyone is wired. However, they are challenged to play a significant leadership role in moving a new ministry forward and establishing the right kind of environment that will draw nonbelievers. Doing this cultivates their drive to live and lead on mission. Something happens in the growth process when we venture out into new territory and are challenged to do something out of our comfort zone where we have the potential to fall flat on our face. No matter what age we are or how long we've been in ministry, I wonder sometimes, "If we're not risking in a way that we're desperate for God to show up, maybe we're not risking enough?"

To jog your thinking, here are a few more brief examples of pre-church ministries:

• I've seen a variety of artistic events like short film festivals, Battle of the Bands events, and even talent show–type events that incorporate spiritual themes.

- David led "Creativity Tours," where people went on a twenty-four-hour outdoor adventure to experience God's creativity and discover their own. He's seen dozens come to faith in Christ through his ongoing efforts.

- Tammy started an annual fashion show that now draws hundreds of people annually, many of whom have now attended church for the first time.

- Scott started a think tank to create intentional dialogues and debates for "intellectually minded, spiritual people."

- Dave started an improv comedy workshop that turned into many more workshops and comedy shows. That then turned into connecting dozens of nonbelievers to our church. Some now follow Christ.

- Charity started an event, and then an organization, that fights human trafficking and brings people from all walks of life and faith together. It establishes common ground and relationship for the gospel to be spread.

I could go on, but the point is that there are endless ideas. And remember, pre-church experiences are not trying to dilute the church experience, but instead are intended to expand the communal spiritual experience for people who aren't quite ready to step through the doors of a church. I challenge you to take responsibility to choose one idea and get started on it. Then, work at it to the best of your ability. Remember to "be wise in the way you act toward outsiders; make the most of every opportunity. Let your conversation be always full of grace, seasoned with salt" (Colossians 4:5-6).

At their core, kingdom entrepreneurs always focus on bringing hope to those without hope, a voice to the voiceless, and love to those who don't know or experience what love really is. They strive to make an eternal impact in our world, whether it's global or local, personal or organizational. And even if we don't change the whole world, we can certainly change our little part of the world! That's what kingdom entrepreneurs do!

IDEAS FOR MENTORS

Experiment with a pre-church experience. Meet one-on-one with a protégé and challenge them to start a pre-church experience. Discuss how this fits into the overall strategy of Christ's mission, as well as the organization or church they are part of. Give them guidance, ideas, support, direction, and don't forget to pray for them. Be their coach and consultant to the measure that they need it. Even offer evaluation, observations, and analysis along the way.

MENTOR TIP:
GET A CLOSER LOOK

Attend a ministry that one of your protégés leads and offer your feedback—both affirmative and constructive. Doing this speaks of your level of engagement and investment in their development. Coach them, but also affirm the good they're doing.

Epilogue

ONE LAST THING

I urge you to live a life worthy of the calling you have received.

(EPHESIANS 4:1)

LEADERSHIP DEVELOPMENT BEGINS WITH acknowledging and trusting the process and the people that God uses to grow us. One of the core processes he uses is testing, refining and shaping the content of our character. This is where the conversation about effective ministry leadership must begin. Our personhood and essence directly correlates to our closeness, depth and surrender to the One who is the Leader of our lives. We cannot lead others where we have not been ourselves. We cannot minister to others by preaching transformation when we are not being transformed. The way we experience true character change first comes through abiding in God. Spiritual depth will always elude us if we are attaching ourselves to things other than Jesus. It is in the abiding that we will see that mystical flourishing in our inner lives that we so deeply need in order to see fruit of the Spirit in our external lives. This is core to ministry. This is core to life. And how we navigate this character journey in our own lives matters now and for eternity.

Once we capture the daily need for God's power and grace to shape our character, and when we take seriously the responsibility of living in the spiritual depths, there are other essential dimensions of God-centered and effective leadership that we can cultivate and build our life and leadership on. Relationships have the power to catalyze or paralyze our leadership. They are the key that unlocks true influence. If we really want to optimize our impact in people's lives for Christ in significant ways, pursuing relational health must remain front and center. All of us have great relational strengths, but all of us have relational deficits too. We must deal with them.

God calls us to a centeredness that holds on to what may seem like opposing relational values, but in reality are complementary, even necessary. Most of us gravitate to certain relational virtues and as a result neglect others. We can easily miss the mark if we are not stretching ourselves, in what seems to be the opposite direction sometimes, as we attempt to *hold on to one without letting go of the other*. One great task of every ministry leader ought to be the pursuit of a more centered relational axis that in turn will create healthier, stronger relationships. When we are committed to this dimension of development, the potential for impact grows exponentially. Not to mention we will be better human beings.

Communication is also critical to leadership development. Words can serve as a bridge that connects with what is unspoken in the human heart, and perhaps not even understood. We have all experienced those moments where a truth is spoken with such power and clarity that it actually changes us profoundly. When articulated well and comprehended, language can allow people to truly know, and even encounter, the God they're really trying to find. Building bridges with words of substance, truth and grace will help others from falling into confusion and ignorance. Protégés are called to be bridge builders through the gift and responsibility of their communication.

Mission is also a core value that no ministry leader can afford to leave behind. Sadly, many do leave it behind. Someone felt the call to share the gospel with us, and that is in large part why we are where we are today. We can now be that someone to the world around us. Mission is and always will be the heartbeat of the gospel because it's rooted in the greatest sacrifice ever made in this world, the very life and death of Jesus Christ. Central to every single Christ follower's calling is to be the living heartbeat in this generation that God has planted us in for this time. Mission starts with the life we're living and can extend into other people's lives through the words we use.

Entrepreneurial leadership is one of the significant and practical ways that mission can be fostered and kept alive, rather than neglected and overlooked. Instead of doing things the way we've always done them, entrepreneurial leadership drives us toward the creative element of who God is and compels us to think strategically, innovatively and biblically about reaching people far from God who stand outside the walls of the church. Creating new avenues where people can see and experience God in new and fresh ways must remain an integral part of how the church moves into the future. Entrepreneurial leadership is about giving people another chance in another way to see God, perhaps for the first time. It's about seeking to save the lost. It's not about serving those who are found, but those who are still lost.

There's a movement that is alive and powerful. It's akin to a tidal wave sweeping us into the Answer to people's deepest searches and longings. It's called the church. And there are people God is using to lead this church. They are called you and me. It is a high calling, one that requires the best of who we are. It demands the kind of devotion this world has never seen and doesn't even think possible. Ultimately, we are all God's protégés, called to learn from the Master and Creator of humanity. Let's follow in his footsteps and give the best of who we are to the One who gave his everything to us.

> For when David had served God's purpose in his own generation, he fell asleep. (Acts 13:36)

Acknowledgments

BEHIND EVERY BOOK THERE IS A TEAM of people who collaborate to accomplish the great task of publishing a book. I am grateful to so many who have given input and advice. And I am thankful for others who, although they didn't give direct or specific feedback to this book, have invested in me, believed in me and shaped who I am today. They've all been invaluable to me, even beyond what I can articulate. Each of them contributed to creating new possibilities in my life, and for that I'm eternally grateful.

Protégés, where do I even begin? I couldn't have gained the experience and insight into leadership development without every single one of you. And more than that, I would've never gained our friendships that are so enduring and meaningful to me. No words can capture how honored I was to be invited to invest in your lives.

And I'll never forget all of your superhero names!

Al Hsu, I'm immeasurably grateful for your input and deeply meaningful expertise. You have that rare blend of giving challenging feedback that pushes me as a writer while also remaining encouraging, kind and tactful in your approach. You remind me of a coach who pushes his players hard, but at same time believes in them and inspires their greatest efforts.

IVP, thanks for taking a risk on me and believing in the message of this book.

Tina Jacobson, you're a trusted agent, ministry partner and friend. Your guidance along the way has been remarkably helpful. I'm much indebted to you.

To each reader of this book, thank you for being a protégé—a humble learner. My hope is that this book is helpful to every one of you, and that it makes a positive difference in your ministry, personal life and future.

Most importantly, God, I pray this book honors you.

Fifteen Things to Do to Develop Leaders:

A SHORT LIST OF TOOLS, EXPERIENCES AND
IDEA STARTERS FOR LEADERSHIP DEVELOPMENT

1. **Learning Labs.** These informal, relational learning environments can simulate real-time pressure situations and offer protégés an opportunity to execute under pressure (e.g., the five-minute talk experience).

2. **Novel Experiences.** This should be a unique experience that will challenge the protégé's normal pattern of thinking or behaving (e.g., the Scientology tour).

3. **Expert Exposure.** Invite seasoned leaders and "experts" to spend time with protégés individually or as a group. It could be via video chat, conference call or some type of social media. Maybe, as a mentor, you can identify people you know in your locale to do a question-and-answer or presentation to your protégés. Remember to use people outside vocational ministry to broaden your protégés' perspectives.

4. **Look for Crisis.** Crisis often creates the greatest opportunity of growth. Pay attention to when someone is going through a crucible or gets triggered deeply by something. Moments like these are when protégés need mentors the most, and coming alongside them in a circumstantial, relational, emotional, spiritual or psychological crisis can help foster substantial growth.

5. **Establish a Concrete Growth Plan.** Teach leaders to develop a concrete growth plan. Evaluate progress, and keep the vision of growth in front of people. Push protégés to set concrete goals for their own growth process.

6. **Create Community Feedback Loops.** Cultivate communal-learning environments for feedback, or utilize other creative ways

to foster feedback (e.g., SurveyMonkey about your character). Don't be someone's sole mentor; rather, leverage the power and insight of community.

7. **Leverage Self-Assessments and 360 Assessments.** Use these as conversation starters and tools to foster self-awareness—or job performance. Here are ones I use frequently: PRO-D, the Birkman method, Myers-Briggs Type Indicator, DISC, Gallup Strengths-Finder, Character Matrix assessment, the Leadership Challenge 360, Relational Intelligence assessment, the Enneagram, etc.

8. **Practice Goal Setting and Accountability.** You may need to start by giving guidance to protégés on how to set goals (the familiar SMART method is a good place to start). Then make sure you are following up with protégés on how their progress is going. This allows the mentor to reinforce the right values, draw out learning and put positive pressure on the protégé.

9. **Create a Map.** This is your guide that enables you to know what your destination is and to figure out how to get there. This ought not to be a rigid structure or system, but it ought to be used as a field guide that helps the mentor (and protégé) clarify what the desired outcomes are for the process they're walking through together. For instance, I have twelve core areas that I focus on in a leader's development process. Around each of the twelve categories, I've identified and categorized resources, books, tools, podcasts, learning experiences and conversations I know I need to have around that arena. I use this map to help cultivate growth according to what God is doing in a person's life and in congruence with where that protégé is developmentally. In short, know and strive to implement your vision for leadership development with concrete clarity.

10. **Classroom Learning.** In certain cases, this may be getting a seminary education. In other cases, it may need to be a classroom environment that the mentor sets up for a group of protégés—or when a senior leader at a church brings someone in for a day-long workshop. Remember to make this experience as interactive as possible, and in ways that enhance learning for all students involved.

11. **Candid Conversations.** From a humble and respectful posture, mentors must be willing to have hard, frank conversations with protégés if they desire to optimize their growth. Doing this wisely, tactfully and humbly ought to be a regular part of one's mentoring process.

12. **Resource Exposure.** Keep protégés informed of the best resources you know about. Send them podcasts, articles to read, people to watch on video, etc. In my view, these resources ought not always be from a Christian perspective because, sometimes, that can limit the scope of learning and development (www.ted.com has some incredible talks on video that I often send to protégés to have them watch/listen to).

13. **Intentionally Guided Retreats.** Retreat experiences often accelerate closeness in relationships and can also foster new kinds of growth if led well. This could be anything from a solitude retreat that you guide or a team-building or strategic retreat. It could even revlove around each person sharing a short movie clip that captures their life story.

14. **Action Learning.** Give teams of protégés a real-time project. For example, plan an event together, build a well in Africa, organize small-group curriculum series for your church and so on. When young protégés get hands-on experience in a team setting with other peers, it often creates a remarkable learning environment.

15. **Establish a Recognition and Reward Culture.** Create a culture of genuine affirmation of what people do well, how hard they work and what they ought to be recognized for. You could give out public praise, awards, superhero action figures or use other creative expressions to execute this. Just make sure you remember how critical positive affirmation and recognition is to a protégé's confidence and growth. This is integral to leadership development.

Notes

The Protégé Narrative

[1]Compiled by Darrin Patrick. See <http://blog.beliefnet.com/jesuscreed/2007/08/burnout-for-pastors.html>.

[2]Jeffrey Jensen Arnett, *Emerging Adulthood: The Winding Road from the Late Teens Through the Twenties* (Oxford: Oxford University Press, 2006).

[3]Some of these churches include National Community Church in Washington, D.C., Ecclesia in Houston, Vintage Faith in Santa Cruz, as well as many others nationally and internationally.

Chapter 1: Building Kingdom Cultures

[1]H. B. London Jr. and Neil B. Wiseman, *Pastors at Greater Risk* (Ventura, Calif.: Regal, 2003).

[2]Ibid.

[3]David Kinnaman, Gabe Lyons and Lloyd James, *unChristian: What a New Generation Really Thinks about Christianity . . . and Why It Matters* (Grand Rapids: Baker, 2008), p. 28.

[4]London and Wiseman, *Pastors at Greater Risk.*

[5]Dallas Willard, *The Divine Conspiracy* (San Francisco: Harper, 1998), p. 26.

[6]Jesus' ministry was always centered on doing the will of the Father (John 4:34).

Chapter 5: The Sin of Entitlement

[1]Richard Foster, *Prayer* (New York: HarperCollins, 1992).

Chapter 7: The Tension of Conflict

[1]*Emotionally Healthy Spirituality* (by Peter Scazzero) and *The Cry of the Soul* (by Dan Allender) are great books to use as starting places to guide someone toward emotional health.

[2]Max Lucado, *When God Whispers Your Name* (Nashville: Thomas Nelson, 1999), p. 44.

Chapter 8: The Tension of Attachment

[1]Brennan Manning, *Abba's Child* (Colorado Springs: NavPress, 2002), p. 56.

Chapter 10: Communicating with a Missional Lens

[1]This use of the term "post-Christian" first appeared in the 1929 book *America Set Free* (New York: Harper) by the German philosopher Hermann Keyserling.

Part 4: Mission

[1]Many of the cities of Judea were placed on the summits or sides of mountains, and could be seen from afar. Perhaps Jesus pointed to such a city, and told his disciples that they were like it. Their actions could not be hidden. The eyes of the world were upon them. (Barnes' Notes on the Bible, online commentary <www.studylight.org>.)

[2]Interim Report on the Books *Jesus and Christ.*

[3]David Jacobus Bosch, *Transforming Mission: Paradigm Shifts in Theology of Mission* (Maryknoll, N.Y.: Orbis, 1991), p. 390.

[4]Alan Hirsch, *The Forgotten Ways: Reactivating the Missional Church* (Grand Rapids: Brazos, 2006), p. 82.

Chapter 11: Gospel Momentum

[1]Adapted from Dan Kimball, *They Like Jesus but Not the Church* (Grand Rapids: Zondervan, 2007).

Chapter 13: Gospel Conversations

[1]For more elaborate detail, read the book *Iconoclast* by Gregory Berns (Boston: Harvard Business Press, 2008).

[2]N. T. Wright, *The New Testament and the People of God,* Christian Origins and the Question of God (Minneapolis: Fortress, 1992), p. 361.

Chapter 14: Gospel Community

[1]There are many resources, scholars and theologians that affirm this idea.

[2]For more exposition, see Al Hsu's *Singles at the Crossroads* (Downers Grove, Ill.: InterVarsity Press, 1997), pp. 34-36.

[3]N. T. Wright, *Simply Christian: Why Christianity Makes Sense* <www.smallgroups.com/downloads/biblestudy/videobiblestudies/simplychristian.htm>.

Chapter 15: Kingdom Entrepreneurs

[1]Warren Bennis, *Organizing Genius: The Secret of Creative Collaboration* (New York: Perseus, 1997).

[2]Henry Cloud, *Integrity* (New York: HarperCollins, 2006), pp. 229-30.

PRAXIS

EQUIPPING LEADERS FOR MINISTRY.

"...TO EQUIP HIS PEOPLE FOR WORKS OF SERVICE,

SO THAT THE BODY OF CHRIST MAY BE BUILT UP."

EPHESIANS 4:12

God has called us to ministry. But it's not enough to have a vision for ministry if you don't have the practical skills for it. Nor is it enough to do the work of ministry if what you do is headed in the wrong direction. We need both vision *and* expertise for effective ministry. We need *praxis*.

Praxis puts theory into practice. It brings cutting-edge ministry expertise from visionary practitioners. You'll find sound biblical and theological foundations for ministry in the real world, with concrete examples for effective action and pastoral ministry. Praxis books are more than the "how to"—they're also the "why to." And because *being* is every bit as important as *doing*, Praxis attends to the inner life of the leader as well as the outer work of ministry. Feed your soul, and feed your ministry.

If you are called to ministry, you know you can't do it on your own. Let Praxis provide the companions you need to equip God's people for life in the kingdom.

www.ivpress.com/praxis